# Imprisoning Communities

# Imprisoning Communities

*How Mass Incarceration Makes
Disadvantaged Neighborhoods Worse*

Todd R. Clear

# OXFORD

UNIVERSITY PRESS

Oxford University Press, Inc., publishes works that further
Oxford University's objective of excellence
in research, scholarship, and education.

Oxford   New York
Auckland   Cape Town   Dar es Salaam   Hong Kong   Karachi
Kuala Lumpur   Madrid   Melbourne   Mexico City   Nairobi
New Delhi   Shanghai   Taipei   Toronto

With offices in
Argentina   Austria   Brazil   Chile   Czech Republic   France   Greece
Guatemala   Hungary   Italy   Japan   Poland   Portugal   Singapore
South Korea   Switzerland   Thailand   Turkey   Ukraine   Vietnam

Copyright © 2007 by Oxford University Press, Inc.

Published by Oxford University Press, Inc.
198 Madison Avenue, New York, New York 10016

www.oup.com

First issued as an Oxford University Press paperback, 2009

Oxford is a registered trademark of Oxford University Press

Library of Congress Cataloging-in-Publication Data
Clear, Todd R.
Imprisoning communities : how mass incarceration makes disadvantaged
neighborhoods worse / by Todd R. Clear.
p. cm.—(Studies in crime and public policy)
Includes bibliographical references.
ISBN 978-0-19-538720-9
1. Imprisonment—Social aspects—United States.   2. Social problems—United States.
3. Urban poor—United States.   I. Title.
HV9950.C55 2007
307.3'360973—dc22   2006034993

Printed in the United States of America
on acid-free paper

To Dina Rose
with gratitude

# Preface

By the mid-1980s, a few penologists, I among them, began to speculate that what had by that time become a 15-year prison population run-up was a trend that had to be nearing an end. We were alarmed at a prison population growth spinning out of control, and because we could find no rational explanation for the growth, unprecedented at that time, we came to the conclusion it was a politically spawned spurt that had about run its course. If you had told us then that the growth in imprisonment numbers was not even half finished, we would have been horrified at the prospect. A generation ago, nobody could have foreseen what was about to take place in U.S. penal policy for the next 35 years. What would have appalled us then to contemplate should appall us now to experience.

About that time, prominent criminologists were touting the crime-prevention potency of incarceration. Never mind that 15 years of prison population growth had been accompanied by 15 years of crime growth, a series of influential studies set an empirical foundation for the crime-prevention value of putting people behind bars. No less an august group than the National Academy of Sciences published a study of criminal careers suggesting that quite impressive suppression of crime might arise from incarcerating "high lambda offenders" (those who were heavily criminally active). Rand had just published Peter Greenwood's conjecture that "selective incapacitation" could simultaneously prevent crime and reduce prison populations. Soon, the National Institute of Justice would widely distribute Edwin Zedlewski's speculation that each new offender locked up prevented literally hundreds of crimes and saved enormous costs of crime. A fashionable theory developed that prisons were efficient crime suppressors. Yet the external validity of these claims was undermined by a fact that nobody seemed to pay much attention to: as prison populations were going up, so was the crime rate.

About that time I wrote a paper for a think-tank retreat (sponsored by the Vera Institute of Justice) entitled "Backfire: When Incarceration Increases Crime." In that paper, I listed 10 ways that incarceration might exacerbate problems and might directly or indirectly lead to increased crime. The paper was received with considerable doubt by scholars, and (as I recall) only the corrections professionals in the audience seemed to like it. (It was published much later in, of all places, the *Journal of the Oklahoma Criminal Justice Research Consortium*, and it has reappeared here and there, mostly cited from being found on the Internet.)

Even though most scholars I knew were lukewarm to the idea—the standard take was that incapacitation effects were so large that they canceled out every concern I raised—I stayed with it, anyway. When I talked about these issues to community groups and within the corrections profession, there was a lot of agreement. The more I read on the topic, the more I thought I was onto something.

In 1995, I met sociologist Dina Rose. What followed was a long and continuing personal and professional conversation, part of which revolved around her interest in social disorganization theory. She had just finished a neighborhood-level study of the impact of churches on crime rates in Chicago, and she convinced me that "backfire" was an idea best housed in social disorganization theory and articulated as a neighborhood effect. Together, we wrote a paper theorizing that high incarceration rates would contribute to the destabilization of poor neighborhoods and, through weakened informal social control, would lead to increased crime. The paper was published in *Criminology* in 1998.

In 1996, we both moved from our then-current positions (hers at the University of Buffalo, mine at Rutgers University) to Florida State University, in Tallahassee, where we continued this work. The Open Society Institute (OSI) gave us a small grant of $35,000 to gather the data we would need to empirically test what we had begun calling the "coercive mobility" hypothesis. We were joined in finishing this work by my former Rutgers colleague Elin Waring. The results of that study, which substantially supported our thesis, were published in *Justice Quarterly* in 2002.

In 1999, Dina and I moved to the New York City area to take positions at John Jay College of Criminal Justice. The campus is less than a city block from the main offices of the Open Society Institute, and we began a lengthy collaboration with the group, and with Susan Tucker as the program director for the After Prison Initiative, exploring ways to expand on our work in Tallahassee. In October 2002, OSI brought together a group of researchers, all of whom were doing work on urban neighborhood datasets, and we asked them to consider ways of incorporating spatial measures of incarceration rates into their research agendas. This group formed the core of what we called the Concentrated Incarceration Consortium. OSI was joined in funding this group by the Jeht Foundation, the Annie E. Casey Foundation, and the Andrew Shiva Family Fund. Eventually, that group grew to include the following researchers, who met three times during the life of the project:

Robert Crutchfield, of the University of Washington, who studied attitudes toward conventional values in Seattle.

Jeffrey Fagan, of Columbia University, who studied voting patterns in New York City.

William Feyerherm and Brian Renauer, of Portland State University, who studied crime in Portland.

Susan George and Robert LaLonde, of the University of Chicago, who studied women's incarceration and crime in Chicago.

James Lynch, then of American University, and William Sabol, then of Case Western Reserve University, who studied crime and informal social control in Baltimore and Cleveland.

Ruth Peterson and Lauren Krivo, of Ohio State University, who studied crime in Columbus.

David Rasmussen, of Florida State University, who studied housing prices in Jacksonville.

Peter St. Jean, of the University of Buffalo, who studied crime and informal social control in Buffalo.

Ralph Taylor, who led a team from Temple University that studied serious juvenile delinquency in Philadelphia.

James Thomas, of the University of North Carolina, who studied sexually transmitted diseases in Durham and elsewhere in North Carolina.

Elin Waring, of Lehman College, who used an expanded dataset to study crime in Tallahassee.

Each research site received a small grant to incorporate incarceration data into existing work. The coordination was quite loose. The teams were free to explore their work in different ways, and each team "owned" the data and was free to publish them in whatever form they wished. Some of this work has been published; some has not. In 1999, Dina Rose and I received a grant from the National Institute of Justice to conduct an ethnography in two Tallahassee neighborhoods, which was reported in

2000 (Award Number: 99-CE-VX-0008; Akiva Lieberman, program manager). Together, this body of research forms the backbone of this book.

The chapters that follow, then, reflect the work of many people over the past decade. Selected portions of chapter 4, the main theoretical chapter, have previously appeared in two published works that extensively covered this ground: the original theoretical study (Dina R. Rose and Todd R. Clear, "Incarceration, Social Capital and Crime: Examining the Unintended Consequences of Incarceration," *Criminology* 36:3 [August 1998]) and a later reprise of it (Todd R. Clear, Elin Waring, and Kristen Scully, "Communities and Reentry: Concentrated Reentry Cycling," in Jeremy Travis and Christy Visher, eds., *Prisoner Reentry and Crime in America*, 179–208 [New York: Cambridge University Press, 2005]). Chapter 6 in this book is a much revised version of a chapter from our report (Dina R. Rose, Todd R. Clear, and Judith Ryder, *Drugs, Incarceration, and Neighborhood Life: The Impact of Reintegrating Offenders into the Community*, a report to the National Institute of Justice [New York: John Jay College 2000], Award Number 99-CE-VX-0008). The opinions expressed in chapter 6 are mine and not necessarily the official positions of the Institute. Details of the sampling methods, content analysis strategy, and results can be found in the report. I have borrowed for the Appendix almost the entire introduction to Todd R. Clear and David R. Karp's *The Community Justice Ideal: Preventing Crime and Achieving Justice* (Boulder, CO: Westview Press, 1999). I am grateful to the publishers who have granted permission to re-use portions of this work.

The list of scholars who have participated in various aspects of this work is an impressive one, and they have my deepest thanks for their willingness to devote their precious time to this agenda. Most of them developed a deep personal interest in the questions the group investigated, and a few of them have continued to work in the area. Their talents are an enormous asset to those of us who hope for a new policy agenda in our penal system. If anything comes of this body of work, it will in large part be due to their unassailable credibility and meticulous attention to the problem.

Along the way, Elin Waring became an indispensable collaborator—a gifted sociologist whose theoretical and empirical contributions to the coercive mobility thesis strengthened every aspect of the work. With regard to the possibilities that arise for community justice, David Karp played a similar role, helping the idea of community justice to be more sharply expressed and contributing no small portion of his own ideas to the mix. Two former students joined in various aspects of the research and writing, Kristen Scully and Judith Ryder; their dedication and skill strengthened the book. My appreciation goes, as well, to Odessa Simms, Cyan Zoeller, and Nicole Kief, who helped with the preparation of the manuscript. As sometimes happens, two former students who assisted at various stages of this work have gone on to become valued colleagues and personal friends, Natasha Frost and Keramet Reiter; I thank them for the effortless way they aided this work.

Friends and colleagues who read drafts of chapters and gave me invaluable comments include Paul Bellair, David Brotherton, Ric Curtis, David Greenberg, Keith Hayward, David Karp, Jim Lynch, Daniel Nagin, Marc Mauer, Andres Rengifo, Bruce Western, and Chris Uggen. Each of them gave me suggestions that came to be reflected in the text.

Allen Beck corrected some of the numbers in an earlier draft of chapter 3, for which I am immensely appreciative; the remaining errors are all my own doing. Michael Tonry offered masterful suggestions about the organization of the narrative in earlier drafts of the book, and his deft touch with argument has strengthened the final version. Linda Donnelly's editorial eye was invaluable. For their several supportive critiques, I am in their debt.

Four project monitors shaped this work: Bart Lubow of Annie E. Casey, Robert Crane of the Jeht Foundation, Akiva Lieberman of the National Institute of Justice, and Susan Tucker of the Open Society Institute. Their able counsel is reflected throughout the book. Of these grant-making advisors, Susan Tucker stands out as having contributed to the strategic and conceptual thinking from the outset. The sagacity of her supportive guidance became even more essential to the success of this work than the funding she arranged to come our way. I thank her deeply and appreciate her profoundly.

None of this would have happened without Dina Rose. She is my partner in thought and feeling, the person who listens with patience to my ideas and helps me rework them and make them better. The fruits of her work show on every page, including the several places where I have used words that originally came from her and elaborated on ideas that were hers to begin with. She has moved her attention on to other topics while, typically, I doggedly have stayed here with this one. But her shining intelligence, sociological acumen, and utter good sense were a secret asset I relied upon time and again.

## The Organization of This Book

I devote a chapter or two to each of the theses mentioned earlier. In chapter 1, I give an overview of the argument presented in this book. The chapter begins by stressing how important it is that the generation-long growth in the U.S. prison population has occurred by removing large concentrations of people from poor places. It then identifies the major ways this high rate of concentrated incarceration intervenes in the life of poor communities, and it summarizes what has happened to social capital, families, community infrastructure, and public safety as a consequence. It concludes with a call for new ideas of justice for poor communities.

Chapter 2 critically reviews what is known about incarceration and crime. After showing the long-term trends in crime and prison populations, I describe the two main ways crime could be suppressed by imprisonment: deterrence and incapacitation. Volumes have been produced on this issue, and my review does not intend to be exhaustive, but rather to both illustrate the range of studies done and point to those that have proved most influential. I give special attention to diverse conclusions that may be derived from these studies, and then try to answer the central question: How can prison populations have grown so extraordinarily for a generation, and yet the crime rate at the end of that period of growth be about what it was at its start?

Chapter 3 describes the growth in the number of people incarcerated in the United States. It begins by showing how three rough policy shifts both produced and sustained that growth, first by reducing the use of nonprison sentencing alternatives, then by increasing the length of sentences, and last by increasing the rate of return to prison for those under community supervision. Special attention is given to changes in sentencing laws for drug crimes, which have been a major factor in imprisonment growth. I then show how this growth in imprisonment has been concentrated in four dimensions: age, gender, race, and place. This concentration has enormous implications for the human capital of young people of color, especially men. It has equally important implications for the social capital of people who reside in those poor places.

Chapter 4 lays out the theoretical argument of how concentrated incarceration affects communities. It builds on the original Rose-Clear thesis of coercive mobility, adding recent theoretical contributions. The chapter opens with a discussion of the importance of "place," and various related concepts are described: human and social capital, social networks, informal social control, and collective efficacy. For each of these concepts, the potential significance of incarceration is explored. The chapter concludes by showing how concentrated incarceration, through various social forces, undermines informal social control and thus leads to more crime.

Chapter 5 offers an empirical investigation of the impact of incarceration on intimate social relations, private (intimate) social control, social networks, and economic and political systems. There is growing interest in the unintended consequences of incarceration, and this has led to several dozen recent studies that examine, directly or indirectly, the impact of incarceration on children, families, and social relations. Many of the studies cited in this chapter have appeared in print, while others I describe are so recent they have not yet been published. The general point of this chapter is to show mounting evidence that sustained high levels of incarceration impair various aspects of community life and damage the community.

Chapter 6 summarizes an ethnographic study of incarceration in two poor communities, based on 100 interviews with individuals and two group interviews of residents in Tallahassee, Florida. Using the observations and experiences of people in these communities, I show that the array of problems described in the preceding chapter are no secret to them. The fact that poor (in this case, almost entirely black) residents of high-incarceration communities are able to identify imprisonment as a *community* problem not only tends to support the main thesis of this book but also shows that there is a social foundation that can become the stage for political action.

Chapter 7 summarizes some studies of the way incarceration, in concentrated levels, contributes to elevated crime rates in the community. It begins with a review of the coercive mobility thesis: that high incarceration rates destabilize informal social control in poor communities. Research in Tallahassee, Portland, Oregon, and Columbus, Ohio, shows evidence of a link between high rates of incarceration and increases in crime. There are, however, methodological weaknesses in these studies, mainly because incarceration and crime are mutually-related—each affects the other—and this makes statistical analysis problematic. Analyses in Baltimore and Cleveland, using a different methodology to take account of this problem, fail to confirm the impact of coercive mobility on crime rates, though other community-level impacts have been found. Recent work in Philadelphia has analyzed the impact of adult incarceration on *juvenile* crime, and has offered support for the coercive mobility hypothesis in the impact on juveniles. Taken together, these research projects suggest that, in high doses, incarceration may well contribute to increased crime.

Chapter 8 proposes solutions for the problem of concentrated incarceration in poor communities. The chapter begins by explaining what initiatives will *not* solve the problem: rehabilitation programs, reentry programs, and alternatives to incarceration. Three types of solutions are then identified. Sentencing reform proposals seek to reduce the number of people going to prison and shorten their length of stay, especially for drug-related crimes, but also for mandatory and extreme sentences. A philosophy of "community justice" provides an excellent starting point for thinking about reform. This then leads to illustrations of potential community justice solutions, some involving the criminal justice system, some not. The chapter concludes with a description of "justice reinvestment" as a way to fund community justice initiatives. For those interested in community justice, I have provided an appendix that gives a detailed illustration of this idea.

## My Hope for This Book

This book was written to inform and persuade. The informational objective is typical for this kind of text. There is growing interest in the problem of mass incarceration, and a specialization within that area is the impact of incarceration on families and communities. Those effects are felt directly, in what happens to social networks when people, especially young men, are removed from their communities and placed in confinement. The impacts are indirect, in the way that incarceration changes, permanently, the life chances of those who go to prison, and as a consequence affect the prospects of the nonincarcerated who are close to them, personally and spatially. My particular interest is in this latter dynamic—the effects on the community—and I hope in this book to bring together a wide range of research to inform the reader of the consequences of high levels incarceration that are concentrated in poor locations.

The second aim, that of persuasion, is less typical for books such as this. I hope to engage the reader in a call to action. The insidiousness of incarceration policies for poor communities of color in the United States is not merely a theoretical problem; it is a stunning impediment to social justice and what we proudly proclaim as a human right in our Declaration of Independence: "the pursuit of happiness." Yet it is nearly impossible to address problems of racial injustice and social inequality without first overcoming one of their main engines: concentrated incarceration.

I recognize from the outset that there is an uneasy fit between the task of informing and that of persuading. The former is best done with studied indifference; the latter cannot abide indifference. There is no obvious middle ground to be taken. Yet, the tone of this book reflects these dual aims by trying, to the extent possible, to stay true to both of them. Where the topic is evidence, I offer reasoned review, with a recognition of the limitations of what we know and the importance of those limitations. When the topic is action, I employ strong words and potent imagery, for I hope the reader will finish this book as persuaded as I am that we must change course.

# Contents

# Imprisoning Communities

# The Problem of Concentrated Incarceration

1

Prison populations have grown mostly through society's locking up ever-increasing numbers of young men, especially black men, largely from impoverished places. The concentration of imprisonment of young men from disadvantaged places has grown to such a point that it is now a bedrock experience, a force that affects families and children, institutions and businesses, social groups and interpersonal relations. With its isolation of people from poor places, incarceration does more damage than good, including increases in crime. In this way, incarceration has become part of its own dynamic. Imprisonment has grown to the point that it now produces the very social problems on which it feeds. It is the perfect storm.

Uninformed public sentiments and practiced political interests have created a malignant foundation for our crime-prevention policy. Legislative changes lean only in the direction of ever-growing punitiveness, drawing more and more young people—especially black men—into the system's clutches. The system clutches them; indeed, people who get caught up in the penal system stay there longer, are subjected to more controls, and suffer a greater chance of failure than ever before in history. Faced with this situation, policy makers think only of becoming more strict and more punitive, more damaging, for an ever wider range of misbehaviors, drawing into the storm an ever larger group. As that group grows, the ripple effects of the damage also grow, crossing the social networks of those poorer communities and extending into future generations. Crime goes up, crime goes down; yet in a weirdly disconnected fashion, prison populations increase regardless.

The concentration of imprisonment among young black urban males is so extreme today that many of us simply assume that, when we encounter a young black man, he has a criminal record; and so we take what seems like appropriate precautions. As a matter of cold, hard facts, often these assumptions are correct. Black people know this and resent (or revel in) it. Resentment and/or rebellion erode the foundation of trust that is essential for public safety and social cohesion. The forces of economic inequality further stratify the geography of our cities, creating a racially segregated residential pattern that has the look and feel of Jim Crow. These dramatically high levels of imprisonment among residents of those communities exacerbate an already intolerable degree of racial disparity. Incarceration is an aspect of life passed on from generation to generation. The confluence of social, political, and penal forces produces a more-or-less permanent stock of prisoners, whether current, former, or future.

Back in 1970, when the prison population began to grow, nobody would have consciously chosen this future. But we have gotten here, surely and precisely, from making a generation of choices, starting about that time. Every year since 1973, the prison population has increased. Thus, during two lengthy periods of increasing crime rates, the prison population went up. But during two periods of dropping crime rates, one in which we now find ourselves, prison populations *also* went up. That is, prison populations have increased during both economic downturns and economic recoveries; while we were at war and also during times of peace; as the baby boomers have aged into crime and then as they have aged out of it; when there's been a national electoral landslide for Democrats and when there was one for Republicans. Through all the experiences that have occurred in the United States since the depths of the Vietnam War, our prison populations have grown. It is the only constant of the post–Civil Rights generation. And no clear path exists—or is at least apparent—out of this morass.

The most obvious consequence of unparalleled growth in the U.S. prison population is that it is now out of line, both historically and when compared with other nations. For most of the twentieth century, the imprisonment rate in the United States hovered at a bit over 100 people behind bars for every 100,000 citizens. But beginning in 1973, the incarceration rate grew annually, and today it is five times that rate (724). According to a report from the Sentencing Project (2005), when the U.S. rate of using prison and jails is compared to that of other countries, especially Western-style democracies as Americans like to think they are, the results are arresting, even stupefying. Consistently, today we are five to ten times more likely to lock up our citizens than are other nations; and among English-speaking nations, we make more use of prisons than does anyone else. South Africa, whose history of apartheid bears a discomfiting similarity to ours of slavery and later Jim Crow, has half our rate, at 344. Russia, unlike the United States in so many other respects, looks like us when it comes to imprisonment, with their rate of 564. And compared to neighbors such as Mexico, with 191, and Canada, with 145, we are out of line, as we are with similar Western-style democracies such as Australia (120), Germany (97), and France (88). Even China, at 118, uses prison less. Many countries have had growing prison populations over the last decade, but none matches our rate of growth (Western 2006, fig 1.2). In recent years, as our imprisonment rate has almost tripled, other nations experienced declines in incarceration owing to a worldwide phenomenon of dropping crime rates. America stands alone among nations in its use of incarceration (statistics from Mauer 2005).

## The Thesis of This Book, in Brief

This book makes four central points:

> The extraordinary growth in the U.S. prison system, sustained for over 30 years, has had, at best, a small impact on crime.
>
> The growth in imprisonment has been concentrated among poor, minority males who live in impoverished neighborhoods.
>
> Concentrated incarceration in those impoverished communities has broken families, weakened the social-control capacity of parents, eroded economic strength, soured attitudes toward society, and distorted politics; even, after reaching a certain level, it has increased rather than decreased crime.

Any attempt to overcome the problems of crime will have to encompass a combination of sentencing reforms and philosophical realignment.

Here is a summary:

## Incarceration and Crime

As a general rule, Americans believe that sending people to prison, especially men, prevents crime. This belief in the crime-prevention power of prison has a good dose of apparent face validity. After all, men behind prison walls cannot commit crimes against society. As a kind of proof, there is the all-too-common news story of a violent crime committed by a person recently released from prison. It seems an unassailable fact that at least *this* crime could have been prevented had the person never been allowed to get out. And if we can just make the prison experience *tough* enough, then surely people will think twice about committing the crimes that put them at risk of going there.

These sustaining beliefs have the support of a body of empirical work. Esteemed economists such as University of Chicago's Steven Levitt (Kessler and Levitt 1999) have argued that tougher sentencing—for example, in California—has reduced crime. Their work is not alone in making the suggestion that prisons reduce crime, and it bolsters the common wisdom about prisons.

In fact, however, the scientific evidence about the relationship between incarceration and crime is by no means uniformly supportive of the prison's capacity to reduce crime. The face validity of incapacitation—if you lock up a person who is actively committing crimes, you prevent the further crimes he would have committed—begins to evaporate upon close inspection. Many crimes still occur, because the person who is now behind bars is replaced by someone else. Almost everyone who goes to prison is eventually released, but the prospects for most of them to live crime-free have been *damaged* by the effects of their prison stay. Moreover, concrete practical and legal limits on punishment establish a surprisingly low ceiling for the potential deterrent power of a prison sentence. A child who is exposed to a parent or sibling who went to prison has an *increased,* rather than a decreased, risk of incarceration, and this testifies to the weakness of the deterrent effect of the sanction.

The limited capability of prisons to prevent crime is surely one of the reasons that, in the 33 years that prison populations have been rising continuously, trends in crime rates have been anything but systematic: they went up in the 1970s; down, then up in the 1980s; and up, then down in the 1990s. Today's headlines raise the fear that after a decade-long drop in crime, the trend may turn upward again (Frieden 2006), even as prison populations continue to rise. There is a puzzling discontinuity between imprisonment rates, which have increased every year since 1973, and crime rates, which have been up and down during that time and are, today, about what they were in 1970, when the prison population was at its lowest level in a generation.

This discontinuity is not discussed very much in the substantial social science literature assessing the impact of prisons on crime rates. Some studies, especially older ones, suggest that the impact is substantial. An equivalent body of studies, many of them more recent, find little or no impact on crime. As weaknesses in the earlier methodology are corrected by newer studies' more careful designs, the results show smaller connections between incarceration and crime prevention. Today, an overwhelming majority opinion is emerging that prison use has probably reduced crime, but only by a marginal amount. Scholars also tend to agree that additional growth in prison populations will produce ever-decreasing marginal returns in public safety (for reviews, see Spelman 1994, 2000).

Nevertheless, the deep-seated belief in the practical value of imprisonment, both as a deterrent and for incapacitation, makes it difficult to change prison policy. When crime was going up—during the entire 1970s and much of the 1980s—this belief fostered public sentiment that we needed *more* use of prison, not less. Now that crime has been decreasing for a decade or so, the public seems loathe to monkey with a system that appears to be working—to many people, the *last* thing we should do is reduce the use of imprisonment. If, as may well be the case, the recent drop in crime is ending, there will predictably be calls for *more*, not less, incarceration, despite the growing body of work that shows increased prison population growth will have little impact on crime rates.

## Black Males

That black men have been put behind bars at higher rates than any other group is not a new observation. But their rate of incarceration, always high, has been growing more rapidly than that for any other subgroup of males, and this is especially true for black high school dropouts. Sociologist Bruce Western has shown that, in the last 25 years, black high school dropouts have been almost five times more likely to go to prison than white high school dropouts, and that this difference in incarceration rates has been growing (Western 2006). This differential rate of incarceration is self-sustaining—first through the way criminal laws are designed, and then how these laws reverberate to affect social relations. Simply put, poor, undereducated, young black men are caught up in a penal crisis.

The main vehicle for the different rate of incarceration for black males is the drug laws. This situation is not because black males are more likely to use drugs. Black high school seniors report using drugs at a rate that is only three-quarters that of white high school seniors, and white students have about three times the number of emergency room visits for drug overdose; this discrepancy in rates has remained steady (or grown) for over a decade (Western 2006, citing Johnston et al. 2004). Blacks, however, are much more likely than whites to be arrested for drug crimes. At the beginning of the incarceration boom (1970), blacks had twice the arrest rate for drugs as whites. As the drug war intensified with a nationwide trend toward mandatory prison sentences for people convicted of drug crime, the arrest rate for blacks grew much more rapidly than for whites, reaching a peak arrest rate in 1989 that was *four* times that of whites. The gap between white and black arrests has declined since then, but the remaining disparity still makes blacks two and a half times more likely than whites to be arrested for drug crimes (Western 2006). Today's laws ensure that most of these arrests will result in some form of incarceration.

The increasing criminalization of black men has meant that, as a group, black men are stigmatized. Many people assume, even as Jesse Jackson has recently admitted, that young black men are "trouble." This image was exploited by the first George Bush in 1988, when he used the infamous "Willie Horton" ads in his election campaign for U.S. president. At that time, there had already been some state-level efforts made toward imposing mandatory sentencing, but once Bush Sr. was in office, he promptly proposed some of the harshest penalties for nonviolent crime in the nation's history. These new penalties were aimed at enforcing federal drug-trafficking laws, thus criminalizing even more black men and reinforcing an image that helped solidify the stereotype. The social concept of the "dangerous young black man," so deeply ingrained in our nation's consciousness, continues to fuel punitive politics (Bontrager, Bales, and Chiricos 2005; Chiricos, Welch, and Gertz 2004). It helps explain why young black men *without* criminal records find it harder to get entry-level employment than do young white men *with* criminal records (Pager 2007).

This is not just a problem of social imagery. Poor, urban black men, especially school dropouts, live in neighborhoods that have been crushed by poverty. They are the men of those neighborhoods—the fathers, brothers, uncles, and sons. When they go to prison, they join many of their neighbors who have already taken that route. Collectively, over time, their high rates of incarceration become the standard for the neighborhood. Sociologist Peter St. Jean has concluded, on the basis of a nearly five-year ethnography, that these men become "part of a cultural attitude which seemed to treat incarceration as a rite of passage" (personal communication, March 20, 2006).

## Damage to Communities

There is a steadily growing body of literature that sheds light on the consequences of high rates of incarceration for individuals from the poorest communities. The level of concentration is substantial: studies estimate that in some of the most impoverished locations, as many as one-fifth of adult men are behind bars on any given day (Lynch and Sabol 2004a). Because these men stay behind prison bars for only a couple of years at a time (jail terms are much shorter, typically much less than a year), they cycle back into their communities, only to be replaced by other cohorts. Many who leave prison come back in a few months. The cycling of these young men through the prison system becomes a dynamic of the poor neighborhoods, so that a family is hardly ever without a son, uncle, or father who has done prison time (Clear, Rose, and Ryder 2001).

The effects on the individual of going to prison are well-documented. Ex-prisoners earn less money during their lifetimes, find it harder to stay employed, are less likely to marry, and suffer a range of medical and psychological problems (see Western, Patillo, and Weiman, 2004). This is important ecologically as well, because the ubiquity of prison touches *almost everybody* in these neighborhoods. Every family has a member who has limited labor-market options; every family knows someone struggling to stay out of jail, many mothers are raising children whose fathers have a prison record. For children in these neighborhoods, merely having a parent or brother who has gone to prison elevates their risk of doing the same; in this way, incarceration serves as its own breeding ground.

Prison is thus woven into the fabric of these communities, with its stark implications for social networks, social capital, and, ultimately, informal social control. Men who are behind bars are the missing links in the social network of those who remain behind. Since these networks have limited strength to begin with, the widespread reality of prison undermines their ability to provide social capital. And neighborhoods with lots of men behind bars are places with especially low endowments of social capital. Because prison saps the limited economic and interpersonal resources of families with a loved one behind bars (Braman 2004), both the families and the neighborhood stay impoverished.

Another consequence of this dynamic is that there are also diminished levels of informal social control when so many members of a community are behind bars or between prison stays. Child-rearing is less likely to implant delinquency-resistant self controls (Weatherburn and Lind 2001), and the pro-social attitudes that usually insulate youths against breaking the law are less likely to develop when they are raised in places where a lot of men go to prison (Crutchfield 2005). Since a neighborhood's level of *informal* social control is far more important for overall public safety than is formal social control, deficits in informal social controls that result from high levels of incarceration are, in fact, criminogenic. The high incarceration rates in poor communities destabilize the social relationships in these places and help cause crime rather than prevent it (Rose and Clear 1998; Clear et al. 2003).

Because over 90 percent of prisoners are men, the social effects of concentrated incarceration are easily seen when a lot of men go to prison from a particular place. But the smaller number of women who cycle in and out of prison from these same neighborhoods does not mean that their *impact* is as small as their numbers. The role women play in their social networks, social capital, and informal social controls, especially in very poor urban neighborhoods, is thought to be more important, per person, than men. Thus, those much smaller levels of incarceration for women seem to produce the same destabilizing results as for men, with an equivalent pattern of increased crime (George and Lalonde 2005).

## The Lack of Strategic Options

It is hard to see how debates on contemporary penal methods can provide a way out of this morass. There are several reasons that present debates will not help us overcome this problem.

First, most of the legislative action toward increasing punishments for crime offers free political capital. Indeed, these laws are often wildly popular, and the legislators who promote them can draw considerable public support for their efforts. When such laws are narrowly drawn, they affect fewer people. On the other hand, the most draconian laws would produce a large number of felony convictions and, as a result, can prove to be quite expensive. But the fiscal impact of these laws is never as immediate as their political benefits, because the fiscal impact of each new wave of sentence-enhancement laws kicks in only after the penalties imposed under the old laws have expired. If people who are convicted of a repeat felony used to serve, on average, five years in prison, then a new law that doubles the sentence for those crimes is actually "free" for the first five years. By the time the fiscal impact of the new sentence enhancements is felt, the politicians who championed them have often left office. Their replacements are left not only facing the new fiscal realities but also meeting pressure to consider even *more* increases in penalties—to be paid for by the next generation of political leaders.

Some state legislatures have tried to place some natural drag on this tendency to grow the penal system by requiring fiscal-impact statements for new penal code legislation, with the fiscal capacity stipulated to cover new costs included in the legislation. But there is no guarantee that fiscal realities will place a meaningful limit on the drive to use reform of the penal code to gain political capital. For example, in the heyday of the get-tough movement of the 1980s, when Pennsylvania's Sentencing Commission produced its first set of recommendations for new sentencing guidelines, it estimated the additional associated growth in costs that they would incur. The legislature sent back the proposals with instructions to increase the penalties, even though this would increase the estimated costs to taxpayers. There is, however, recent evidence that the severe budget crunch the states faced in the early 2000s has led to some attempts to downsize prison populations (Jacobson 2005).

Second, there is almost no political capital to be gained from an elected official taking on this problem. While there are some quite active prison-reform groups, such as Families Against Mandatory Minimums, there is no large and broad-based citizen's group lobbying for prison reform. There are vocal and active opponents to prison reform, representing victims' groups and other conservative political forces. So, in terms of pure political sapience, a prison reform agenda will not go far.

The travails of California's governor, Arnold Schwarzenegger, in trying to confront the California prison system provide ample evidence that this is an issue not easily confronted. Few governors have arrived in office with a clearer mandate to clean up a broken correctional system. The state's prisons were nearing double capacity, the courts had held that the prisons' health-care system was so bad it violated the rights of prisoners to basic medical care, and a titanic struggle was about to ensue with the correctional officers' union. Recent public referenda had supported drug-treatment alternatives for people arrested on drug charges, and a proposition to rescind the "three strikes" legislation was barely defeated. Governor Schwarzenegger made the corrections system a priority from the day he took office, and penal reformers were optimistic about making progress. Yet within a few months, Schwarzenegger's corrections agenda was in tatters. Talks with the corrections officer's union had broken down, and plans were afoot to rent prison cells in other states to hold California's additional prisoners. That California's brief window of opportunity has appeared to close does not bode well for other elected officials who want to reform prisons (Rau 2007).

Third, and most important, the most commonly suggested reforms in today's penal landscape are unlikely to have much to do with the growth of incarceration, whether they are adopted or not. Rehabilitation programs, even if they become wildly successful, will reduce prison return rates only at the margin. The same goes for the new interest in "reentry programs." Three decades of experience with "alternatives to incarceration" suggest that they, likewise, will not reduce the size of the prison population. These are each good ideas, worth our investment on grounds of humaneness and practicality, but they are largely irrelevant to the central need to slow the growth of incarceration.

There are signs that the seemingly overwhelming political obstacles to reform are becoming less daunting. Crime as an important issue of concern has been missing from public opinion surveys for the last several years, and it has played almost no role in the last three presidential elections. Local leaders, such as Chicago's Mayor Richard Daley and

New York's Attorney General (and now Governor) Eliot Spitzer, have successfully embraced correctional reform as important priorities. President Bush's Second Chance Act has received wide bipartisan support. As Vera Director Michael Jacobson puts it, "the current environment . . . is the most conducive to reform . . . in decades" (2005, 280). There is a sense that politics today provides a different foundation for reform than has been the case for many a year.

Yet there are limits to what can be done within the current paradigm. Partly because there is so much social stigma for young black men, it is hard to use their plight to generate much enthusiasm for penal reform. Aside from a general lack of sympathy for this group—people might be wont to say "you do the crime you do the time"—there is the vexing problem of realistic alternatives. As a group, young men, black and white, who go to prison are responsible for violent crime in vastly disproportionate numbers compared to their fellow citizens. This is not to say that they are all "dangerous"—only about one in five parolees is rearrested for a violent crime (Langan and Levin 2002). But people released from prison account for 6 to 7 percent of all arrests for violent crime during the three years following their release. If we want to do something about the penal crisis for young men, especially black men, leaving them alone is clearly not an option. Yet there is no denying a central truth: the prison population is produced by sentencing policy, and the problem of mass incarceration cannot be addressed without changing sentencing law and practice.

In the end, we cannot reform sentencing procedures without reconceptualizing the correctional project itself. It goes without saying that the narrow range of concepts about corrections that we hold currently cannot help. Phrases such as "getting smarter rather than tougher," "providing more programs," and "investing in reentry" are not bad ideas, they are just irrelevant to the problem of mass incarceration of people from poor communities. To deal with that problem, we will have to make community well-being a central objective of our penal system. We will have to embrace an idea of community justice.

# Incarceration and Crime

2

There is a commonsense idea that the size of the prison population has something to do with how much crime there is. It would be silly to argue otherwise. Prisons house people who were active enough in their criminal behavior to be caught and serious enough in their crimes to be sent there. Common sense tells us that while they are behind bars, their criminal activity is interrupted. Further, having so many people behind bars seems likely to convince at least some of us not to take the risk of committing a crime in the first place.

We thus think that prisons prevent crime in two ways: incapacitation and deterrence. *Incapacitation* occurs when the crimes a person would have committed are averted because the person is in prison. As Ben Wattenberg put it, "a thug in jail can't shoot my sister" (DiIulio 1995). To achieve incapacitation, prison sentences must incarcerate a person during the active years of criminality, with release occurring only after the person has "aged out" of the crime-prone years. *Deterrence* occurs when the thought of going to prison is sufficiently undesirable that people shape their behavior to comply with the law in order to avoid going there. To enhance the deterrent power of prison, we must make prison sentences a more likely consequence of committing criminal acts, and we must make the likely unpleasantness of those sentences greater than the likely benefits of the crimes. These simple ideas offer a kind of face validity that cannot easily be disregarded.

If it is absurd to think that prisons have *nothing* to do with crime, it is equally difficult to determine precisely how prisons *do* affect crime. It may be that locking up a prisoner averts the crimes that prisoner might have committed had he been free. It might also be that the desire to avoid prison makes some people decide against the temptation to engage in crime. But it cannot be the case that these are the only—even the main—ways prisons are related to crime. Indeed, this is the only conclusion we can draw from the generation-long experiment in greater use of imprisonment in the United States.

Figure 2.1, which tracks changes in incarceration rates and crime rates between 1970 and 2004, displays that relationship in its broadest pattern (King, Mauer, and Young, 2005). As the figure shows, the U.S prison population began to rise in 1973 and grew every year thereafter. The crime rate, on the other hand, behaved quite differently. Since 1973, there have been three periods of growth in crime and three periods of dropping rates of crime. In all, there have been about as many years with an increase in crime over the previous year as there have been years when crime decreased from the prior year. During this period of high-incarceration policy, the rate of state-level imprisonment grew from just under 84 (per 100,000 citizens) in 1972 to 432 in 2004—an overall growth of 400 percent. The crime rate, as measured by the FBI crime index, started out at just under 4,000 crimes (per 100,000 citizens) and finished the period at just over that number—a growth rate of about 3 percent. Whatever the relationship between prison population and crime rate, it is not a simple one of more prisoners meaning more crime prevention.

In fact, there is a two-way relationship between imprisonment and crime. That is, in times of rising crime rates, we would expect the number of prisoners to grow, if for no other reason than that the number of candidates for prison has grown. But if the idea of prison suppresses crime, then we would expect any growth in the prison population to be accompanied by a reduction in crime. The fact that the actual pattern has, for this period, been substantially more complicated means that the crime-suppression capacity of prisons is not straightforward. How did the United States have over 30 years of sustained growth in imprisonment in the face of periodic fluctuations in crime? The answer to this question takes us on the first step toward understanding the limits of imprisonment as a technique for crime control.

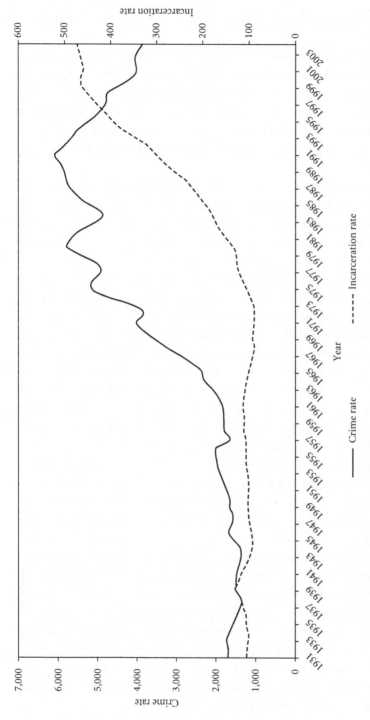

**Figure 2.1** U.S. Unified Crime Report (UCR) crime trends and sentenced prisoners in federal and state institutions, 1931–2004, showing an increasing incarceration rate and a rising and falling crime rate. Rate of crime and rate of incarceration given are per 100,000 resident population.

## How Changes in Incarceration Ought to Affect Crime Control

The prison population count on a given day is produced by two statistics: the number of people who go in and the length of their stay. All else being equal, prison populations grow if there are more prisoners going in or if those going in stay longer. To the extent that more prisoners go in *and* stay longer, prison growth is accelerated. An assessment of prison population growth in the United States shows the importance of these dynamics.

Blumstein and Beck (2005) have argued that the 33 years of growth in imprisonment can be broken down into three different policy periods, roughly corresponding to each decade. The 1970s was a period of slow increase in incarceration (about 40 percent) accompanied by a similar increase in crime (about 50 percent). During this period, most of the increase in the number of prisoners can be attributed to a growth in crime: there were simply more felony convictions available to result in more prison commitments. The 1980s began and ended with about the same crime rate as the previous decade (crime first dropped by about 20 percent over four years, but then by 1991 it had returned to its 1980 rate). Yet the state-level incarceration rate more than doubled, from about 140 to about 310 per 100,000 citizens. During this period, the growing incarceration rate was due, in equal parts, to growth in the length of time served and growth in the probability of a prison commitment for those convicted of a felony. Most of this latter change was a consequence of the increased likelihood of a prison sentence for drug felonies (often, but not solely, as a result of laws that mandated prison time for these crimes). The third period, essentially the 1990s, was a time during which prison populations continued to grow, though less rapidly (an increase of about 80 percent between 1990 and 2000), while the crime rate was steadily dropping (about 30 percent). There was an increase in the rate of felony sentences to prison, and despite declining crime rates, there was an increase in the number of people entering prison each year. Thus, the prison populations grew during this period partly as a consequence of increased admissions, but also because of increases in the amount of time served by those going to prison. (As an aside, a new era may be upon us. Beginning around the year 2000, growth in incarceration seemed to be slowing down, and the big drop in crime also seemed to be ending.)

Regarding the period between 1980 and 2001, Blumstein and Beck conclude:

> Growth in incarceration is attributable first to the 10-fold increase since 1980 in incarceration rates for drug offenses. Beyond drugs, no contribution to that increase is associated with increases in crime rate or increases in police effectiveness as measured by arrests per crime. Rather, the entire growth is attributable to sentencing broadly defined—roughly equally to increases in commitments to prison per arrest ... and to increases in time served in prison, including time served for parole violation. (2005:50)

The two sources of prison population growth have important implications for crime control. For instance, the probability that a given crime will result in a prison commitment is closely associated with the idea of deterrence. Theories of deterrence hold that people modify their behavior as they grow convinced that a negative consequence is likely. As prison commitment rates grow, the deterrent power of prison is expected to grow. Obviously, any time a person goes to prison, there is an expected incapacitation effect. But the degree of incapacitation is thought to be more closely connected to the length of stay in prison. As the period of time a person is removed from society grows, so does the period of time when that person cannot be committing crimes in society.

Applying Blumstein and Beck's three periods, we would expect that in the 1970s, when prison population growth was mostly a consequence of increases in crime, the deterrence power of the prison system would have been roughly stable. In the 1980s, prison populations grew partly as a consequence of increased nondrug felony convictions and partly as a result of greater likelihood of a prison term for an arrest, and significantly as a consequence of increased incarceration rates for drug offenses. If deterrence were at work then, we would expect fewer people to engage in drug crimes. In the 1990s, when prison growth was due much more to increases in the length of prison stays, we would expect incapacitation to have had a greater effect. People who were inclined to engage in crime would have been locked up longer, released when they were older, and thus less prone to committing a crime again.

The data on arrests for drug crimes and the data on age of commitment to prison provide a simple test of these expected outcomes. Regarding the former, arrests for drug crimes not only failed to decline but actually increased almost fivefold between 1970 and 2004 (Bureau of Justice Statistics 2006). Regarding the latter, if longer prison terms reduced crime through incapacitation, then we would expect prison commitments to have been for younger people, as the older criminal population sat behind bars. But the average age of prison commitments actually *rose* during this time, especially for those receiving long sentences (Mauer, King, and Young 2004). We would also expect that the arrest rate of those released from prison would have gone down, if for no other reason than that they were older when they get out. Again, the evidence is not very persuasive: in 1983, about 62 percent of people released from prison were arrested again within three years, but for those released in 1994, the proportion had grown to 68 percent (Hughes, Wilson, and Beck 2006). Thus, the average age at prison commitment has not become younger, and the failure rate on community supervision has actually *increased*.

This is a simple first example of a theme that runs through this chapter. As we look for evidence that incarceration reduces crime, we find weak results more often than otherwise. It is not that the evidence fails to prove that prisons reduce crime, but rather that the effects are small, contrary to expectations, or the findings are in other ways problematic. The inescapable conclusion is that incarceration is not a simple antidote for crime. Far from it, prison has a problematic relationship to crime control—so much so that the desire for crime control, by itself, cannot reasonably be used to justify expanded use of the prison system in the United States.

### Prisons as Means of Crime Control

When it comes to deterring crime and incapacitating criminals, the modern prison is a blunt instrument. It does not offer a panorama of finely calibrated experiences designed to surgically counteract the forces of evil. Rather, when a prison sentence is imposed, the action is basically a one-size-fits-all decision to remove someone from his or her community. The only matters to be determined are the kind of prison experience it will be and its duration.

Studies of the crime-reduction capacity of the typical prison thus consider the deterring and incapacitating effects of these two elements of imprisonment. Yet there are almost no true experiments among these studies. For mostly obvious reasons, researchers do not randomly assign various people convicted of crimes to different lengths and types of imprisonment and then observe the impact of these differences. As a result, the effects of length and type of prison sentence cannot be directly observed; rather, conclusions have to be derived from social science models that estimate true effects; and as we shall see, different models provide different estimates. These models all compare the *potential* or *inferred* benefits of prison sentences compared to other types of sanctions. They compare longer prison sentences to shorter ones—typically within some small range of time that is reasonable for the offense. And they compare different levels of intentional discomfort *during* the sentences, usually assessing the effects of harsher prison experiences compared to less onerous ones.

## Deterrence

Deterrence is a simple idea with important nuances. The simple idea is that people want to avoid pain and pursue pleasure—an assertion that is unremarkable at face value. From this simple idea people conclude that if prison is made painful, people will be better persuaded to avoid it. What makes the idea of deterrence complicated is that the ratio between two uncertainties—the pleasure of crime and the pains of incarceration— varies from person to person. Pain sufficient to persuade one person to avoid the possibility of prison may not be enough to persuade another person. That fact does not invalidate prison as a deterrent; it just suggests that prison is not a panacea.

Much is made, for example, of the fact that in London in the 1800s, pickpockets worked the crowds assembled to watch public hangings of pickpockets. Ernest van den Haag (1975) has wisely questioned whether there would have been *more* pickpockets had the crowd been assembled to view, say, a flogging or a public berating instead of a hanging. He reminds us that some people may be deterred by the threat of a hanging while others are not. Hanging is, by this view, a beneficial crime-prevention tool but not an all-encompassing one.

Why does the threat of punishment as severe as public hanging fail to deter the most intransigent thieves? Deterrence theorists have suggested two possible answers. The first is strategic, suggesting that deterrence fails as a consequence of being supplied in insufficient doses. The second is more fundamental, suggesting that deterrence fails because the context within which it operates limits its capacity to inform action.

Deterrence proponents recognize that the human trait of intransigence is variably distributed across the population. Some potential lawbreakers think they will not be caught, or they have trouble imagining the likelihood of punishment, or they do not see how the painful experiences of others have any relevance for their own choices. Moreover, some rational calculators may incorporate the cost of punishment into their decisions and still feel that crime is a preferable option. For these people, crime pays well—at least in comparison to the other options reasonably available to them. A version of this idea is the well-worn argument of "three hots and a cot," meaning that for poor people who face limited life prospects, prison is not that much of a step down from everyday life and it certainly is not enough of a reduction in the quality of life to overcome the temptations of illicit gain.

These limitations do not present a fatal problem for deterrence theory. Its advocates have an easy answer: make punishment more severe. If a certain level of punishment is sufficient to deter some potential lawbreakers but is so low that it leaves others undecided, an increase in punishment will change the thinking of at least some of the undecided. The punitive solution is thus an apt reply to the most prominent challenges facing deterrence as an idea. This is one of the reasons policy makers made punishments more severe in the 1970s and 1980s, even in the face of crime rates that continued to rise. To the proponents of deterrence, increases in crime were not evidence that punishment had weak deterrent power but, rather, that punishment was not severe enough to deter. What they called for was not a new approach to fighting crime but a way to ratchet up the existing strategy.

Enhancing the severity of the penalties for crime is only one of the mechanisms of deterrence. Theorists point out that the *certainty* and *celerity* of punishments also matter. By certainty is meant the likelihood that a given decision to break the law will result in a penalty, however severe. By celerity is meant the speed with which the penalty is imposed. Logic holds that when penalties are more certain to be imposed and are more rapidly imposed, they are more likely to deter. This is true, but it highlights the problem of operational criminal justice. According to the National Criminal Victimization Survey, about 60 percent of the

25 million victimizations in 2002 were never reported to the police. In 2002, there were about 1.8 million violent victimizations reported, with about 600,000 convictions for violent crimes resulting in about 150,000 sentences to prison (BJS 2006). Even with very friendly assumptions, to achieve meaningful increases in the likelihood of being penalized for doing a crime, there need to be wholesale changes in the rate at which victims report crimes and the police clear them with arrests. It is therefore doubtful if the certainty of punishment can ever be increased except at the margins. The same can be said for celerity, because almost all the mechanical and practical constraints of criminal- justice procedure result in delays that cannot be eradicated within the existing requirements of due process of law. It is perhaps for these reasons that most penal reform initiatives designed to achieve greater deterrence focuses on the severity of the penalty rather than on the certainty or celerity—the latter two elements of criminal deterrence cannot easily be leveraged.

Further, critics of deterrence have suggested a limitation that is a direct challenge to the deterrence model and might explain why increased punishments have done so little in the way of crime reduction. Lawrence Sherman has called this the Defiance Hypothesis (1993). He argues that potential lawbreakers are not merely rational risk-reward calculators, but are also moral and cultural reasoners. Borrowing from the work of legal theorists such as Tom Tyler (1990), Sherman has said that when a potential lawbreaker sees a sanction as unfair, and experiences its imposition as a personal rejection rather than a consequence of a violation of law, then the threat and experience of severe punishment generate not compliance with the law but defiance of it. Sherman's critique of deterrence is fundamental, for it suggests that the limited potency of punishment cannot be overcome merely by increasing the penalty, because the heavier penalty will be perceived as unfairly harsh, generating further defiance.

## Studying Deterrence

The simple idea of deterrence—that people will mold their behavior to avoid the painful consequences of the criminal justice system—is complicated by a host of practical and theoretical considerations. Studying the effectiveness of deterrence faces all of those practical problems mentioned earlier, to which may be added the difficult mechanics of studying complex social phenomena. For example, penal codes vary in the amount of punishment they impose, but how can these variations be linked to the amount of crime that results, when we know that states *also* vary in such factors as poverty and inequality and we believe *these* also contribute to crime. In essence, how do we isolate the effects of a penalty when so many social factors also cause crime? Likewise, how do we know the relative importance of punishment severity, when certainty and celerity are also thought to be important, and the latter vary from place to place? In short, when we see differences in crime rates, how do we link them to differences in the penalties for crime?

Nothing intrigues the social scientist more than an important question that is hard to penetrate. So the problem of evaluating deterrence has motivated a substantial body of empirical work. Studies tend to be of two general types: surveys/experiments and statistical assessments of patterns of crime and punishment.

The surveys and laboratory experiments are useful because they allow the scientist to control for certain social factors that can confound the ability to interpret results. For example, respondents can be given a certain crime–penalty scenario to determine how much of a penalty is required for subjects to overcome the temptation of committing a crime. Similarly, laboratory experiments allow the scientist to cancel out the effects of real-world uncertainties and to isolate factors that can be used to evaluate the importance of severity of penalties as compared to, say, their certainty. These techniques enable investigators relatively easily to isolate the deterrence factor in which they are interested and measure its impact. Surveys and laboratory experiments are thus useful because the investigators control extraneous factors. But they tend to create conditions that are more or less different from the real world in which crime and punishments occur. They measure the way people *reason* about crime or choose it in pristine settings. They do not measure the way people *actually* behave in the social settings that give rise to crime.

Statistical assessments of crime and punishment patterns have the advantage of providing data about the way people actually behave in the routine world. Actual crime rates and punishment levels are measured and correlated. The problem with these studies is that they have to *model* the effects of various confounding factors on the correlation between the level of crime and the amount of punishment, and this often requires assumptions about society and people's behavior that may be more or less problematic. It is rarely possible to include in the model *all* the potentially confounding factors.

Each kind of study has its advantages. Surveys and laboratory studies tend to give a good picture of the decision-making processes that underlie the way penalties influence decisions to commit crimes. But the way people behave reflects their perceptions of the world, and the effect of penalties on behavior is shaped by those perceptions in ways that surveys and experiments have trouble taking into account. A nuanced understanding of deterrence comes with considering these studies in light of their strengths.

For our purposes, deterrence investigators ask four important questions: (1) How does a prison sanction compare to other (nonprison) sanctions? (2) How much specific deterrence is produced by increasing the likelihood of a prison sentence for a crime? (3) How do longer prison terms compare to shorter prison terms? (4) How do more harsh prison terms compare to less harsh terms?

### Studies of Prison versus Other Sanctions Such as Probation (Specific Deterrence)

*Specific deterrence* refers to the ability of a sanction to deter the person who has experienced it from continuing to engage in criminal behavior. With recidivism rates so high for those who leave prison, the question of the deterrent power of a prison sentence seems slightly academic. Langan and Levin (2002) studied over 200,000 prisoners released in 1994. They report that of those who "were serving...their first-ever prison sentence,...63.8% were rearrested following their release. Among those who had been in prison at least once before,...73.5% were rearrested" (1). Hughes, Wilson, and Beck (2001) found a similar pattern—that parolees with prior incarceration actually did worse than parolees leaving prison for the first time. Gottfredson (1999) followed for 20 years a cohort of people sentenced in Essex County, New Jersey, and found that 70 percent of them were rearrested at least once during that period. Prisons clearly do not communicate a message about the need to conform to the law that is fully understood and accepted.

Yet as van den Haag reminds us about the pickpockets who worked public hangings, the question is not the recidivism rate *per se* for individuals who are incarcerated on felony crimes, but how that rate compares to people convicted of felonies who did *not* go to prison. Indeed, studies of probation have found very high rates of recidivism, as high as a 65 percent rearrest rate in California (Petersilia et al. 1985) in a three-year follow-up. California may be a special case, as other researchers have reported much lower recidivism rates for probationers elsewhere (Vito, 1986).

Nonetheless, the question is how probation failure rates compare to prison failure rates. This is not a pure deterrence question, of course, since both probationers and prisoners are penalized. Moreover, it is not obvious that probationers and prisoners can easily be compared. Presumably, prisoners are more likely to have been convicted of more serious crimes, and they might require more punishment to be deterred from further crime. The best method would be to randomly assign some people convicted of felonies to prison and some to probation, but that kind of study has never been done, at least because it is unethical, if not for other reasons.

Absent a strong experimental design, one of the methods for determining how well a program works is to compare systematically the various study results across a large number of studies, averaging the effects. This approach, referred to as meta-analysis, was used by Smith, Goggin and Gendreau (2002) to summarize the significance of 117 different studies of recidivism rates. They found no evidence of a difference in recidivism rates between prison sentences and sentences to probation, and that null effect held for samples of adults, juveniles, and women.

There have been a few notable attempts to create comparable groups of prisoners and probationers by matching them (in one way or another) on the basis of their personal characteristics and criminal history. These studies then follow up the matched samples to see how they perform. The results have been fairly consistent across different types of samples and different analytical strategies. When comparing probationers and prisoners who look much alike, follow-up studies find recidivism rates that are either not different or are *lower* for probationers. The former was true of a comparison of prisoners to a sample especially diverted from Florida prisons (Smith and Akers 1993) and a large 20-year follow-up of prisoners, probationers, and those who went to jail in New Jersey (Gottfredson 1999). The latter was found in a study by Petersilia et al. (1986), comparing a matched sample of California probationers and prisoners. The study found that probationers had lower rearrest rates than the prisoners, as Dejong (1997) found in a comparison of pretrial releasees to jail detainees. Spohn and Holleran (2002) studied a Kansas City sample of people convicted of drug felonies, and also found that people on probation had lower rearrest rates than people who went to prison.

This last study is interesting in several important respects. First, the authors consider felony drug offenders, the group for whom the growth in incarceration in the 1980s was most marked. Second, they "used several different measures of recidivism, tested for the effect of imprisonment on different types of offenders... and examined recidivism rates for a relatively long follow-up period" (Spohn and Holleran 2002:350). They find "compelling evidence that offenders who are sentenced to prison have higher recidivism rates and recidivate more quickly than do prisoners who are placed on probation" (329).

There may, then, be a difference between probation and prison in deterring criminal behavior. If there is, probation gets the advantage. Yet this is not what the deterrence hypothesis would suggest. There is no room in the logic of deterrence theory for a preference for probation over prison. There can be little doubt that prison is a worse experience than probation, so deterrence theorists could explain a finding of "no difference" by saying that prison sanctions need to be toughened up. There is also the argument that comparisons between prison sentences and probation are methodologically problematic. But there is solid evidence to suggest that probationers do "better" than prisoners. Prison—at least when compared to probation—does something to people that damages their chances of staying out of prison.

There are two possible explanations for this difference in deterrence effect. The first is obvious and has been the subject of much discussion: being in prison is a brutalizing experience, and people who are subjected to these experiences find it harder to adjust to free society again. To make this assertion is to join a long list of prison reformers, going back at least to John Howard and the 1700s and continuing almost without interruption through the luminaries of the 1800s and 1900s. None of them would be surprised to hear that people exposed to prison do less well adjusting to society than do those who have been exposed to a different kind of sanction. The uneasy conclusion from this thinking is that prison, far from being a deterrent, disables those who experience it.

The other explanation is cousin to the brutalization hypothesis: once exposed to prison, the person learns how to adjust to prison life and the fears it would provoke are no longer as salient. This idea leaves open the possibility that prison is not distasteful enough, and we will return to this idea in a few paragraphs.

*Studies of the Probability of a Sentence to Prison*

If the actual experience of prison may have limited deterrent value for those who experience it, what about general deterrence—the power of the threat of such a penalty to influence the behavior of people who have not yet experienced prison? In deterrence research, analysts measure the impact of different *rates* of incarceration on crime. Many of these researchers use surveys or do work in the laboratory. They try to control for potential confounding influences by designing them out of their studies, either by providing an experiment in which these confounding influences (such as the economic or political situation) are not present, or by specifying them as conditions in a survey scenario. Other studies compare jurisdictions that vary in the likelihood of incarceration for a felony crime. The researchers posit that, all things being equal, areas that make prison more likely will experience less crime as a consequence of general deterrence. A final kind of study investigates what people report as their perceived *risks* of being punished, so as to determine if risk is correlated with rates of involvement in crime.

There are two major conceptual problems in these studies. First, much of the research rests on measuring *perceptions* of the risk of being punished. It goes without saying that a person's *perceptions* may well influence his choices, but those perceptions may also be inaccurate in various ways. That is, people may think that they are more likely—or less likely—to be caught and punished, yet those thoughts may bear little relation to what the actual risks are. Thus, it is not clear that changing *actual* risks of punishment will result in a change of *perceived* risks. Second, studies that investigate *actual* variations in rates of incarceration confound a potential incapacitation effect with a general deterrence effect. That is, places that impose prison sentences may more readily have lower crime rates, not as a result of general deterrence, but because more of the potentially active lawbreakers are being incapacitated while they are behind bars. We give sustained attention to this idea in the next section on incapacitation, but because studies of higher sanction rates posit deterrence effects, they are worth dealing with separately.

It is not necessary to review here all of the various and diverse studies of deterrence. Several reliable reviews already exist (see, for example, Nagin 1998 and Paternoster 1987). In general, these reviews of deterrence research find evidence of a general deterrence effect based on risk perceptions; that is, people who perceive punishments for crime to be more likely or more severe are less likely to say they have (or will) will engage in crime. This result is found in simulations that systematically shift the likelihood and severity of sanctions (Klepper and Nagin 1989) and in studies of self-reported perceptions of sanctions (Nagin 1988). Interviews of active burglars show that the likelihood of apprehension affects their decision whether or not to burglarize a particular home (Wright and Decker 1994). The way perceptions of punishment shape criminal conduct is not certain, however. There is some dispute as to how these perceptions are affected by *actual* experiences of sanction likelihood for those who have successfully engaged in crime. In panel surveys, it seems that risk perceptions of punishment change based on experience, and active criminals fail to be deterred by punishment after a period of successfully engaging in crime (Paternoster 1983, 1985). There is also evidence that there is "no significant association between perceptions of punishment levels and actual levels, . . . implying that increases in punishment levels do not routinely reduce crime through general deterrence mechanisms" (Kleck et al. 2005:623). It is clear that people who think they will probably get caught are less likely to commit crimes. What is not clear is how this perception is related to personal experiences and perceptions of the *actual* level of punishment.

Perceptions, then, are one thing and actual experiences are another. Economists who have sought to investigate the latter approach punishment as a "cost" of committing a crime. They calculate the likelihood of going to prison per offense, which they refer to as the "expected payoff" of a crime. They then correlate the changes in crime rate with changes in this expected payoff. There are several ways of doing this, but a good illustration is provided by economist Morgan Reynolds (1996). He calculates the expected prison stay per crime for people convicted of felonies in Texas counties and then correlates this with crime rates. Reynolds finds that counties with higher prison stays per crime have less crime, and he concludes that this is evidence of deterrence at work. This result is not unusual for studies of this type. Yet this "cost of crime" model fails to take into account the fact that the likelihood of being apprehended for a crime is a far more important determinant of a person's evaluation of penalty risk than is the punishment severity, and has a powerful impact on the "expected payoff" of a crime. For instance, a situation in which 30% of burglaries result in an arrest leading to a prison sentence of 1 year has the same "expected payoff" as one in which 2% are arrested and get 15 years each. These situations have the same payoff, but they would likely have quite different deterrent power. As Nagin and Pogarsky put it, "punishment certainty is far more consistently found to deter crime than punishment severity" (2000:865).

So here is the overall problem: perceptions of punishment risk seem to matter, but people's perception of their risk is neither accurate nor is it related to official sanctions. Moreover, those who commit crimes without being caught seem to adjust their perceptions of risk downward, to the point that criminal activity may seem a reasonable choice. Actual risk may also matter, but it is very hard to affect by obtaining more arrests. The probability of arrest for serious crimes has been more or less stable for 30 years (Blumstein and Beck 2005). The probability of confinement, once someone is convicted of a felony, has changed dramatically, from less than one in three cases in the 1970s to more than two in three today. But because most criminal actions never result in an arrest, the event-specific probabilities of being punished remain quite low. In each case, the foundation needed for efficient deterrence by controlling the *risk* of punishment is missing or attenuated.

### Studies of the Harshness of Penalties

Because it is so difficult to influence the likelihood of punishment for crimes, some have thought that making the *experience* of punishment more onerous will deter repeat crime. This is an argument for *specific deterrence*—that making punishments more unpleasant will convince people who experience them to refrain from committing the crime again. Advocates of this view face two problems. First, there is again the problem of recidivism rates: about two-thirds of those released from to prison are rearrested, and half of them are reincarcerated within three years (Langan and Levin 2002). Second, there is the repeated finding that people who go to prison for *longer periods* have higher recidivism rates (Smith, Goggin, and Gendreau 2002; Gottfredson 1999). Still, those who want tougher sentences may say that prison is simply not a difficult enough experience, so "more" of this kind of weak sanction would not matter much. So what if we made prison more difficult?

The best example of this line of reasoning is the "boot camp" prison movement. This idea, which became popular during the Clinton administration, was that prison time was "easy" time, and people who did easy time had no reluctance to repeat the experience. What we needed instead, the argument went, was "hard" time that was physically and emotionally demanding. There was also a "rehabilitative" argument for boot camps: that a major underpinning of criminality is the undisciplined life. If prison time could be redesigned to teach discipline, the people who go to prison would develop the tools that could form the foundation for a life of productive work. Boot camp advocates often recalled the character formation that occurs in military boot camps, and they sought to recreate that experience in penal institutions. As a high priority of the Clinton Justice Department, dozens of federally funded boot camps were set up across the nation. Evaluations were a standard part of the package underwriting these projects, and so few correctional programs have received the level of study afforded to this idea.

The results of the boot-camp experiment have been notoriously bad (for a summary, see MacKenzie 2006). With isolated exceptions (Kurlycheck and Kempinen 2006), studies find that boot-camp graduates fare no better than non-boot-campers after release, and often they seem to do worse. A few studies find that boot-camp attendees show evidence of slight changes in their attitudes, but the fact that these changes seem not to translate into behavioral changes on the streets makes the case for boot camps almost silly; at best, they produce a more well-adjusted criminal. A few boot camps saved money when some people were diverted from regular prisons to shorter stays in the camps, but this kind of diversionary boot camp was the exception rather than the rule. Overall, the idea that a tougher prison experience will better deter those who experience it— either as a matter of punitiveness or as a softer idea of rehabilitation—has simply not panned out.

Other forms of "tough" prison time have not been evaluated with anything near the rigor of the boot-camp movement. There have been plenty of these other ideas, however. We've seen a rebirth of chain gangs working alongside the roads in some southern state prison systems, in some places prisoners have been made to wear pink underwear, and some prisons have prohibited such amenities as smoking and weight lifting. The thrust of these wide-ranging indignities is to make prison time as unpalatable as possible, as a way of convincing those who experience it to give up their lives of crime. It is hard to imagine that this kind of thinking will lead to anything but more brutal prisons, and the track record for brutality is not good. Finckenauer's (1982) classic study of the "scared straight" program serves as a model lesson. Juvenile court judges in New Jersey thought they could scare young delinquents out of crime by exposing them to adult prisoners, who would taunt them and threaten them about what would happen if they ended up in prison if they did not mend their ways. The kids who were "scared" did not go straight—they did worse than those who were not exposed to the scare.

A study by Chen and Shapiro (2006) investigates the impact of routine prison conditions on recidivism among federal prisoners. Because the federal classification system determines the prison conditions to which a person is assigned, researchers are able to test whether the onerousness of the prison setting has any impact on the rate of recidivism. Their findings that harsher prison conditions are associated with significantly more post-release crime "... are difficult to reconcile with policies in which specific deterrence or in-prison rehabilitation play a central role" (132).

Making prison tougher seems more likely to backfire than to pay off in reformed prisoners. The result is not people who are determined to avoid prison because it has been so unpleasant, but merely a larger body of people who have been treated harshly by the state. Some scholars have speculated that the long-term prospects of these tough methods are not merely neutral, but are actually negative (see Nagin 1998; Sherman 1993), because when people are treated badly, they are more likely to learn the norms of bad treatment than the benefits of compliance with the law.

The idea that people obey the law because they are afraid of its power is deeply ingrained but simplistic. Fear of the consequences of breaking the law undoubtedly leads many of us to refrain from crime. Those who have broken the law are not made more compliant by heavy-handed enforcement, however. The irony is that fairness, not toughness, seems a more important quality for engendering compliance with the law (Tyler 1990). The worrisome question is whether harsh treatment not only fails to reform its target but also undermines the legitimacy of the law itself.

People report that their behavior is shaped by their understanding of the sanctions they face for the choices they make. And people are not wholly illogical in the decisions they make. This basic fact gives deterrence theorists great optimism in deciding how to devise penalties in order to minimize the benefits of criminal behavior. Some of this optimism has meant that the deterrence theorists place significant value on the use of prison. They reason that if people shape their behavior based on the likely payoff of those choices, it is wise to organize prison policy to maximize the negative payoff for engaging in crime.

As we have seen, the question is not *whether* deterrence exists as an idea; the question is what ability there is to enhance deterrence by expanding the use of imprisonment. Here, the evidence is not as encouraging as deterrence theorists might want. *Specific deterrence* gets little empirical support. People who are exposed to prison do not behave much differently from people who are exposed to less onerous correctional programs, and they may even behave worse. Multiple exposures to prison appear to have little effect. More brutal experiences in prison also have little effect, and again may be counterproductive. The entire deterrence agenda hangs on *general deterrence*, or the impact of the threat of prison. On this, one recent comprehensive review concluded that "a reasonable assessment of the research to date—with a particular focus on studies conducted in the past decade—is that sentence severity has no effect on the level of crime in society. It is time to accept the null hypothesis [that penalties do not deter]" (Doob and Webster 2003).

The threat of imprisonment for crime has grown dramatically in the United States. In 1985, the averaged time served for those released from prison on a robbery conviction was 32 months; by 1993, it was 46 months; and in 2002, it was 53 months (Beck, personal communication; National Corrections Reporting Program 2002). Economic models of the crime-suppression impact of this growth in time served consistently find evidence that it worked, though it is impossible to know whether the impact results from deterrence or from incapacitation (which we consider in the next section). There are reasons to doubt that deterrence is at work. In recent years, the per-crime increase in prison time served has been produced, *not* by increasing the chances that a person will experience that penalty, but by increasing the penalty a person experiences once caught. The per-crime expected penalty becomes a matter, not of certainty of punishment, but of severity of punishment. All deterrence theorists agree that altering the severity of the penalties for committing a crime has less promise than altering its certainty.

Even in the best-case scenario, however, there seems little play in the certainty side of the punishment argument. Police are not likely to clear more felonies; the felony clearance rate has remained stable for almost as long as we have been measuring it. The likelihood of a prison sentence for each felony conviction has grown to a point that it now may be increased only at the margins. Any wholesale change in the likelihood of prison, given a conviction, will take place only with a near eradication of sentences for probation and other nonprison sanctions—an exceedingly unlikely (and also unwise) possibility. To the extent that there is a deterrent effect for imprisonment, it is hard to envision how much of an increase in deterrence can be squeezed out of the law under currently feasible scenarios. As Doob and Webster (2003) have observed:

> Simply put, if penalty structures are irrelevant to potential offenders, it does not matter how severe they might be. Or more broadly, the deterrence process—as a perceptual model—is not nearly as simple as that which one might assume or the economist might contemplate when employing utility functions to explain why the chicken crossed the road against the red light. (190)

There is another issue, one that has worried deterrence theorist Daniel Nagin: the problem of diminishing returns. The idea of deterrence rests, at least a bit, on the social disapprobation that the sanction implies. Deterrence works, ironically, partly because punishment is not common. The uncommon nature of public punishment means that fear of receiving the stigma of punishment is one of the main mechanisms by which the threat works. Nagin and Pogorsky (2000) make the point that this less tangible result of punishment—what they call "extra-legal consequences"—are of considerable importance in making the threat matter. From this basis, many observers worry that as punishments become more common, they become less stigmatizing and their threat may thus become less behavior-shaping. In the next chapter, we consider how U.S. growth in punishment has been concentrated among poor men of color, to the point that it is almost a commonplace experience. As punishment becomes the norm, even diehard deterrence advocates agree that its power to influence behavior diminishes. Under today's regime of the prison, to what extent have we already reached a point of diminished returns?

## Incapacitation

The idea of incapacitation is a simple one: people who are behind bars cannot commit crimes. To measure the degree of incapacitation, it seems all that is necessary is to estimate the number of crimes people would have committed had they not been locked up. It is, of course, not that simple. There are three problems with incapacitation as a theory and three problems with it in practice.

### Problems with Incapacitation as a Theory

It turns out that people behind bars report high rates of involvement in crime prior to their incarceration, and this is a promising fact for advocates of incapacitation. All things being equal, if people who are locked up had high rates of criminal activity when they were on the streets, then it is plausible to assume that high rates of criminal activity would be prevented by locking them up. The number of crimes an active criminal commits in a year is an unknown that scholars who study incapacitation refer to as *lambda*. The bigger the lambda, it is thought, the greater the incapacitation effects of imprisonment.

One of the first studies to try to estimate lambda, carried out by a team from Rand, did so by asking a sample of serious male California prisoners the number of nondrug crimes they had committed in the year prior to their current incarceration (Petersilia, Greenwood, and Lavin 1978). The estimates were astoundingly high; even after eliminating the highest numbers as unlikely (some numbers were so high that they were not credible under the most bountiful criteria), the average number of crimes this group admitted to having committed was thought to be as high as 287 per year. The researchers concluded that this provided evidence of a potentially enormous incapacitation effect. A later paper by one of these researchers suggested that by focusing on a few factors that identified the most criminally active in their sample, they could simultaneously reduce the size of the prison population and decrease crime (Greenwood and Abrahamse 1982)

The results caught lightning in a bottle, coming as they did at a time of severe prison crowding nationwide. A National Institute of Justice economist, Edwin Zedlewski (1987), used the Rand study estimates to show that the growth in U.S. prisoners, which at the time was only a fraction of what it is today, had *both* reduced crime and saved tax dollars over and above the expenditures on new prison beds. The incapacitation movement hit something of an apex, when this official government report of the Reagan administration promised that more prison beds would reduce crime and save money.

If these numbers seemed too good to be true, they were. At the time, *both* the prison population and the crime rate were going up. If the new prisoners represented reductions in crime, it was hard to see how. Indeed, Franklin Zimring and Gordon Hawkins's (1988) analysis, which they entitled bitingly, "The New Mathematics of Prison Expansion," showed that if Zedlewski's numbers were correct, the growth in the number of prisoners from 1971 should have resulted in a such a substantial reduction in crime that the United States would, within a few years, have experienced a *negative* crime rate—which, obviously, it did not.

Why are these optimistic estimates of crime diverted by prison expansion so far off? There are three reasons, two of which are a kind of replacement. First, many (perhaps most) crimes are committed by young men in groups, and locking up one member of the group may not stop the remainder from continuing their criminal activity. Indeed, losing a member of the group to prison may not only leave the group's criminality undisturbed, it may also encourage the group to recruit a new member to take the recently incarcerated person's place. In this sense, imprisonment can actually *expand* the networks of active criminals (though not their number of crimes) through processes of recruitment and replacement. This is particularly true for imprisonments for drug crimes, which were the main engine for increases in imprisonment in the 1980s and most of the 1990s. But it is also true of other kinds of crime. A recent study (Felson 2003) found that "about 40 percent of juvenile offenders commit most of their crimes with others, and that co-offenders are more likely than solo offenders to be recidivists" (153). Felson has shown that most criminally active youth groups do not fit the *West Side Story* model of criminal gangs. They do not have leaders, they do not engage in planned criminal events. Instead, they remain loosely formed with fluctuating sets of members participating in a range of episodes, some criminal, some not. The prospects of disrupting the group's criminality by finding and incarcerating the leader are, he says, not great. While there are also studies that find that criminally active groups have "idea men" and "instigators" (see Reiss 1988; Sherman 1992), and that interventions with these leaders may bear fruit, the long-term, crime-reduction benefits of locking up putative "gang leaders" has not been demonstrated empirically.

Second, incapacitation theory makes an assumption that the period of time a person is behind bars creates a gap in the criminal activity that represents a net loss in overall criminal behavior. That is, the well-known age-crime curve suggests that people "age out" of crime (a point to which we return below), and incapacitation theory assumes that the aging-out process continues unabated by the time behind bars. But what if this is not so? What if the experience of a typical prison stay of a couple of years or so amplifies later criminality upon release from prison? What if the prison period is little more than a "time out," and people resume their previous levels of criminal activity once they return to the streets? There is not much research on this question, but what there is poses problems for the incapacitation model. Canelo-Cacho and his colleagues (1997) found evidence that the period in prison does not deteriorate the rate of offending at the same pace as might be expected for a free population. Evidence referred to above (Spohn and Holleran 2002), that people who are sentenced to prison have higher rates of new arrests upon release than those with similar criminal records who do not get sentences to incarceration, also suggests that prison amplifies criminal careers. In short, the period of imprisonment may not translate into the expected level of fewer crimes *by that person* over the person's lifetime.

Third, and just as crucial, is that analysts rely on deceptively large lambda estimates to project incapacitative effects. Zedlewski, for example, based his cost-saving estimates on the average of 287 crimes per year that prisoners in the Rand study admitted to having committed in the year before their incarceration. But this is a *mean* number of crimes the prisoners admitted committing per year. It is misleadingly high because a few cases admit to several thousand crimes per year, driving up the group's overall average number of crimes. By analogy, anytime Bill Gates walks into a room of people, the *average* wealth per person in that room is immediately well over a billion dollars. But even if the room were filled with the well-to-do, the amount of money a *typical* person in that room has available is much less than the average amount, a figure much inflated by Gates's presence there. Once Bill Gates arrives, you cannot use the average wealth as an accurate picture of the economics in the room anymore because his enormous holdings distort the number to be misleadingly high. In the same way, the average number of crimes of 287 was made misleadingly high by the small number who reported crimes per year in the thousands. The much more typical case reported single- or double-digit number of crimes in the year preceding incarceration. Zedlewski would have obtained a more realistic (and much lower) estimate had he used a different number, such as the *median* number of crimes per person in the sample.

### Problems with Incapacitation in Practice

There are practical upper limits to the effectiveness of incapacitation, two of which involve the problem of age (for a discussion, see Spelman 2000). First, for both boys and girls, criminal activity peaks in the late teenage years, 17 or 18. The median age of first prison admission is, however, much later, 29. About half of the arrests for felony crimes occur for people who are younger than this median imprisonment age. The number of crimes committed by people who are in their early years is uncertain, but it is both large and not affected by the incapacitation of adults who are older. It is unlikely in the extreme that the average age of first prison admission will drop very much. Prison is reserved for the people who are repeatedly convicted of felonies and those whose crimes are the most serious. There are enormous social pressures not to extend imprisonment to youngsters who, it is widely thought, need a second chance, and for whom it would be unwise to apply this expensive and intrusive sanction since many will soon age out of their criminal behavior. So long as this pressure remains, there will be no meaningful incapacitation for youngsters. Because the criminal justice system tends to find the most criminally active youngsters eventually, there is a feeling that the policy of incarceration in the later years makes good sense and will eventually select the most criminally active for imprisonment. But it will occur only after some substantial number of crimes have already occurred.

A second problem with age has to do with the declining rate of crime as people grow older: the age-crime curve. Once a person is caught and sentenced to prison, the criminal career is interrupted, but in many cases the career is waning anyway. Racheting up the incapacitation effect can be done only by increasing the length of incarceration. If the point above is correct—that *earlier* incarceration is not a very plausible policy option in most cases—then the only choice is to lock people up longer. Since it is reasonable to assume that people tend to be incarcerated as their careers in crime are peaking, adding time in prison, even with the best of scenarios, offers a decaying payoff in the incapacitation effect for each additional year of time in prison. The most extreme examples are provided by life-without-parole sentences. On the whole, once people who are serving their natural lives in prison reach their forties and fifties, the incapacitation effect becomes minimal, if not zero.

The growth in U.S. prison population has been sustained by retaining an increasingly aging prison population. In 1974, there were 10,700 state prisoners serving time who were 50 or older, about 6 percent of the population. Parole systems and shorter sentences meant that most prisoners, by far, were released before reaching this age. Changes in recidivist sentencing statutes, three-strikes laws, and limitations on parole for violent crime have changed that picture. In 2004, there were 125,700 people in state prisons who were 50 or older, almost 10 percent of the population. For them, the incapacitation effects are not very great. A good example of this practical limitation on incapacitation is provided by the violent-recidivist statutes passed in the 1990s in New Jersey. These laws imposed a mandatory life-without-parole sentence on all people convicted of their third violent offense. The rationale was purely incapacitation—to prevent these people from committing more violent crimes. But the new law replaced a statute that imposed a sentence of 25 years, with a minimum stay of 15 years. If the average age of people convicted of a third violent offense was, say, 25 (and it is usually quite a bit older than that), then the old law kept them behind bars *at least* until they turned 40. The net gain of the new law was to prevent crimes past the 40th birthday. This is not likely to be much of a payoff.

Finally, there is the problem of the shape of the *lamda*, which all studies show is highly skewed—that is, a small number of people account for the vast majority of crimes. These *very* active criminals tend to get caught, tend to end up in prison, and tend to be eligible for the enhanced penalties when they get into their most criminally active years. Under almost all conceivable systems of justice, these highly active criminals will always get caught, convicted, and placed in prison for healthy chunks of their potential criminal careers. The *growing* prison system comes about because of the increasing willingness to incarcerate other criminals who are less active and, under other regimes, might not have ended up in prison. In other words, prison systems may be able to grow, *especially in times of declining crime*, by society's becoming increasingly more willing to lock up people with ever-shorter criminal records. The result is that incarcerating more of those who are less criminally active decreases the efficiency of the prison sentence in preventing crime, because each new prison admission represents a declining incapacitation effect.

There is another possible explanation, suggested to me by justice statistician Allen J. Beck: the whole apparatus of criminal justice—police, courts, and corrections—has grown so much that a prison population can be sustained that has *not* necessarily dipped into an increasingly less criminally active crowd, but simply by growing the capacity to apprehend and detain those engaged in serious crime (personal communication 2006).

The Rand study that set the stage for an era of incapacitation illustrates the problem of accurately defining lambda. Their estimates of lambda were made on a sample of "habitual criminals," not a random sample of California prisoners, already biasing the results toward higher estimates. The original work was based on interviews of 49 prisoners (Petersilia, Greenwood, and Lavin 1978). "On the average, these offenders committed 20 felonies per year of street time and were arrested for only about 9 percent of them. The seriousness and frequency of their crimes declined during their careers" (http://www.rand.org/pubs/reports/R2144/). Based on this work, Greenwood and his colleagues (Greenwood and Abrahamse 1982) designed a survey that they gave to approximately 2,100 men in prison and jail in three states—California, Michigan, and Texas. This latter survey produced the astonishing estimates of the potential benefits of "selective" incapacitation—that is, identifying the "high-rate" group and making sure they are locked up for a long time.

Problems with this latter survey soon became apparent, however. The high *average* number of offenses attributed to each member of the high-rate group was produced by a very small proportion of that group, who reported committing thousands of offenses per year—a monumentally dubious number. Even if this number were accurate, the high-rate sub-group is so criminally active that, under the practicalities of the normal criminal justice system, they would end up behind bars anyway. Thus, analyses have found that the robbers in the Rand sample were more than ten times as criminally active as all other robbers (Blumstein, Canelo-Cacho, and Cohen 1993). When the extreme, dubious cases are omitted from the high-rate category, the number of crimes preventable by selective incapacitation drops markedly. To use imprisonment to *extend* the incapacitation effect requires dipping increasingly into this much less active group; that is, a growing prison system similarly taps an increasingly less active group of criminals with a decreasing payoff per person locked up.

For these reasons, several analysts (see, for example, Donohue and Siegelman 1998; Zimring and Hawkins 1997; Spelman 1994) have concluded that the potential selective incapacitation effects originally reported in the early 1980s and heavily influential throughout the 1990s were unreasonably high, a conclusion eventually reached as well by Peter Greenwood himself (Greenwood and Turner 1987).

## Studying Incapacitation

Even in the face of these daunting theoretical and practical problems, scholars have sought to estimate the size of the incapacitation effect. A paper by Spelman (2000) reviews these studies, and the discussion here follows his lead.

There are two general approaches to estimating the size of the incapacitation effect on incarceration. One approach—an individual-level strategy—investigates the characteristics of people convicted of crime and, based on those characteristics, seeks to estimate the amount of crime prevented by a prison term. The other approach—an ecological strategy—analyzes changes in crime and incarceration across time to see how an increase in one affects a change in the other. The earliest approaches (following the Rand study) used individuals as the unit of analysis. Later studies have tried to infer from crime and punishment trends the nature of the incapacitation effect.

These individual-level studies must model the problems of crime replacement, aging out of crime, and the potential amplification of crime that arises from going to prison. Sometimes these studies make no effort to incorporate these constraints into the analysis, but when they do, the ordinary strategy is to estimate the way these processes work (rather than to observe them) and incorporate the estimates in the analysis. Early studies devoid of such constraints lead to estimates of incapacitation effects that are very large, following Zedlewski's work. Various re-analyses of this kind of approach uncovered important weaknesses in these earlier studies that resulted in an overstatement of the incapacitation effects. The more recent individual-based studies of incapacitation find solid evidence of an incapacitation effect, but the size varies from quite small (Zimring and Hawkins 1988) to fairly large (see, for example, Piehl and DiIulio 1995). When corrections are made for problems of replacement and aging out, the size of the incapacitation effect diminishes even more (Spelman 1994). A recent review (Piquero and Blumstein 2007) of these offender-focused analyses concluded that "... estimates about the incapacitation effect on crime vary considerably, and most are based on very old and incomplete estimates of the longitudinal pattern of criminal careers."

Ecological studies follow this same pattern. Earlier studies find larger effects, but as constraints are included in the ecological models, the size of the effect diminishes. Early studies using national-level data tend to find an effect that is quite large. For example, using national-level data, several economists have derived estimates of enormous crime-reduction effects, much of it due to incapacitation. In two studies, Marvell and Moody (1997, 1998) estimate that a 10 percent increase in the prison population results in a reduction in crime of *more than 1 percent*. Levitt (1996) analyzes national data and finds a similarly large effect of imprisonment on crime. Spelman's results (2000, 2005) have tended to be in the same range. Liedka, Piehl, and Useem (2006) summarize these studies as estimating that "a 10% increase in the prison rate will result in a 1.6% to 5.5% drop in the crime rate" (247). But critics point out that these estimates are "implausibly high ... so high that some scholars have dismissed them as not being reasonably interpretable" (Kovandsic and Vieraitis 2006:104, citing Levitt 2001 and Spelman 2000). In fact, while prison populations have increased several hundred percent since 1970, crime has not dropped at anything near the rate these models would predict.

The noncredible results of studies using national-level data have led to the use of state-level data as an alternative. In this vein, Kessler and

Levitt (1999) analyze California crime data to assess whether Proposition 8, which required mandatory prison sentences for people convicted of certain felonies, had an effect on crime. They conclude that the crime rate showed evidence of both deterrent and incapacitative effects. Yet even these state-level studies are subject to dispute; in the case of Proposition 8, for example, Webster, Doob and Zimring (2006) have shown that crime started dropping in California in years *prior* to its passage, casting substantial doubt on studies that conclude the new law was responsible for the drop in crime. Using a state level of analysis, even when problematic, leads to effect-size estimates that are one-third to one-tenth the size of the national-level studies (see Spelman 2000: table 4.1, 102). Thus, as the question becomes more precise, the effect size gets smaller. In general, state-level studies support a belief that a 1 percent increase in the prison population results in a decrease in crime of perhaps .2 percent. But here again, the external validity of these estimates is problematic. States with the most monumental increases in imprisonment have not experienced relatively more monumental drops in crime. Spelman, reading these results and offering his own analysis, concludes that about only about one-fourth of the drop in crime since 1990 has resulted from expansion of the size of the prison population. Spelman is not surprised:

> [K]eep in mind that crime has been among the most persistent problems over the past twenty-five years, and that prison construction has been our principal response to this problem. About as many police officers per capita are employed today as were employed twenty-five year ago; only a tiny fraction of probationers and parolees are assigned to intensive supervision programs; the courts behave about the same as they did in the 1970s. But four times as many people are in prison. Even if imprisonment were an incredibly inefficient means of reducing crime— and there are strong arguments that it is exactly that—it could hardly have helped but have a substantial effect on the crime rate, given the scale of the difference. (126)

There is reason to believe that even these effects are either overestimated or not nearly as systematic as they sound. Western (2006) has recalculated the national-level estimates presented by Levitt (2001), for example, while taking into account the impact of crime rates on incarceration, and he concludes that the estimate "is almost certainly too large"

(182). His analysis suggested a much smaller effect, "that a one percent rise in the state imprisonment rate reduced the rate of serious crime by .07 of one percent" (Western 2005:185). His results are consistent with other recent economic analyses (see Besci 1999).

Those who doubt there is a substantial incapacitation effect are fond of comparing contiguous (or nearby) states' incarceration rates and crime rates. Such comparisons invariably show patterns that question the existence of any meaningful incapacitation effect (see King, Mauer, and Young 2005; Fabelo, Naro, and Austin 2005). These gross comparisons are provocative, but critics of such comparisons point out that they lack the statistical controls used in more widely cited (and more influential) studies. Yet the debate is far from over. Kovandzic and Vieraitis (2006) apply the usual econometric models others have used to study prison growth and crime in 58 Florida counties, from 1980 to 2000. They find "no support for the more prisoners, less crime thesis . . . Florida counties that relied most heavily on imprisonment as a tool to control crime did not as a result experience greater reductions in crime" (30, 33). No doubt, findings such as these will fuel more state-level studies.

A final way to think about the size of the incapacitation effect is to estimate what happens when people are released from prison. Rosenfeld, Wallman and Fornango (2005) analyze arrest histories of a cohort released from prison in 13 states in the 1990s and estimate that they accounted for 16 percent of violent crimes and 10 percent of property crimes in the year following their release. These figures are about twice as high as the state-level study of Alabama by Geerken and Hayes (1993). Neither estimate should be read as indicating an amount of crime that would have been averted had this group remained behind bars; the problem of replacement exists here in the reverse, and doubtless some of this crime would have occurred no matter. Yet this figure gives credibility to the commonly cited incapacitation estimates. Prison stays are for people who are criminally active and who would have remained criminally active had they not been in prison, on the average. The bitter irony, of course, is that some of the crimes committed by those released from prison can be attributed to the criminogenic effects of going to prison in the first place. One state-level study Veiraitis, Kovandsic and Marvell 2007) of the patterns of crime and incarceration between 1974 and 2002 found that ". . . while prison population growth appears to be associated with statistically significant decreases in crime rates, increases in the number of prisoners released from prison appears to be significantly associated with an increase in crime... [a result they] attribute... to the criminogenic effects of prison" (1).


## Discussion

This chapter has reviewed the question of how imprisonment affects crime. We began with the assertion that it would be silly to argue that prisons have nothing to do with crime. Our review of the evidence suggests that it would also be contrary to what we have learned from 30 years' study of the growing prison population. The size of the prison population undeniably has something to do with the amount of crime: the more prisoners we have, the less crime. Myriad studies have shown that growth in the size of the prison population is associated with a decline in the crime rate. Some studies suggest a fairly sizeable effect, others offer a much smaller, even trivial effect.

Surprisingly, however, when the body of evidence is considered as a whole, the fairest conclusion is that the effect of imprisonment on crime is not very large and is probably declining as the prison population surges. Some of this has to do with how weak the deterrent effect of prison is, especially the *specific deterrence*. In fact, some evidence on specific deterrence suggests that, if anything, going to prison makes people more likely to engage in crime rather than less so. There is problematic evidence in support of a small general deterrence effect, having more to do with the certainty of punishment than its severity. Evidence in support of an incapacitation effect suggests that there are substantial upper limits to that effect that may already have been reached by a large prison population. While it is clear that prison growth has played a role in the recent downward trend in crime, the role of incarceration during earlier periods of prison expansion is not a settled matter. As more studies are published, evidence mounts that the effect of incarceration on crime via incapacitation is less than has been popularly believed. As a recent review by Vera Institute of Justice (Stemen 2007) concluded, "... criminal justice policymakers appear to have placed too much emphasis on incarceration." (13)

There are methodological problems with all studies that purport to measure the impact of penalties on crime (for a discussion, see Spelman

2000; Nagin 1998). These problems apply both to studies that seem to uncover an effect and to studies that find little effect. In general, however, older studies find a substantial crime-prevention effect, while more recent studies find either a much smaller effect or none at all. Why are these more recent studies so likely to find diminished impact? At least one study of national prison and crime trends between 1972 and 2000 (Liedka, Piehl, and Useem 2006) suggests that as the prison population has grown, its crime-control effect has declined. As a consequence of "diminishing marginal returns…prison expansion, beyond a certain point, will no longer serve any reasonable purpose." They go on to conclude "that point has been reached" (272). Certainly, the early growth in incarceration, from 1981 to 1985, was linked to serious crime rates in a way that later growth has not been linked. The fact that for nearly two decades the increase in imprisonment has been substantially a product of the way we enforce drug laws means that the crime-prevention dynamics of the prison population are potentially quite different now from how they were in the middle of the 30-year increase in imprisonment (Shepherd 2006).

How important are the research findings reviewed here, and what can they tell us about future prison growth as a crime-control policy? Not as much as might seem, for two reasons. First, continued growth in the prison population of the magnitude we have seen in the last 30 years is almost unthinkable. (I say "almost," because most of us would have thought that a 400 percent increase in prison population, sustained gradually over a 30-year period, would have been unthinkable; see Blumstein and Cohen 1973.) A fourfold increase in the amount of incarceration we have now would mean *8 million prisoners* in 2035—if this happens, there will have been an astounding historical narrative about other social processes that went along with it. If the changes are much smaller, then it follows that the crime control prospects will have been limited, as well.

Nagin put the situation this way:

> [T]he collective actions of the criminal justice system exert a very substantial deterrent [and incapacitation] effect…[but] this conclusion is of limited value in formulating policy. Policy options to prevent crime generally involve targeted and incremental changes. So for policy makers the issue is not whether the

criminal justice system in its totality prevents crime, but whether a specific policy, grafted onto the existing structure, will materially add to the preventive effect. (1998:3)

Second, there is evidence that expansion of the prison system has reached a new and potentially more stable threshold nationally. Crime, after dropping for a decade, appears to be leveling off. The burgeoning size of the prison system is now being sustained, not by new criminals coming in, so much as by holding the existing set of criminals much longer than ever before and by recycling those released from prison at a somewhat higher rate. Nationally, the ratio of prison admissions to prison releases, which has for a generation favored the former, shifted in 2001 and projects to an increasing imbalance in favor of the latter for the coming decades (Rosenfeld, Wallman, and Fornango 2005). These are all signs that the great prison experiment of the twentieth century is starting to be behind us.

There is a glimpse of change in the political dynamics of prison policy as well. It used to be that the growth of incarceration was built on an idea that we needed more prisoners because we wanted less crime. But that idea makes sense only if (1) prisoners get the message of prison and mend their ways, and (2) the undesirable side effects of prison are at least neutral. Neither point seems to be sustained by evidence or experience. The crime-prevention capacity of an expanding prison system has come at a cost. The fiscal costs are well known; we are beginning to encounter other, less direct costs, and it is this problem to which we now turn our attention.

Our thinking about the collateral consequences of prison growth is tweaked by the idea that returning prisoners are a public risk. Going to prison did not make them better citizens—arguably, it made them (at least on average) worse. We have so many of them coming back because we locked so many of them up a few years ago. Locking them up did not deter many others from committing crimes, nor did it do much to convince them to live differently now that they are released. There was a benefit to not having them around—a small benefit, given the investment. But that benefit has the uneasy side effect that we now must find places in society for this much larger cohort of past law violators. It increasingly seems to look like a problem of our own making.

The purpose of this review has been to set the stage for the discussion to which the remainder of this book is devoted: the community-level effects created by the growth of the prison system. We had to begin with this review because no discussion of prison policy in the United States can go far without first considering the role of prison in suppressing crime. This assignment is the main one we have given to the prison system. The reason we have grown the prison system systematically for a generation is that we have wanted to fight crime. For better or worse, the story of prison as a crime-fighting device has now mostly been told.

We are left to consider the long-term and more structural aspects of this growth in prison populations, and this is the topic of the remainder of this book. As we lay out in the following chapter, we will see that growth of the prison system has been a concentrated social policy felt by people of color who live in poor places. We will now consider how prisons have affected them.

# The Problem of Mass Incarceration Concentrated in Poor Places

## 3

We begin with a description of how the prison population has grown in the past 33 years. Most of that growth has had little to do with crime; rather, it has been the product of a series of policy choices. Those policy choices have had distinct implications for the way prison populations have come to reflect a concentrated experience among certain subgroups in the U.S. population—in particular, young black men from impoverished places. This concentration is, in some ways, the most salient characteristic of incarceration policy in the United States, since the social consequences of incarceration are dominantly felt among those people and in those places of concentration.

To illustrate this concentration, I describe imprisonment both nationally and in Tallahassee, Florida. Tallahassee provides a useful illustration because a team of researchers has been investigating incarceration patterns there for almost a decade, and some of the studies reported in later chapters of this book have been done in that city. That there is nothing particularly special about Tallahassee—nothing to make us think that it is in any way an unusual place with regard to incarceration—makes it a particularly useful illustration. When it comes to prison, there must be many places in the United States like Tallahassee.

Here is the bottom line: there is nothing "equal opportunity" about prison. Rather, accidents of birth play an enormous role in determining the possibility of imprisonment during a person's life. This is, of course, a potent challenge to philosophers of social justice. Indeed, the theme of social justice runs throughout the remaining chapters of this book. The single most disturbing aspect of incarceration policy in the United Sates is its inequitable social consequences.

## How the Prison Population Has Grown

Recall that the prison population has increased annually every year since 1973. Blumstein and Beck (1999, 2005) have shown that for this entire period of growth, police arrest rates for felony crimes and prosecutorial conviction rates for those crimes have remained essentially stable. So why did prison populations grow? (For a compelling history of penal code reform in the United States, see Tonry 1996b.)

As we saw in the preceding chapter, for the first decade or so, the bulk of this rise had to do with increasing crime. But during that same time, public concern about crime also began to grow. By the late 1960s, there began to be the earliest glimmers of a tough-on-crime movement in many areas of the country, and in fact, crime concerns became a national theme during the second Nixon presidential campaign (1972). For a brief period in the 1970s, a consensus of conservative and liberal intellectuals argued that the "rehabilitation" era of penology had failed and that the proper purpose of prisons was to punish those who broke the law. There was a difference of opinion about the value of prisons for anything else, however. It is hard to believe today, but at the outset of the 1970s, the Left was excited about the growing irrelevance of prisons in crime policy (American Friends Service Committee 1971). Meanwhile, the Right was convinced that prisons were a central weapon in the War on Crime (van den Haag 1975; Wilson, 1975). They agreed that the next step in penal policy should treat prisons as primarily an instrument of punishment.

In those years, there came to be a hard edge to public sentiment about crime. Crime rates began to rise in the 1960s and continued their rise throughout the 1970s. Public opinion polls consistently found that crime was at or near the top of people's worries about the country (Flanagan and Longmire, 1996). This concern about crime also served as a symbol for other, less easily voiced worries about civil-rights unrest, antiwar disturbances, and bubbling reaction to the underlying principles of the welfare state and Lyndon Johnson's Great Society. In the public mind, the social fabric of American society had broken down and disorder and disruption were rampant. A strong response—law and order—was required.

Public debate was accompanied by political action. Predictably, the action started where consensus was greatest, so by the end of the 1970s, seven states had abolished parole release—sometimes for everyone and sometimes for people convicted of certain "serious" crimes—by establishing a "presumptive" sentence to be served (minus good time). For the most part, public debate about these laws lacked any defenders of the status quo, and debaters differed only in the degree to which the sentences should get longer. States that did not abolish parole instead passed sentence enhancements for some types of crimes. In short, the 1970s was a period of penal upheaval, and almost no state ended the decade with the sentence structure it had started with. Almost every change in penal code was passed with the firm intention of increasing the frequency and duration of prison terms for those convicted of felonies.

By the 1980s, the effects of these reforms began to be felt in the prison system. Crime rates dropped in the early years of the decade, leading to a round of self-congratulation among those who had wanted to use prison to fight crime. When crime started to rise again in the mid-1980s, these advocates redoubled their efforts. Fueled by "an epidemic" of crack-related crime, the reform movement set about on another round of sentencing changes, this time focused on drug-related crimes. The landmark Rockefeller drug laws, passed in New York State in the mid-1970s, had provided extended sentences for people convicted of possessing large amounts of "hard" drugs. But they did not hold a candle to the wave of changes in sentencing for drug-related crimes that characterized the politics of the 1980s. Federal drug laws passed first in the Reagan administration and then enhanced under the first Bush administration eventually provided for mandatory prison sentences of five years for drug possession of shockingly small amounts (for example, 5 grams of crack cocaine), which when found in someone's possession, were presumed to be "for distribution." States such as New Jersey passed "school zone" laws that enhanced and made *mandatory* prison terms for possession of illegal drugs within 1,000 feet of a school zone, ostensibly to counteract drug sales to schoolchildren. (Alabama, not to be out-toughened by liberal New Jersey, made the drug-safe school zone a three-mile radius, effectively designating the entire city of Birmingham a drug-safe school zone.) Delaware passed the "three will get you three" drug law, providing that possession of 3 *grams* of any controlled substance called for a mandatory penalty of three years, with no parole. Even though studies have found that the school zones "laws had failed entirely to accomplish their primary objective... [but instead] were creating unwarranted racial disparity of in the use of incarceration," (Green, Pranis and Ziedenberg 2006:4) they remain popular and on the books.

The 1980s was also a period of systematic reform designed to decrease judicial discretion in sentencing. By the end of the decade, a dozen states had passed some form of sentencing "guidelines," which enabled either the executive or the legislative branch of government to write more stringent standards for sentences to be imposed. Those who first developed the idea of sentencing guidelines in the 1970s did so with the belief that sentencing disparity was a core problem (see Gottfredson, Wilkins, and Hoffman 1978), but the impetus for the sentencing-guidelines movement shifted in the 1980s to a desire to eliminate judicial leniency.

In the late 1980s and early 1990s, a series of vicious crimes by former prisoners recently released from prison shocked and outraged the nation. As was common during this period, presidential politics set the tone. Willie Horton, a violent criminal given work release in Massachusetts, killed a woman in her home in Oxen Hill, Maryland. This event came to symbolize recidivist crime, the first in a series of awful incidents to make the national news. A few years later, Polly Klaas was abducted from her bedroom by a recent parolee in California; and in 1993, little Megan Kanka was abducted, raped, and killed in New Jersey. The man who did it had been previously convicted of a sex crime. Similar events occurred in other places, so that public outrage soon fueled legislative actions to lengthen terms for repeat crimes. There is now a Web page devoted to news about these events and the laws that were passed as follow-ups to them (http://www.klaaskids.org).

Thus, hot on the heels of drug-law reform, states began to pass enhanced penalties for people convicted of violent crimes, especially repeat crimes and sex crimes. A Clinton-era "truth-in-sentencing movement" called for people to serve at least 85 percent of their sentences— this movement especially targeted people convicted of violent crimes.

Life-without-parole statutes for repeat convictions and some types of violent crimes were also passed, with the hope that some people convicted of particularly heinous crimes would never see the outside of a prison again. By 2000, every state had some form of a registry statute for people convicted of sex crimes; Internet Web sites were set up for people to find former prisoners in their neighborhoods; and 24 states had passed some version of a three-strikes law, the most extreme of which was California's statute, which made a third felony conviction of *any* type subject to a mandatory 25-to-life sentence. Most of the sentence-enhancement statutes for recidivists were passed in the 1990s, just as crime began to drop nationally. It commonly happens that dramatic legal changes are enacted just as the problem they are designed to address has begun to diminish (Musto, 1999; Tonry, 2004).

Prison population growth thus has come in three broad waves. The first wave was a result of the abolition of parole and related statutes in the 1970s, and it had a moderate effect on prison populations, though it had a major effect on the prisons themselves (eliminating parole changed the incentive structure for providing rehabilitation programs and eventually became a basis for closing them down). The second wave was a result of drug-law reform that began under Ronald Reagan and got a boost from the rise in concern about crack cocaine. People who used to receive probation, including a new segment of people with no previous conviction, now went to prison. The third wave was the result of get-tough sentencing for violent crimes and for recidivists. We now have 132,000 lifers in our prisons, 28 percent "without possibility of parole." By contrast, there were only 42,000 lifers in 1980. A recent study released by the Vera Institute of Justice (Stemen, Rengifo, and Wilson 2005) summarizes the effects of sentencing reform between 1975 and 2002. They find that the biggest influences on prison-system growth were produced by mandatory sentencing laws, especially minimum terms for cocaine, and by truth-in-sentencing statues for people convicted of violent crimes.

These three waves of penal-code reform have produced a prison population that is different from the general U.S. population in important ways. It has always been true that people in prison hail disproportionately from the lower social classes. That is still true, but the penal-code reforms that produced the waves of prison growth we just discussed have each, in their own way, exacerbated that historical disparity. Here is how.

## Drug Crime versus Other Crime

None of the story being told about prison changes in the United States would be possible without the seismic changes that were made in drug laws. In the 11-year period beginning in 1980, before most drug-law changes had been enacted, and ending in 1991, by which time the last of the straggling states had finished changing their drug laws (and attention began to shift to frenzied concern about violent crime), the offense characteristics of those sentenced to prison changed markedly. The number of new court commitments to prison for drug crimes went from about 12,000 in 1980 to about 102,000 in 1991—a ninefold increase. The number of people incarcerated for drug crimes increased tenfold between 1980 and 2001 (Western 2005: table 2.3). No other type of offense had incarceration numbers rise at anything close to that rate (assault commitments, the closest competitor on terms of rate of change, doubled from about 12,000 in 1980 to about 24,000 in 1991). In 1980, of the major types of crime (murder, sexual assault, robbery, assault, burglary, and drugs), only sexual assault had fewer new commitments to prison. By 1991, the number of new prison commitments for drug crimes had reached a new level and has remained there for over a decade, with three times more commitments than the next largest category, burglary (calculations based on Blumstein and Beck 2005:62, fig. 3.4).

Drug use is widely distributed in the population, but any sensible observer would have known that these changes in penal practices would affect people of color disproportionately to their numbers in the drug-using population. Drug *markets* are concentrated in poor, urban areas. Street-level drug *distribution* is an occupation dominated by poor African-American (and to a lesser extent in some regions, Hispanic) males who live in areas where other legitimate labor-market choices are limited. While it is commonly speculated that drug cartels have racial and ethnic diversity at the top, it is beyond speculation that most visible street-level distributors are dominantly young men of color. Enforcement practices that concentrate undercover work on apprehending street dealers in impoverished neighborhoods, where open-air drug markets tend to operate, further guarantee that those arrested on drug-distribution charges will be disproportionately young males of color who live and work their trade in the poorest locations. The highly elastic nature of the employment market in drugs—every time a young black man is arrested and sent to prison for drug crime, a new recruit can be found to take his place—guarantees a nearly inexhaustible supply of prison candidates.

All of this was well known at the time the War on Drugs got underway, and it could have convinced us that the negative consequences of the war would fall disproportionately on poor minority males (Tonry 1996a). Astoundingly, the rules regarding drug-law enforcement were gerrymandered to show an even greater bias against poor minorities. Under federal drug laws, the amount of powder cocaine it takes to trigger mandatory prison penalties is 100 times greater than the crack cocaine equivalent. The putative rationale for this disparate treatment under the law is the fear engendered by "the crack epidemic" and the specter of crack-crazed criminals out-of-their-minds high and doing "anything" to get money for drugs. Yet all the available research shows this to be a myth—the physical effects of powder cocaine are no different from those for the rock (crack) version. And neither form of cocaine leads to the frequency of uncontrollable violence associated with addictive levels of alcohol abuse (Fagan 1990).

Because the crack form of cocaine is cheaper, its use is more prevalent among the poor. Middle-class (and upscale) whites who want to get high prefer the powder version. The enormous difference in penalties, not justifiable on the basis of any scientifically known criteria, ensures that the racially differential *enforcement* of drug laws described above will be augmented by the racial differences in *penalties* imposed. In fact, the blatancy of the racial disproportion is almost impossible to overstate. It is all the more unfathomable that Congress has twice acted to sustain this disparity, first in 1995 when it voted overwhelming to reject a recommendation of the U.S. Sentencing Commission to eliminate the disparity in penalties, and more recently in 2002, when legislation introduced to amend the law's racially potent differences died in committee. The only conclusion to be drawn is that the racially disparate results of drug laws are unimportant to policy makers.

Numerically, the drug laws have been a powerful engine to bring young minority men into the prison system. But the *proportional* impact has fallen even more heavily on minority women. Frost (2006) points out that rates of growth in the incarceration of African-American women have actually been higher than for African-American men. This is almost exclusively due to the heavy involvement of minority women in drug crimes, particularly as cocaine addicts. If we should have foreseen the differential impact of the new drug laws on young black males, we equally should not have been surprised to see that these laws are even more aggressive in moving minority women into prison.

## Length of Stay: Recidivist Statutes

A bit of sympathy is natural for drug-addicted lawbreakers, even crack user-dealers. But this is not as easy for repeat criminals, especially the violent ones and those convicted of sex crimes. We can understand a person who makes a mistake, even sometimes when the mistake leads to a serious crime. But we have trouble with the persistent criminal who seems never to learn a lesson. Repeat victimizing is all the more opprobrious when we have previously been lenient with the first-timer, who turns around and does it again.

Yet we do not have to be forgiving of recidivists to recognize the inherent distortions that arise from broad recidivist statutes. California's three-strikes law is as good an example as any. The law makes no distinctions regarding the types of felonies that activate the enhancements. According to public coverage of the law, one of the first people prosecuted under the enhancements got 25 years *flat time* for stealing a pizza on the Santa Monica pier. Zimring, Hawkins and Kamin's analysis of the law (2001) suggests that it is being applied to people convicted of property and lower level crimes as a matter of course, and that there are statewide disparities in its application. While every person under California's three-strikes provisions is indeed a recidivist, the vast bulk of those targeted by the law are far from dangerous.

This points to an anomaly in recidivist statutes. If they are carefully drawn, the statues apply to only a small number of people. New Jersey's law, for example, covers only three kinds of offenses on the third felony and as a consequence is "rarely invoked" (Clark, Austin, and Henry 1997). The net crime-prevention value of this kind of law is, by necessity, small though not necessarily unimportant. Broadly drawn laws, like the California version, have the capacity to prevent more crime, if only because they apply to more people, but they are inefficient. They imprison a large number of people for what might be thought of as nuisance crimes, and in California's case, they are partly responsible for major increases in the size of the prison population. The only way to write a recidivism statute that can prevent many crimes is to make it so broad that it overreaches, covering well beyond recidivists who are likely to be dangerous.

Broad recidivism laws differentially affect the poor and the marginalized who struggle to find meaningful lives in free society. They create a population of aging prisoners who spend so long in prison that their ties to society deteriorate to the point they can't sustain a decent reentry plan. Like killing a housefly with a bazooka, these laws do a lot of collateral damage when trying to solve a troubling problem.

It is troubling, too, how much recidivist statutes rely on suspect stereotypes as their justification. Willie Horton's blackness helped the Bush campaign fuel white fear of dangerous black men in order to gain momentum at a time when Dukakis had a big lead in the polls. News stories that give prominence to minority males engaging in repeat criminal activities feed the racial stereotype of the dangerous black man, especially in the South (Barlow, Barlow and Chiricos 1995). These recidivist statutes tend to apply more to African-American men because they make up a disproportionate share of those with criminal records; by simple math, then, they are disproportionately more likely to face three-strikes laws when they are rearrested.

Statutes related to sex crimes use images of wanton and uncontrollable urges—for sexual violence or perversions against children, or both—in order to support laws that stigmatize and isolate those convicted of sex crimes. The portrayal is that we and our neighbors need to be ever-vigilant against the possibility of someone, once convicted of a sex crime, moving near us and threatening our kids. Yet the most recent studies show that those convicted of sex crimes, as a group, have *low* recidivism, even when the criterion is new sex crimes. It is correct that when they are rearrested, people convicted of sex crimes are more likely than others to be rearrested for a sex crime. But only a scant 5.3 percent of those convicted of a sex crime are rearrested for a sex crime within four years, and overall they have a rearrest rate of 43 percent compared to 68 percent for people convicted of other crimes. (Langan, Schmidt and Durose 2003)

Irrespective of these factual outcomes, sex-offender statutes have been passed because of exacerbated public fears of repeat sex-related crimes. These statutes have made it harder for those convicted of sex crimes to find places to live, relegating them to low-standard, undesirable housing because only that is available in the areas where they can get permission to live. There are reports that landlords rent dilapidated housing to people who with prior sex convictions in concentrated numbers because the tenants cannot complain about the conditions of those apartments or else they are evicted. The result for many who are covered by sex-offender registration restrictions is a kind of ghetto, and studies of the poorest urban zip codes find that people required to register often tend to migrate there, in part because going anywhere else is too hard.

### Reentry Cycling: Piling on the Collateral Consequences

You would think that public policy would accord a high priority to helping those who have been released from prison find the support they need to avoid going back. Yet this is far from the case. People released from prison face collateral consequences of their convictions, and their list of restrictions is growing rather than diminishing (Samuels and Mukamal 2004). Mauer provides an illustration:

> [A]n 18-year-old with a first-time felony conviction for drug possession now may be barred from receiving welfare for life, prohibited from living in public housing, denied student loans to attend college, permanently excluded from voting, and if not a citizen, be deported. (2005:610)

This is not the whole of it. Every state imposes employment restrictions on those released from prison, and felony convictions usually bar obtaining certain types of paraprofessional employment and professional licenses. Some of these restrictions have face-validity; for example, people convicted of child abuse are prohibited from working in child care and related areas. But other restrictions seem to make little sense, such as prohibition of employment in the beauty industry or in transportation. The labor-market consequences of incarceration are explored in more depth in chapter 6, but here we can make a simple point. Being poor, a minority group member, undereducated, under-skilled, and having a criminal record makes it hard enough to get and keep a job that provides a decent wage. The many statutes—in New York, there are 283 restricted jobs for people with prior felony covictions—that eliminate job options make a difficult situation even worse.

The conditions of post-release supervision faced by most of those who leave prison add to these pressures (Travis 2005; Petersilia 2003).

Supervision strategies have shifted away from the longstanding models of support and assistance to an emphasis on surveillance and control. There has been an increase in regular drug testing. Several states have instituted supervision fees that charge parolees for some of the costs of their supervision. Reporting and other requirements are more stringently enforced. The predictable effect of this piling on of new rules, greater restrictions, and closer surveillance has been an increase in technical parole failures (returns to prison not because of new crimes but because of breaches of one or more of these rules; Jacobson 2005). In 1980 there were about 24,000 prison admissions for technical violations of parole—about one-fourth of all prison admissions. By 2001, this number had grown to almost 150,000 and constituted about 40 percent of all prison admissions nationally. It is argued by some that many technical violators are recidivists who have committed new crimes—perhaps as many as 20 percent of them—but who are being handled administratively because it is simpler to do so (Petersilia in press). This is almost certainly true for a portion of this group, but it is by no means true for all—or even perhaps most—of them.

The net effect of this regulatory practice is to sustain a large prison population, even in the face of declining felony convictions, by creating a large group of quasi-permanent prisoners who cycle through the prison system, are out on parole supervision, and are back in again after failing a drug test or violating some other rule. There is, of course, enormous state variation in this practice; in California, for example, 57 percent of prison admissions in 2000 were for technical failure on parole (Travis 2005). Blumstein and Beck (2005) summarize the effect of this policy on California prison cycling. Of those California prisoners who are released from prison the first time, about 40 percent do not return to prison. Of the 60 percent who do return, nearly all are eventually released again, after about six months behind bars. For this latter group, only 25 percent are able to remain free, and the 75 percent failure rate continues to apply for each subsequent prison return and release cycle.

The great irony of all this is how little the prison-cycling process has to do with crime. We should not be surprised about this, since studies of drug testing show that neither the frequency of testing nor its randomness seems to affect the amount of drug use (Haapinen and Britton 2002). Likewise, studies of the connection between the technical revocation of parolees and their criminal activity suggest that the former has little to do with the latter (Jacobson 2005). Blumstein and Beck (2005) compare California's heavy reliance on technical revocation to three other large states (New York, Florida, and Illinois) that use this kind of revocation less than half as often. They show that California's parolees do not experience fewer commitments for new crimes, and this leads the researchers to question "to what degree a policy of aggressive use of technical violations provides any clear-cut advantage in enhancing public safety" (Blumstein and Beck 2005:79).

It does, however, create a subgroup of more or less permanent prisoners. Their status as subjects of state surveillance and control persists despite the limited payoff in public safety. They are different from their fellow citizens in that once caught in this net, they find it difficult to escape the control of the state and most find it impossible to ever put their convict status behind them. Nor is this the only way in which they are different.

## Who Goes to Prison? The Four Loci of Concentration

It is estimated that one in 20 U.S citizens has experienced a stint in prison. This alone makes these individuals different from most other Americans. But they are different in other ways, as well. Prisoners are young men of color who have substantial deficits in human capital. They are more than 2.5 times more likely to have failed to complete high school (Uggen, Wakefield, and Western 2005:212), three to four times more likely to have speech and hearing impairments (Maruschak and Beck 2001), twice as likely to have a serious disease such as HIV (compare Maruschak 2001 to World Fact Book 2006), and two to five times more likely to be diagnosed with a mental illness such as schizophrenia, posttraumatic stress disorder, or moderate depression (National Commission on Correctional Health Care 2002). Clearly, this is a group at substantial disadvantage compared to the rest of society.

But these broad characteristics tell only part of the story. The imprisonment experience in America is concentrated in four ways that have crucial implications for the social consequences of incarceration: socioeconomic status, gender/age; race/ethnicity, and place.

## Socioeconomic Status (Human and Social Capital)

As a rule, poor people go to prison and others do not. This pattern is as old as prison itself. What it really means is that imprisonment is a kind of social welfare policy. There have been plenty of theoretical analyses of the social function of prison (see Melossi, 1998; Pettit and Western 2004). For our purposes, the underlying social mechanisms that move poor people behind bars are less important than the fact that it is true.

Because prisons house poor people, several implications follow. First, poor people do not have much of a political constituency, and neither do prisoners. Historically, prison-reform movements have been cyclical, and they usually involve elites who speak from the point of view of moral consciousness. They rarely involve grass-roots efforts by people who have themselves been locked up. There are notable exceptions (Charles Colson, the Christian evangelist, and Families Against Mandatory Minimums), but the prison population comprises mostly poor people who cannot vote and who do not matter politically. It is therefore difficult for the prison population to have a public voice.

## Gender and Age

Young men go to prison, entering at an average age of 29 and being released for the first time at an average age of 32. A majority will return to prison for another period of their lives. These are prime years for young men, years when other men are building the foundation for a lifetime of work and social connections. For most men in this age group, marriage, children, and careers are dominant concerns. Men who go to prison also have families—there are more than 1 million children under age 18 whose parents are behind bars (extrapolating from Hagan and Dinovitzer 1999:138). Nearly half of all men who go to prison were living with their children at the time of their admission to confinement (Western, Patillo and Weiman 2004:10). Going to prison is like a hole in the life span of most men who go there, and the hole spreads to others in their social group.

Those who study the life course think of the late twenties and early thirties as some of the most important building-block years in a man's life. This is the time when men settle into places to live and people to live with. These are the entrepreneurial years; men shift through work assignments until they find an occupation to which they can commit, earn Social Security and health benefits, and locate themselves within their social networks. For a person who goes to prison, the effects of this missing period of time are felt as interruptions in earnings, breaks from family (especially children), and lost opportunities to advance socially. There is stigma, of course, associated with going to prison, but there is also a hole in the person's adulthood. The collateral damage for a young man who goes to prison is not only lost freedom but also delayed functions of young adulthood, if they are not passed over altogether. None of this is meant to romanticize the lifestyles of so many men who go to prison. With perhaps only rare exceptions, they serve a prison sentence their misbehavior has fully earned. But the loss of freedom that comes with a prison sentence obscures the equally great loss of potential for a man in his prime years. Going to prison reduces life chances in ways we will discuss in greater detail in chapter 5.

It is also true that young women go to prison, though in much smaller numbers. The drug laws have helped shrink the gap between prison-bound men and women. And the collateral legal barriers for women, which often include constraints related to children, can exceed those for men. People who argue for heightened concern about women prisoners point out that the women represent, on the whole, a much smaller risk to society and at the same time a much greater loss of parental and familial support for those they leave behind as they enter prison.

Taken together, the 700,000 men and women sentenced to prison or jail annually represent substantial collective social and economic losses. By 2000, more than 1.5 million minors (more than one-fifth of them less than 5 years old) had a parent in prison, (Mumola 2000), and the "number if children who have ever had a parent incarcerated is much higher" (Uggen, Wakefield, and Western 2005), perhaps five times that figure. For many, there will never be a reconciliation. (Chapter 5 considers the complexities of these issues in greater detail.)

While they are in prison, prisoners do not count as unemployed. Western and Beckett (1999) have shown that U.S. labor-force participation statistics (especially unemployment figures) are distorted by a failure to take into account those who are behind bars. For young men, especially young black men, overall labor-force participation is much lower than official statistics show. Counting those who are behind bars, Western

(2006) has shown that "as the unemployment rate sank to historically low levels in the late 1990s, jobless rates among noncollege black men in their twenties rose to their highest levels ever. This increase in joblessness was propelled by historically high incarceration rates" (97). Because the people we put behind bars have most of their lives ahead of them, the effects of their incarceration are felt for many years after, even for those who never go back to prison.

*Race and Ethnicity*

Imprisonment happens for all social groups, but it is far more prominent an experience among minorities. Black men are seven times more likely to go to prison than are white men; black women are eight times more likely to go than are white women. The lifetime likelihood of incarceration for Hispanic men and women falls in between that for blacks and whites. The aggregate numbers require some getting used to. If today's imprisonment rates stay stable, nearly one-third of the black males born annually will go to prison at least once in their lives (Bonczar and Beck 1997).

This racial concentration of imprisonment interacts with concentrations of age and gender. All told, 12 percent of black men between ages 20 and 40 are behind bars. White males are equally as likely to be in prison or jail as they are to be in labor unions or on welfare; blacks males are at least ten times more likely to be behind bars than in labor unions or on welfare (Western 2005; table 1.2).

In our society, there is already an economic and social burden associated with race. The overwhelming frequency of imprisonment in the African-American community, especially among men, means that we often unwittingly associate blackness with criminality. Research shows that prohibiting potential employers from being able to run criminal-history background checks on African-American applicants actually *decreases* their chances of being hired, probably owing to employer suspicions that a young black male may have been in trouble with the law (Holzer, Raphael, and Stoll 2001). Deva Pager's (2003) research shows that young black men who report having *no* criminal record in job interviews are less likely to be hired for entry-level jobs than similarly situated white males who *do admit* their criminal backgrounds.

The strong association between race and involvement with the criminal justice system has spawned a large body of research on the topic of racism in the system. Some studies seem to show that small racial biases at successive stages in the criminal justice process may result in substantial racial differences at the end of the process (see Walker, Spohn, and Delone 2006). Other studies find that the racial differences wash out after legally relevant background variables are accounted for, suggesting that the system is not so much overtly racist as it is covertly racially insensitive (see Blumstein 1993). To these studies, critics point out the implications of racially disparate drug laws, which were described above. Though this is an important research problem, for our purposes it does not matter. The difference in incarceration rates for different racial and ethnic groups is such a stark fact, with such substantial social and personal consequences, that we have to worry about this even if the system is making its decisions in a racially unbiased manner.

*Place*

Socioeconomic status, race, age, and gender interact to produce an extreme concentration of incarceration demographically. Economist Richard Freeman "has estimated that *over half* of young, poorly educated black males were in prison or jail in 2001" (Thomas 2005:1, citing Freeman 2003). Because housing in the United States is economically and racially segregated, incarceration that concentrates by socioeconomic status and race also concentrates by location. Some neighborhoods have dominant numbers of residents either on their way to prison, in prison, or recently released. Sections of Washington, D.C. have been estimated to have one in five adult males behind bars on any given day. In Cleveland and Baltimore, there are neighborhoods with more than 18 percent of the males missing because they are behind bars (Lynch and Sabol 2004). For black children living in poor urban neighborhoods, having a close family relative in prison or jail is commonplace. A study in Tallahassee, Florida, interviewed over 100 people in two poor, almost exclusively black neighborhoods, and every resident reported having had a family member in prison during the previous five years. In 1998, large sections of Brooklyn, New York, had one person go to prison or jail for every seven males age 20 to 45 (Clear and Cadora 2001). One study (Clear and Rose 2003) estimates that in Brooklyn neighborhoods that are overwhelmingly African American, the incarceration rate of adult males is 12.4 per 1,000 residents; by contrast, in predominantly white Brooklyn neighborhoods, the rate is 2.7 per 1,000 residents.

The emerging interest in reentry has shed light on this concentration of citizens in the criminal justice system. In Chicago, more than half of those returning from prison go to just seven of Chicago's 77 communities (Visher and Farrell 2005). These neighborhoods tend to have higher crime rates and more families in poverty than other Chicago communities, and their rate of female-headed households is consistently about double that of the Chicago average (Visher and Farrell 2005: table 1:3). Slightly more than half of those in reentry go back to their former neighborhoods. New neighborhoods may be better places for former prisoners who choose to go there, but they are not necessarily better places overall: they believe their new locations pose less risk for reinvolvement in crime, but they do not see them as good places to get work or otherwise live for the long term.

Figure 3.1 shows incarceration rates for New York City community districts in 2003 (Swartz 2007). The map shows how some areas contribute heavily to the prison population, and within those areas some sub-sections (similar to census block groups) dominate the prison admissions. The high-incarceration areas have an annual imprisonment rate that is more than 60 times higher than the low incarceration areas. In these high-rate places, upwards of 2% of the adults males enter prison in a given year.

## Tallahassee as an Example of Concentrated Incarceration

Place is the final destination for any analysis of the way incarceration is concentrated, because places are organized by the factors that predominate the incarcerated population. Places that have concentrations of prison incarceration are also places where "a number of social problems tend to come bundled together... including, but not limited to, crime, adolescent delinquency, social and physical disorder, low birth weight, infant mortality, school dropout, and child mistreatment" (Sampson, Morenoff, and Gannon-Rowley 2002). As a consequence, place has enormous implications for the social meaning and practical consequences of incarceration; in these places, incarceration is a dominant dynamic.

The various ways that incarceration concentrates can be illustrated by data from Tallahassee, Florida. Among Tallahassee residents either going

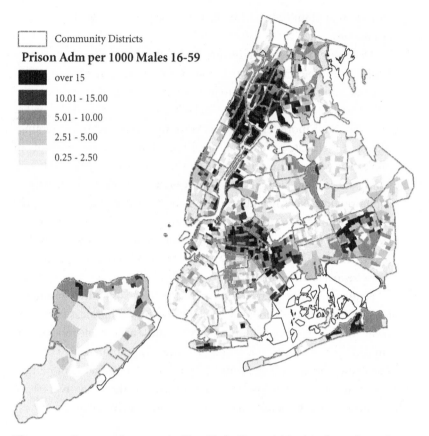

**Figure 3.1** Incarceration rates in New York City neighborhoods as shown by prison admission rates in 2003.

Map created by Eric Cadora and Charles Swartz at the Justice Mapping Center with the Spatial Information Design Lab, 2007.

to prison or returning from prison, from 1994 to 2002, 89 percent were men, more than two-thirds of whom were black, with an average age of 30. There were 88 neighborhoods in Tallahassee in 1998. Two of them—Frenchtown and South City-had more that 1.5% of residents entering prison in that year (these locations are described in detail in Chapter 6). While most other places had a person or two going to prison, these two places were well-known in the city for crime and for having residents who go to and return from prison.

These data from Tallahassee underscore the way incarceration policy is a concentrated social force. Those who to go to prison are overrepresented by young men of color; these young black males tend to come, in concentrated ways, from certain disadvantaged neighborhoods. In short, these neighborhoods are "prison places." For them, incarceration is not just a common theme, it is a constant one. The question considered by this book is: In what ways does the cycling of young poor men into prison and then back into poor communities affect those communities, especially the quality of life and public safety?

## Conclusion

In the preceding chapter, we saw that growing prison populations play a limited role in suppressing crime rates. In this chapter, we saw that shifts in crime, upward or down, have had little impact on the size of the prison population. Instead, policy variables account for the growth in prison populations far more than crime. Prison populations have remained high because penal policy has ensured a continual supply of prison admissions, through sentencing laws and community supervision practices.

The prison population is produced by two factors: the number of people who enter prison and how long they stay. The number of people charged with crimes is a constraint on the prison population, but it does not determine it. There is enough crime that the number of people *eligible* for prison is large. When the enforcement of drug laws becomes a main source of prison sentences, the capacity to maintain a sizable prison population, even when crime drops precipitously, is substantial. Because there are *three* prison pressure points—the in/out ratio, length of stay, and the return rate—the number of policy options available to grow prison populations without regard to the number of people eligible for prison is large indeed.

That is what has happened in the United States. For a 33-year period, policy makers have enacted the precise laws needed to keep prison populations growing, given changes in crime rates and the nature of those eligible for prison. The prison population in the United States is not a natural consequence of the amount of crime nearly so much as it is a studied consequence of consciously chosen policies.

These laws have fallen disproportionately onto a subgroup of the larger population: young men of color who come from impoverished neighborhoods. In these neighborhoods, the possibility of prison is so ubiquitous that we can think of them as "prison places." For the remainder of this book, we will consider the ways incarceration affects these places.

# Communities, Coercive

# Mobility, and Public Safety

4

The concentration of young, disadvantaged males of color in prisons has been the subject of substantial empirical work and policy commentary. Their concentration in impoverished, minority neighborhoods has not received the same amount of attention. This is unfortunate, because neighborhoods, "places," matter. Neighborhoods are the building blocks for community life, and community life is an important wellspring for a good quality of life. Clearly, however, the nature and quality of community life varies from one neighborhood to another. That is one reason there has been a resurgence of interest in the influence of neighborhood and community contexts (Gephart and Brooks-Gunn 1997).

Neighborhoods are places where people live or work in proximity to one another. While plenty of heterogeneous communities exist, in most poor communities the shared characteristics of people who reside and work there are far more important than their differences (see Saegert, Thompson, and Warren 2001). Thus, these communities typically comprise people who share one another's experience and social circumstances. In this way, the communities provide concentrations of certain experiences and proximity to certain people who are alike in important respects.

Empirical investigations of neighborhoods must define their boundaries. The different methods used to do so variously include census block groups, census tracts, indigenous "neighborhoods" defined by cultural norms, the geography of voluntary associations, or state-created political boundaries. In fact, the precise spatial definition of a given place is not critical; typically, it depends on the social indicators being investigated. When crime is the social indicator of concern, the method used to determine the neighborhood's boundaries may be immaterial (Wooldredge 2002; Sampson, Morenoff, and Gannon-Rowley 2002). This suggests that we may accept the importance of a neighborhood as an analytical construct without worrying too much (within reason) about the different ways the term may be operationalized in research.

## Why Places Matter

It is obvious that the place where a person lives is an important aspect of the quality of that person's life. People try to live in places that offer them the social amenities they most want in their lives. They tend to live in the best places they can afford, moving away from less desirable locations when they can. People who live in undesirable locations are often stuck there, not liking where they live but unable to change the fact. These places then become concentrated with poor people who have few options. This circumstance has been referred to as "concentrated disadvantage," and its presence in a location "is associated with . . . infant mortality, low birth weight, teenage childbearing, dropping out of high school, child maltreatment, and adolescent delinquency" (Sampson, Morenoff, and Gannon-Rowley 2002).

The nature of the places people live may actually matter more to very poor people than to those who are better off. For those who have means, there are social options away from their neighborhoods. Most urban Americans are employed away from their homes and commute to and from work. They maintain friendships and have business relationships with people who live away from their areas. This means that their networks extend well beyond the narrow confines of their neighborhoods. For the very poor, this is not the case. As William Julius Wilson (1987, 1996) has pointed out in his classic studies of entrenched poverty in urban minority areas, the people who live in the most impoverished areas of inner cities are isolated politically, socially, and economically. The sphere of their lives is largely bounded by the streets and alleys of their hope-starved neighborhood. The options for support are limited to whatever resources their neighborhood can provide; they are not as able to travel elsewhere to get what is not available locally. Wilson also shows how this urban spacial isolation of the poorest city residents is more prevalent today than it was a decade ago.

We are used to thinking about this neighborhood isolation as an aspect of urban communities of color, and indeed for the places where concentrated poverty and disadvantage converge with minority group status, the image is accurate. Economic inequality is increasingly expressed as a spatial residential phenomenon in America's cities, and color is clearly a correlate of this spatial/economic pattern, with high levels of crime concentrated in these very poor places. But historical patterns of racial injustice are not the only factor: studies show that "when African Americans and whites have similar levels of concentrated disadvantage, the effects of disadvantage . . . are relatively comparable" (Krivo 2000:547).

The importance of this isolation stems from the "channels through which neighborhoods can shape or constrain opportunities" (Turner and Acevedo-Garcia 2005:2). Research has identified six ways that a person's place of residence affects social and economic opportunity. They are (summarizing Turner and Acevedo-Garcia 2005)

- *Local service quality.* People look to local schools, retail establishments, social child-care providers, health-care providers, and grocery stores as sources of support for their quality of life. In the poorest locations, these are substandard or nonexistent.
- *Shared norms and social control.* Public behavior, especially by young people, shapes what it feels like to be in public space where social relationships develop and are nourished. When people think the streets are unsafe or disordered, they abandon public activity and isolate themselves in their homes, ceding the streets to deviant behavior (see Skogan 1990).
- *Peer influences.* Young people make their friendships with those who live near them and come to emulate the values and perspectives that dominate their peer groups. In the poorest places, this can promote a shared culture of antisocial values, such as indifference to school, teenage pregnancy, and

interpersonal violence (see Anderson 1999; Weatherburn and Lind 2001).

- *Crime and violence.* One of the most persistently identified neighborhood-level effects is crime, especially violent crime (Sampson, Morenoff, and Gannon-Rowley 2002). This results not only in greater chances of victimization but also elevated stress levels and trauma.
- *Job access.* As jobs leave the inner city, the poorest places stop offering nearby employment to residents. Those who are able to find work elsewhere have to rely on public transportation, which is often problematic and always an expense (see Wilson 1996).

For reasons such as these, the quality of a neighborhood is an important condition in the quality of life for those who live and work there. This is particularly true for the prospects of children, because children are affected not only directly by the neighborhood conditions but also indirectly by the way the neighborhood's conditions affect their parents. Studies show that "resource-poor families in relatively rich environments may benefit from community ties...[but] in resource-poor environments, children in relatively well-functioning families may suffer when their families maintain strong ties to the neighborhood" (Darling and Steinberg 1997: 130). Indeed, even though "the importance of families cannot be overstated...[p]arents must interact with community-level agencies and institutions to garner resources for their children" (Leventhal, Brooks-Gunn, and Kamerman 1997: 186). When those agencies and institutions are weak, there is little upon which parents can depend. Community disadvantage "amplifies the effects on crime of problems in the family environment." (Hay et al 2006: 326)

Moving away from problem places is a potentially powerful solution to these problems. As said before, people who can, usually do. When people are given the opportunity to change their living areas, their circumstances often change for the better. In the famous Gautreaux project (Rosenbaum and DeLuca 2000), families that were moved from the poorest sections of inner-city Chicago to integrated suburban locations experienced substantial improvements in their children's school performance. The results of similar mobility programs (Goering and Feins 2003) have not been as impressive, but they still tend to show that changing a family's residential location can change that family's lifelong prospects. The people who are fortunate enough to be able to move away from problem places improve their lives, but those who remain face ever diminishing prospects with each new departure.

## Social Disorganization and Coercive Mobility

Clearly, places matter. The neighborhood you live in is a crucial aspect of how you live. How is neighborhood related to crime, and how is incarceration an important consideration in neighborhood life? To answer this question, we begin with one of the oldest and most respected theories in criminology: social disorganization.

In its original formulation (Shaw and McKay 1942), social disorganization theory sought to explain why certain neighborhoods in Chicago sustained high numbers of delinquents over time. They observed that these neighborhoods had high levels of poverty, ethnic heterogeneity, and mobility. They argued that poverty and ethnic heterogeneity established a basis for norms to develop that enabled criminal values to be transferred to children from one generation to another. High mobility, they said, meant that people felt little long-term attachment to their communities, did not form sustaining relationships with neighbors, and did not invest in maintaining their property. This trio of forces produced "social disorganization," a condition under which crime flourishes because informal social control is weak.

Incarceration can operate as a kind of "coercive mobility," destabilizing neighborhoods by increasing levels of disorganization, first when a person is removed to go to prison, then later when that person reenters the community. In high-incarceration neighborhoods, the processes of incarceration and reentry create an environment where a significant portion of residents are constantly in flux—perhaps as many as 15 percent of parent-age, male residents a year (CASES 1988). Upon release, ex-prisoners continue their pattern of residential instability, frequently relying upon local shelters for lodging (Fleisher and Decker 2001). Consequently, when we combine the number of people admitted to prison with the number who are released annually, we can see how coercive mobility decreases residential stability.

Coercive mobility also adds to residential mobility because it increases the likelihood that family members and other residents will move, too. Family members often move owing to the financial hardship that results from incarceration of a loved one. Studies show that children, especially those whose mothers are imprisoned, frequently move to live with a new caregiver during the incarceration of one of their parents (O'Brien 2001; Sharp and Marcus-Mendoza 2001). Siblings sometimes are separated from each other (Sharp and Marcus-Mendoza 2001) and sent to new homes to live. Families sometimes move as a strategy to help relatives returning from prison, hoping that by moving to new areas away from the old "bad" influences they will decrease the likelihood of a return to crime. At the same time, residents without incarcerated family members sometimes seek to escape a neighborhood they view either as deteriorating or as limited in its ability to provide opportunities for them and their children (Rose, Clear, and Ryder 2000). Thus, in high-incarceration neighborhoods, imprisonment produces high rates of residential mobility and therefore disrupts social networks and diminishes community stability.

Communities that experience turnover are thought to be less stable in a number of ways. First, there is a large amount of literature examining the relationships among residential mobility, social disorganization, and crime. High rates of residential mobility are thought to create a social environment in which residents isolate themselves from one other. This reduces the collective sentiment that promotes pro-social community action (Sampson 1991). In these environments, there are low levels of integration and high levels of anonymity that impede social cohesion (Crutchfield 1989; Crutchfield, Geerken, and Gove 1982). Mobility is also thought to reduce the commitment residents have to the area, making those who live there have less stake in collective action. In this sense, mobility contributes to an atmosphere of anonymity that impedes informal social control (Warner and Pierce 1993).

As a form of residential mobility, incarceration disrupts social networks in a variety of ways. Some are straightforward: incarceration removes people from their family members and friends. Some are more complex: relationships are strained when residents withdraw from community life to cope with financial problems or to manage stigma. Reentry, however, does not automatically remedy these problems; sometimes it might exacerbate them. Fractured families may be repaired with the return of a loved one. They also may disintegrate under the strain of trying to reabsorb a member who has been absent. Neighbors may welcome back old friends or they may withdraw, out of fear. Other effects are more indirect. For instance, residents stop socializing when groups of people are targeted for increased police surveillance in neighborhoods with reputations as hotspots for ex-prisoners. In this way, networks of nonincarcerated individuals are disrupted, too (Rose, Clear, and Ryder 2000).

## Human Capital, Social Capital, and Public Safety

That extreme poverty is a correlate of high crime, especially violent crime, is now an established fact (see Krivo and Peterson 1996). Increasingly, studies also report that various other characteristics of neighborhoods affect rates of crime. Recent examples include Bellair (1997), who showed that "getting together with neighbors" had a negative impact on burglary, auto theft, and robbery in 60 urban neighborhoods. His related analysis (Bellair 2000) found that greater amounts of informal property surveillance by neighbors reduced some types of crime. Analyzing the British Crime Survey, Markowitz and his colleagues (2001) found that lower levels of neighborhood cohesion predicts greater crime and disorder. Studies of Chicago neighborhoods (Morenoff, Sampson, and Raudenbush 2000) suggest that informal social controls—voluntary associations, kin/friend networks, and local organizations—can reduce crime. New research now suggests that these neighborhood-level crime effects are most pronounced for "socially isolated communities" (Stretesky, Schuck, and Hogan 2004). What is it about poor communities that makes them so susceptible to crime?

In a discussion of public safety in the context of community life, five constructs provide useful insights for understanding how differences among communities contribute to differences in public safety. These constructs are human capital, social networks, social capital, collective efficacy, and informal social control. In the discussion below, each is defined and its relevance for concentrated incarceration is described. When reading this discussion, bear in mind that incarceration is not simply removal of a person from the community; in almost all cases, it is a reentry cycle involving both removal and return, often more than once. Each aspect of coercive mobility—the removal and the return—has its own destabilizing aspects for those who live in impoverished communities. The cycle of removal and return, or the reentry cycle (Clear, Waring, and Scully 2005), adds up across people and events to become a dominant dynamic in the community. As Jeremy Travis (2005) has pointed out, they all come back—to which we might add, "often more than once."

### Human Capital

The basic building block of community well-being is human capital. *Human capital* refers to the personal resources an individual brings to the social and economic marketplace. Typical forms of human capital are education and job skills that potential employers value. Others include intelligence and ease in social situations. People with generous endowments of human capital have personal talents and attributes upon which to call in order to advance their personal interests, especially in the realm of the competitive marketplace: a good education, a solid job history, an array of skills, and so forth.

Human capital is a quality of individuals. Communities whose residents possess good amounts of human capital tend to be more successful, if only because the people who live there are themselves more successful. But human capital is not a community-level attribute, and places where there is a wealth of human capital may struggle to be effective communities when residents give little importance to community life. For example, people of wealth and social status may enjoy only superficial connections to those who live near them; conversely, places whose residents are bereft of human capital may generate a strong social basis for collective action. In either case, however, the endowment of human capital enjoyed by a place's residents serves as a constraint upon community life. Even so, places where there is great human capital tend to enjoy a degree of safety, even if community life does not thrive, because those with human capital would not live there otherwise. In this way, communities rich in human capital tend to be places where street crime is rare.

As a group, people who end up going to prison are substantially lacking in human capital. The existence of a criminal conviction is itself a debilitating factor for ex-prisoners, since felony convictions can make ex-prisoners ineligible for housing assistance, welfare, and certain types of employment (Petersilia 2003). But criminal conviction is only a marker on a population already bereft of human capital. Only about half of those who are behind bars have graduated from high school (Hughes, Wilson, and Beck 2001). This poor educational history makes them an enormously high risk for criminal justice involvement. Of black males age 20 to 35, an estimated 36 percent were incarcerated in 1996; of black males born in the 1960s who dropped out of high school, 60 percent were incarcerated before reaching their thirties. By the end of the 1990s, 16 percent of black male high-school dropouts age 20 to 39 entered prison each year (Western 2005: table 1.2; fig. 1.4, fig. 3.3).

Nearly three-fourths of prisoners have histories of drug or alcohol abuse (Beck 2000), almost one-third have histories of substantial physical or mental illness (Maruschak and Beck 2001), and nearly one-third were unemployed at the time of their arrest (Petersilia 2003). The people who end up going to prison have such poor job prospects to begin with that the impact of imprisonment on their future employment prospects is not large, though the negative impact of incarceration on lifetime earnings from employment is quite substantial (Western, Kling, and Wieman 2001; Nagin and Walfogel 1998). Ex-prisoners who started out as intermittently employed in unskilled daily-wage jobs tend to remain in that situation. Thus, places that are crowded with people who go to prison are crowded with people who have deficiencies in human capital.

## Social Networks

People use their human capital to compete for goods and services, but they rely on their social networks to accomplish goals otherwise unattainable through human capital alone. *Social networks* are essentially the array of relationships in which a person lives, works, and engages in recreation. For most of us, our dominant social networks consist of family members and people in our workplace. Social networks can also contain friendships, attenuated or even distant acquaintanceships, and other atypical interpersonal relationships. One reason disorganized communities are so is that they do not have the strong bonds and dense social relationships so important to social control (Kornhauser 1978). This makes the fragile links in those areas even more important.

The unit of analysis for the social network is the "tie"—the nature of the bond between the person and the other member of the network. Poor people tend to have what is referred to as "strong" ties—that is, ties that are mostly reciprocal and are formed within tight networks. These kinds of ties are very useful for meeting needs of intimacy and mutuality, but they are not very useful for activating sources of support from outside the network. For example, strong ties do not help people learn of jobs that are about to become available or help people find services to deal with problems (Spaulding 2005). "Weak" ties, by contrast, tend to generate contacts outside the close interpersonal network. These ties are capable of bringing new resources into the person's life by expanding the network (Granovetter 1993).

People living in impoverished communities tend to have sparse networks that are dominated by strong ties rather than weak ones. Those who go in and out of prison have networks that are reduced to the few people who have kept close associations while they were away. For the most part, these are strong ties, limited in scope and restricted in their potential to generate material support outside of what is directly available from those in the network. Because many who live in the poorest neighborhoods—especially those who have gone to prison—lack so much in the way of human capital, they are a potential drain on the support capacities of the few strong ties upon which they can rely. One of the most pressing tasks facing those involved in the criminal justice system is to develop social ties that will marshal the new resources needed for a better life: a job, a place to live, and educational skills. At least initially, the ex-prisoner who can rely on his family for these supports does so. There are not very many alternatives.

As might be expected, removing people from a community and sending them to prison affects the networks of those who remain. Andres Rengifo and Elin Waring (2005) have been interviewing a systematic sample of Bronx, New York, residents to learn more about their social networks, including how incarceration affects their size, shape, and nature. They hypothesize that incarceration creates a "hole" in people's networks, with the idea that high rates of incarceration damage the networks as a consequence. Their preliminary results suggest that removal for incarceration may generate losses in the efficiency and heterogeneity of the social networks of residents in high-incarceration areas. Their simulations suggest that the removal of individuals as a consequence of incarceration affects primarily weak ties as opposed to the more robust ties generated by close kinship relations and longstanding friendships. Perhaps more significantly, results from the Bronx interviews suggest that residents regularly adapt to the high mobility of network contacts (owing to incarceration but also to more general reasons, such as the search for affordable housing). This adaptation leads to network configurations with a high number of weak ties versus strong ties and relative instability in the provision of social support, information flows, and personal advice (i.e., "If Joe is not around to hang out, I will hang out with Luis. Joe may be out of circulation for a day, a week or a year; it doesn't really matter. There is always someone to hang out with. When Joe shows up again, he will join the crowd again") (Rengifo, private communication).

Those who become involved in the reentry cycle experience the existing arrays of social networks in one of two general ways. Many are extremely isolated from these networks. As a consequence of their criminal behavior, they may have alienated their families. As a consequence of their desire to stay out of trouble, they may have isolated themselves from former associates. This kind of reentry can be lonely, a process devoid of support systems and detached from social connections. Yet this existence is highly visible to the community: many idle ex-prisoners spend their nights sleeping in public places and loiter on street corners during daylight hours; they take their place in the various social-service lines, waiting for work, health care, and public assistance; they add to the numbers of people who are disconnected from the broader social and economic forces of society (see Fleisher 1995).

Others who have inclusive kinship networks are more fortunate. Because they typically have such limited human capital to offer employers and other social contacts, they are forced to rely upon their families for help. These families, usually also poor and with few resources available to divert for the ex-prisoner's needs, are typically systems of strong ties. Whatever can be done to ease the disruption that occurs because of reentry cycling, few new resources can be brought from outside the existing family system. When families welcome ex-prisoners home, they are forced to devote sometimes considerable resources to dealing with the removals and reentries. Mothers, siblings, or others may give ex-prisoners money during their prison stay to pay for commissary items and after release to cover expenses until a job is secured; children may shift their attention to new adults or face the prospect of reduced adult supervision; new housing arrangements may be needed; and always, there is the potential for conflict when people whose lives are already stressful deal with the consequences of further disruption.

It is important to recognize the demands that disrupt the homeostasis both before removal and in the face of return. Imprisoning young people of parenting age who are in their early years of adulthood removes parents, income earners, and interpersonal supports. People who had ties to the person who is sent to prison are affected by that removal, and they find ways to reorganize their lives to make up for the person's absence. The ex-prisoner's return changes this new interpersonal homeostasis and forces a renegotiation of expectations and relations. This, too, absorbs the resources of the network.

*Social Capital, Human Capital, and Social Networks:*
*Creating Social Support*

While *human capital* refers to the capacity of individuals to compete in the marketplace, *social capital* is the capacity of a person to call upon personal ties (usually within social networks) in order to advance some personal interest. Social capital can be activated to solve myriad problems. It can be the ability to use friends and acquaintances to find out about job openings and gain access to potential employers in an advantageous way. Social capital can also mean access to health-care resources or helpful information about housing and child care, as well as contacts to obtain this kind of care. Social capital and social networks are closely related. Social networks define the underlying structure of interpersonal relationships that hold the capacity for providing social capital; social capital is the capacity of networks to provide goods for people within these networks.

Social capital works by facilitating certain actions and constraining others. It stems from a sense of trust and obligation created through interactions among community members and serves to reinforce a set of prescriptive norms (Portes and Sensebrenner 1993). Thus, social capital effectively unites individuals within a neighborhood, thereby initiating and enhancing a sense of collectivity (Coleman, 1988). High levels of social capital augment the ability and efficacy of the community to sanction transgressors. Thus, in communities with large supplies of social capital, adolescents are encouraged to complete their education, are discouraged from stealing cars, and are sanctioned appropriately in informal and intimate relationships. Sampson and Laub (1993) conclude that social investment (or social capital) in institutional relationships dictates the salience of informal social control at the individual level. More important, they find that trajectories of crime and deviance can be modified by these bonds. It follows that communities rich in social capital also will experience relatively low levels of disorganization and low levels of crime. It has been shown, for instance, that immigrant groups rich in human and social capital are more able to promote self-employment than their more capital-poor counterparts (Sanders and Nee, 1996). This, then, insulates the neighborhood from making the link between unemployment and crime.

Social capital relies upon (and in turn promotes) human capital. It contextualizes human capital (and vice versa) because neighborhoods rich in social capital exert more control over individual residents, thus helping to produce more highly educated, employable, and productive members of the community. Neighborhoods deficient in social capital are conducive to crime because they have many individuals who are under-educated, unemployed, and more likely to be criminal. Thus, communities rich in social capital also are communities rich in human capital. Conversely, those communities lacking one tend also to lack the other. Recent research provides evidence to support these relationships. For instance, disrupted network ties (the basis for social capital) that limit access to noncash resources have been shown to be a primary determinant of whether women are working or are on welfare (Edin and Lein 1997). Farkas et al. (1997) recently found that differences in cognitive skills (human capital) explain a large part of the pay differences between ethnic groups, but those differences also arise from social sources such as school, family, and neighborhood experiences.

Neighborhoods are the focal point for satisfying daily needs through the creation of informal support networks. Thomas Lengyel (2000) points out that people who live in the poorest neighborhoods are forced to rely on informal social supports when formal agency services fall short. For instance, place of residence is an important source of informal networks of people who provide important products and services (such as child care) and alter life chances with job referrals and political connections. While this informal marketplace sometimes operates through monetary exchange, more often it works through barter, where reciprocity is the currency of exchange (Logan and Molotch 1987).

Reciprocity is especially important for the poor, who rely more upon each other for these social supports because they tend to be less spatially liberated than the well-to-do (Wellman 1979). They live in neighborhoods where community-based and civic organizations are lacking, which means that they fail to have places where they can meet people and thus form weak ties. As a result, poor people draw upon their network of strong ties more frequently than do people in affluent areas, and poor people are particularly damaged when their interpersonal networks are disrupted. Further, this type of endogenous exchange becomes irrelevant if it does not carry with it the external connection to economic and political structures that foster community (Logan and Molotch 1987). In the aggregate, the impact of social disruptions on the neighborhood can be devastating.

At the community level, a minimum number of healthy networks are needed for the neighborhood to function effectively. When a sufficient number of individual networks are disrupted, the community is disrupted, too. There may be a tipping point; that is, a small number of people may be removed to prison or jail with little ill effect because the remaining networks are minimally concerned. But after some point of having males removed, the remaining networks lose their capacity to function as ordinary social controls. Indeed, this threshold may be lower in the most disorganized communities, where networks are thin to begin with and thus more vulnerable. In other words, social capital contextualizes the impact of network disruption through incarceration. Not only do disorganized communities have more networks disrupted through incarceration, the impact may be stronger in these neighborhoods because they have lower thresholds owing to depleted supplies of social capital.

### Collective Efficacy and Informal Social Control

*Collective efficacy* is the capacity of a group of people who live in the same vicinity to come together to solve problems or otherwise take action that affects their collective circumstances. Collective efficacy is a normative concept. It assumes a shared understanding of what the collective problem is and what is needed to solve it, and it relies upon the community's sense of a shared interest in each other's prospects.

Studies have demonstrated that collective efficacy is a factor in crime rates (Morenoff, Sampson and Raudenbush 2001).

In many of the most economically disadvantaged places, where reentry cycling is concentrated, normative dissensus exists. Anderson's studies (1999) of poor inner-city neighborhoods describes the normative conflict between the older leaders and the younger males. Exposure to the criminal justice system has been shown in some studies to be associated with lack of confidence in authority (Tyler 1990). To the extent that collective efficacy is built on a normative foundation, impoverished areas may lack that normative foundation. Many of the people who live in these places have had experiences with legal authority, as represented by the criminal justice system, that may undermine belief in conventional authority. The mix of experiences may lead to mixed regard for authority and so may serve as a poor collective normative foundation.

For people to come together in collective efficacy also requires a degree of stability to undergird the shared normative views. The original work of Shaw and McKay (1942), articulating the problem of social disorganization, defines the problem of residential mobility and documents its importance. That is, places that lack a stable population have difficulty developing the interpersonal relationships that promote collective efficacy. As noted above, though, the places where incarceration is concentrated today may be where there is some measure of traditional residential stability, but only because people are unable to move elsewhere (Wilson 1987). Voluntary mobility out of undesirable areas is replaced by the coercive mobility of incarceration, however, which means there is turnover in population despite the inability of residents to find other places to live. There is also a tendency toward withdrawal among people who live in these undesirable places, and this isolation has several sources. People who fear crime withdraw from their neighbors (Skogan 1990), as do people who struggle to find time to meet family obligations. Those who have family members in prison report responding to this circumstance by isolating themselves from others (Rose, Clear, and Ryder 2000).

The most powerful source of public safety is the array of informal social controls that suppress deviance. These are the forces that sustain order and compliance with norms that are outside the formal agency of the state. There are principally two levels of informal social control

(Hunter 1985). *Private social control* is the influence exerted by families and loved ones to get people to conform to social expectations (in particular, not to break laws or violate norms). Private social control is typically the result of strong ties. *Parochial social control* is the influence of nonintimate social relations to get people to conform to the expectations of voluntary social groups, employers, religious institutions, and so forth. Thus, strong ties are the foundation for private social control. Weak ties are the basis of parochial social control, because they develop as a result of relationships outside the family and friendship networks.

Informal social-control capacities are strained by removal and reentry (Clear, Rose, and Ryder 2001). This is in large part because families, the main source of private social control, are directly challenged by a family member's removal, and later are challenged again to become part of an ex-prisoner's adjustment. In places facing high-volume incarceration, this can be a dominant problem. As people turn attention to the resuscitation of their strong networks, weak ties are neglected.

It is for these reasons that reentry cycling poses a challenge to the public-safety capacities of collective efficacy and informal social control. When oversubscribed social networks are forced to adjust first to a person's being removed, and then must accommodate the person's re-turn, they are even less likely to shift attention to collective action at the community level. People often isolate themselves when their loved ones go to prison, just as they frequently move. Locations also have to absorb large numbers of ex-prisoners who do not return to welcoming family systems. For these reasons, the capacity for meaningful collectivity is limited by incarceration.

In short, the normative consensus and interpersonal connectedness that are the foundation of collective efficacy are undermined by high levels of concentrated incarceration and reentry. Residents come to distrust authority, and they become alienated from basic political institutions. Family units redirect their resources to adjust first to the removal of family members and then to their return. Little capacity exists for the formation of or participation in informal organizational entities—social clubs, religious institutions, and neighborhood associations—that serve as the main source of parochial social control. Increasingly, residents turn to the formal agencies of the state for what they need—the police, welfare systems, and public health agencies. Community life as a force for social order deteriorates.

## Communities and Incarceration

Criminologists have, in recent years, begun to recognize the importance of the community as a dimension of crime. An important exploration of neighborhood-related processes and crime was offered by Robert Bursik and Harold Grasmick (1993), who integrated concepts of social control into the social disorganization framework of Shaw and McKay (1942). Social control, they argue, represents an effort by neighborhood residents to regulate the behavior of both locals and outsiders to achieve a safe living environment. They called their model "systemic," because they sought to show how social disorganization creates constraints on social networks, which in turn activate or impede the capacity of social control. Drawing from Albert Hunter's (1985) classification of social controls described above, they show in some detail how social disorganization impedes them.

The Bursik-Grasmick Basic Systemic Model suggests a traditional form of the crime-control relationship: communities that experience less social disorganization have less crime. They make the argument that residential mobility and racial and ethnic heterogeneity affect the relational networks that are the basis of control, because both conditions make it difficult for residents to establish and maintain ties within the neighborhood. These forces decrease the ability and willingness of individuals to intervene in criminal events on behalf of their neighbors, owing to individual anonymity and alienation and, possibly, to hostility or mistrust between groups. In addition, mobility and heterogeneity potentially impair the socialization of youths, who are presumably exposed to multiple standards and forms of behavior rather than to one, unified code (Bursik and Grasmick 1993).

Clearly, however, crime is not only a consequence of social disorganization but also one of the causes of it. That is, crime is one of the factors producing fear of one's neighbors and isolation from others, a foundation for social disorganization (Skogan 1990; Taylor 1997). Just as clearly, social controls, especially public controls (in the form of incarceration), feed back on most of the elements of the Basic Systemic Model. Indeed, Bursik and Grasmick themselves note that their systemic model may be incomplete because of a failure to incorporate the degree to which crime and delinquency affect a neighborhood's capacity for social control. Rose and Clear (1998) adapted the Bursik-Grasmik approach to describe a social- control feedback affecting crime at the neighborhood level. A modified version of that argument is shown in figure 4.1.

This conceptual model helps explain how high levels of incarceration, operating as a kind of coercive mobility, can lead to an increase in crime. Communities hardest hit by incarceration already suffer from depleted social supports (Wilson 1987), so that each resource they do have is vital. But incarceration causes those resources to deteriorate for members of the social network of the person going to prison. Compared to healthy neighborhoods with sufficient supplies of human and social capital to overcome this deterioration, impoverished areas suffer exponentially with each additional network disruption. We expect, then, a negative effect of coercive mobility on informal social control in these communities.

A great deal depends, of course, on whether the person is viewed as a neighborhood asset or a liability. It is logical to assume that the loss of criminally-active males benefits communities simply because they are residents who are committing crimes. Their removal, then, could be seen as a positive act by the state: criminals are gone, communities are safer, and informal controls are now free to blossom.

But if people convicted of crimes are not solely a drain—if they are resources to some members of the community and if they occupy roles within networks that form the basis for informal social control—their removal is not solely a positive act but also imposes losses on those networks and their capacity for strengthened community life. There are

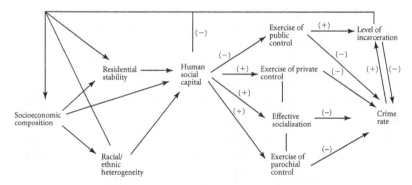

**Figure 4.1**   A nonrecursive model of crime control, social disorder, and crime.
Source: Modified from Rose and Clear 1998.

two potential ways that people who are involved in criminal behavior can serve as assets to their communities, such that when they are removed, their communities lose those assets. First, they can provide direct support to those around them; they can provide money, perform child care, give emotional support, and so forth. Second, they can provide indirect support through the way they link those around them to others, in the traditional way networks provide social capital. As Sampson puts it, "the removal of young males from vulnerable communities serves to undermine key aspects of local social capital" (2001:100).

The point is not that people who break the law be romanticized as good citizens but, rather, that they not be demonized. A view of them as "merely bad" is a one-sided stereotype that not only ignores the assets they present to the networks in which they engage but also fails to account for the ways they benefit their environments. It also fails to recognize the damage done to other relational networks when they are incarcerated—networks often consisting of nonoffending family members, relatives, and friends. To be sure, people active in committing crimes are often not very good at these supports and almost always absorb emotional and tangible resources from those who care about them. To say that people who break the law contribute to their communities is not to say that they are ideal relatives and neighbors. It does recognize, however, that their contribution exists, and in disorganized areas with low levels of control partly due to weak ties, the contributions these residents make may not be that much less than their law-abiding neighbors.

## A Framework for Identifying the Community Effects of Concentrated Incarceration

The consequences of imprisonment to the community are embedded in three important legitimate systems of neighborhood order: family, economic, and political. Familial systems are the most important source of private social controls. Economic and political systems set the context within which parochial social controls flourish or wane. These systems are the building blocks of neighborhood order. Chapters 5 and 6 present research on these areas in more detail. Here, we simply make the point that disruptions of the family, of economic viability, and of civic life by incarcerating consequential portions of a neighborhood's population can promote, rather than reduce, crime.

### Familial Systems

Communities that contribute greater numbers of people to incarceration experience higher rates of family disruption, single-parent families, and births to young, single adults (Lynch and Sabol 1992). This close association suggests a plausible hypothesis that one is, in part, a product of another (or at least that they are mutually reinforcing phenomena). Disruptions are numerous: parenting is interrupted, role models are removed, families move and change school districts, mothers go on welfare, children receive less supervision, the number of single-parent families increases, incarceration experiences are models for children, and so forth. This chain of negative effects on the family—the socialization unit of private social control— contributes to a gradual reduction of social capital within the community. None of these changes by itself "causes" delinquency, but such disruptions are associated with earlier and more active delinquent careers. Their effects would be expected to be additive and, in more extreme levels of removal of males, interactive. Moreover, these occur in addition to the destabilizing effects of crime.

### Economic Systems

The microeconomics of concentrated incarceration and reentry create neighborhoods of (mostly) men who have depleted their labor-market prospects in places where labor markets are weak to begin with. Imprisonment in large numbers ravages the supplies of local human capital and leaves a gap in employable residents. Prior to incarceration, most prisoners are an economic resource to their neighborhoods and immediate families. For example, in impoverished neighborhoods, a work-age male generates economic activity from a variety of endeavors, including off-the-books work, intermittent illicit drug trade, theft, welfare, and part-time employment. When he goes to prison, some of this economic activity is taken up by others who replace him, and some is not. When he comes back from prison, his legitimate labor-market prospects are even more bleak than they were before.

Also, the macroeconomics of crime policy damage inner-city communities by shifting government funding away from improving those communities and toward penal institutions instead. Once they are arrested and incarcerated, these peoples' economic value is transformed and transferred into penal capital—the demand for salaried correctional employees to provide security. It is also transferred to the locality of the prison, where the penal system's employees reside. The harsh budgetary politics of the 1990s have corresponded to equally harsh punitive politics, in which correctional expenditures have grown by billions of dollars annually while money to support schools, supplement tuition, provide summer jobs for teens, and so forth was cut. The latter funds had provided meager support for communities already hard hit by crime and justice, but the funds became more meager still. Whatever role these social programs play in propping up informal networks of social control is eliminated with the depletion of funding. A neighborhood experiencing economic loss as a result of increased incarceration will also experience an increase in crime.

## Political Systems

The overwhelming presence of the American criminal justice system in these impoverished communities goes a long way to defining the meaning of the state for this segment of society. The state is most likely encountered as a coercive agent of control rather than a fair agent of justice; and when this perception is true, people are less likely to conform their behavior to the requirements of the law (Tyler 1990). Most minority-group children can tell stories of racism in the criminal justice system, and validation of these tales is apparent to the eye. This is one of the reasons it is no surprise that many inner-city young people define the power of the state as a nemesis to be avoided rather than an ally to be cultivated. In the community, disillusionment with the political structure often erodes residents' feelings of empowerment and reduces their willingness to participate in local politics. As a result, the call for citizen involvement may fall on deaf ears.

Furthermore, there has been a systematic move to bar people who have felony convictions or who have been to prison from political participation (Uggen and Manza 2005). Laws that disenfranchise citizens with felony convictions have disparate impact on African Americans, many of whom are already alienated from politics. These laws make certain that inner-city areas with many disenfranchised residents are underrepresented in the vote. One result is that policies friendly to inner-city constituencies have disproportionally poor political payoff for those who run for office.

## Discussion

This chapter argues that high levels of incarceration can damage social networks and social capital, increasing disorganization by impeding other forms of control. High incarceration rates may contribute to high rates of criminal violence by the way they foster social problems such as inequality, deterioration of family life, economic and political alienation, and social disorganization. When incarceration is concentrated at high levels within certain communities, the effect is to undermine social, political, and economic systems already weakened by the low levels of human and social capital owing to high rates of poverty, unemployment, and crime. Further impairing these damaged systems means that communities with scarce supplies of human and social capital are unable to produce the resources they so greatly need. The result is a reduction in social cohesion and a lessening of those communities' capacity for self-regulation.

There is reason to think that this pattern applies primarily (perhaps even exclusively) to the most resource-poor communities. These areas suffer from the most crime partly because they lack social and human capital. As a result, they suffer the most from incarceration and its unintended consequences. Stronger communities produce fewer people who break the law because they have fewer of the environmental conditions conducive to crime. Also, because stronger communities have larger supplies of human and social capital, they have stronger foundational structures and, as a result, suffer from less crime.

Incarceration is a crime-control strategy that works best for communities where few people are removed and the disruption caused by their absence is minimal; indeed, in such places many of those who are convicted stay in the community on non-prison social control systems such as probation. By contrast, high-crime neighborhoods are also high-incarceration neighborhoods. In these latter places, children are more likely to experience family disruption, lack of parental supervision, property devoid of effective guardians, and all other manner of deteriorated informal social controls that otherwise deflect the young from criminal behavior. This is the point Etzioni (1996) made when he argued that overreliance on external control agencies weakens the capacity of communities to exert their own self-management. The prison can never be a substitute for absent adults, family members, and neighbors in making a place safe.

# Death by a Thousand Little Cuts

Studies of the Impact

of Incarceration

5

The preceding chapter offered the conceptual case that high levels of incarceration would be damaging to impoverished communities. It turns out that from what we *already know* about social networks and social supports, especially in impoverished places, high rates of imprisonment ought to create challenges for those places. It is obvious that going to prison creates problems for the people who go there; after all, one of the reasons we use prison is to impose a deficit on the lawbreaker's life. We do not use prison in order to diminish the prospects for those who remain behind, however; to the contrary, we justify prison in part because it is expected to ameliorate the problems faced by those who live in high-crime communities. Yet cycling a large number of young men from a particular place through imprisonment, and then returning them to that place, is not healthy for the people who live in that place. There are sound theoretical reasons to expect high incarceration rates to make many of these places worse, not better. This is, to many, a surprising, even counterintuitive, conclusion. It certainly demands empirical support.

This chapter provides that support. In it, I review dozens of studies showing that different aspects of incarceration make life harder for those who live in places that experience high rates of incarceration. The chapter is organized around the three domains identified at the close of chapter 4.

It begins with a review of studies of the impact of incarceration on families and children. Incarceration, it turns out, affects marriage prospects, parenting capacity, family functioning, and even sexual behavior. These effects add up to alter the way a community functions. The result of this collective impact on child, family, and community functioning is a reduction in the capacity for informal social control. (I explore studies of the public safety consequences of reduced informal social controls in chapter 7.) Compared to the large number of studies of families and children, there are few exploring the impact of incarceration on economic activity. But here again, the way imprisonment diminishes the individual's economic viability translates into substantially reduced economic viability at the community level. Finally, I summarize the small number of studies of the political consequences of incarceration. These effects are profound for poor places; through the way disenfranchisement has affected electoral politics, the impact has reached all Americans.

None of these effects is particularly large by itself. But each effect, no matter how small, cannot be considered in isolation from the others. It is not just a single effect, like reduced rates of marriage, that is important, but rather the sum of reduced marriage rates, more teen-age motherhood, diminished parental supervision, and so on in those communities where incarceration is so concentrated. The review of these studies reads like a nonstop monologue of difficulties, one after another, building a sense that incarceration slices its way into almost every aspect of community life. The studies help us see how various negative effects of incarceration, many of them small, are cumulative; taken together, they are like suffering death by a thousand little cuts.

## Children and Families

We were walking around the South City neighborhood of Tallahassee, the summer of 2001. As summers always are in the Florida Panhandle, it was steamy hot. People stay inside; there may be a threesome of pre-teens playing basketball in the schoolyard, or a couple of pre-schoolers yelling exuberantly, playing in the shade of a tree. But for the most part, the out-of-doors is empty. School's out, so it would be natural to wonder where the kids are. We enter a two-story housing project, go upstairs to knock on a door in the door of a household in our sample, and explain why we are there. We are invited in. It is dark inside, the television is blaring. Four children at various ages, maybe ranging from 4 to 9, are sitting—no, bouncing—on the couch. That is where the children are, we realize, inside. Hidden or hiding. Watching TV. It becomes a theme in almost every house we visit. Mothers, children, television, noise...and no fathers.

Families are the building blocks of a healthy society, and family functioning is the key ingredient in child development. Adults in the family socialize their children about the normative rules and behavioral expectations of society. Family members connect one another—especially children—to networks of social supports that become the foundation for later social capital as adults. Families are the central mechanism of informal social controls, bolstering the limited capacity of formal social controls to shape behavior. And the interpersonal dynamics of families are the source of later psychological and emotional health (or maladjustment). There is no single institution that carries more importance in the well-being of children than the family, and the prospects for healthy social relations in adulthood rely heavily on the existence of a vibrant family life.

There are indications that family life in America is changing, especially among people who are poor. In this group, changes over the last 40 years have been devastating: divorce rates are one-third higher and births to unmarried mothers have doubled, as has the rate of households headed by single mothers (see Western, Lopoo, and McLanahan 2004). Small wonder that so much attention has recently been given to strengthening and sustaining the family life of poor families in America.

Incarceration policy has been a fellow traveler in the deterioration of poor American families. For example, almost three out of five African-American high-school dropouts will spend some time in prison, a rate five times higher than for equivalent whites (Pettit and Western 2004). Two-fifths of those African-American high-school dropouts are fathers who were living with their children before they entered prison (Western, Patillo, and Weiman 2004). One-fourth of *juveniles* convicted of crime have children (Nurse 2004); locking up these fathers increases the chances of divorce and damages their bonds with their children. Counting both adult and juvenile parents, there are probably close to 2 million children in the United States with a parent currently behind prison bars (extrapolating from Western, Pattillo, and Weiman 2004). Between 1991 and 1999, according to Murray and Farrington (forthcoming), the number of children with a mother in prison was up 98 percent, and the number with a father in prison rose by 58 percent. Half of these children are black, almost one-tenth of all black children (Western 2005: fig. 6.2).

That incarceration affects families and children in deleterious ways should be obvious. There is a long and rich literature showing that removal of a parent from the home has, on the average, negative consequences for the partner and the children who remain (see, for example, Bloom 1995 and Hairston 1998). This is the average picture, of course, which masks considerable variation in outcomes. Some families do well in the face of loss; others fare disastrously. What is not clear is the nature and extent of the disruption that follows an adult's incarceration, though numerous negative and positive effects can be posited from the literature (see Hagan and Donovitzer 1999). Phillips et al. (2006) point out that:

> There is evidence... that the arrest of parents disrupts marital relationships, separates children and parents, and may contribute to the permanent legal dissolution of these relationships. It may also contribute to the establishment of grandparent-headed households and, upon parents' return home from prison, to three-generation households. (103)

They go on to say that, "One must be careful... in attributing these family risks to parents' involvement with the [criminal justice system] because these same situations (e.g., divorce, parent-child separation, economic strain, instability, large households, and so forth) also occur when parents have problems such as substance abuse, mental illness, or inadequate education" (104). Thus, while it is known that the incarceration of a parent (especially the mother) increases the chances of foster care or other substitute-care placement, and that substitute (i.e., foster) care is associated with poorer long-term life outcomes, "we know remarkably little about whether children placed in substitute care fare better or worse than similar children remaining with their own parent or parents" (Johnson and Waldfogel 2004:100). And while there is a host of behavioral and emotional problems associated with being a child of an incarcerated parent (see Hagan and Dinovitzer 1999), there are but a few studies showing that the parent's incarceration *causes* this kind of distress.

Having an adult family member go to prison has been shown as a source of problems, not the least of which is increased risk of juvenile delinquency (Widom 1994). Myriad studies show that children and partners of incarcerated adults tend to experience other difficulties, as well, compared to children of nonincarcerated parents. These include school-related performance problems, depression and anxiety, low self-esteem, and aggressiveness (see Hagan and Dinovitzer 1999). The studies show that the negative psychological, behavioral, and circumstantial impact on children from the removal of a parent for incarceration is similar in form, though not always in degree, to that produced by removal owing to divorce or death.

It might be argued that removal of a criminally active parent *improves* the environment of the remaining children. This is clearly not true. Studies (Nurse 2004) have found that substantial positive parental activity has often preceded incarceration. Garfinkel, McLanahan, and Hanson concluded that even though young fathers may have trouble holding a job and may even spend time in jail, most of them have something to offer their children (1998).

A brief review of studies of incarceration and family life helps illustrate the array of problems that arise.

## *Marriage*

There is consistent evidence that poor neighborhoods in which there is a large ratio of adult women to men are places where female-headed, single-parent families are common, and that incarceration is one of several dynamics that have removed black males from their neighborhoods, producing this ratio (Darity and Myers 1994). This may be a race-specific effect; in a county-level analysis for 1980 and 1990, Sabol and Lynch (2003) found that *both* removals to and returns from prison increased the rate of female-headed households in the county.

Being incarcerated reduces marriage prospects for young men. Analyzing the National Longitudinal Survey of Youth (NLSY), Harvard economist Adam Thomas (2005) found that going to prison substantially reduces the likelihood of being married. The effects hold across all racial and ethnic groups, but are strongest for black males over 23 years old, whose likelihood of getting married drops by 50 percent following incarceration. Thomas concluded that "past imprisonment is associated with a lower probability of marrying not only in the near term but also over the long run... [and] it is certainly the case that, among blacks, the relationship cannot easily be explained away by casually controlling for economic, family background characteristics, and neighborhood effects" (2005:26–27). He does find, however, that men with past incidents of incarceration who do become involved with women are more likely instead to cohabit without marriage. These unconventional living arrangements contribute to intergenerational family dysfunction. Cohabitation is associated with previous parental divorce, suggesting an intergenerational pattern, and it carries the risk for future abuse or neglect (called "troubled home"). Western's (2006) analysis of the NYSL confirms these patterns, and his analysis of the Fragile Families Survey of Child Well-Being estimates that going to prison cuts the rate of marriage within a year of the birth of a child by at least one-half and about doubles the chance of separating in that same year (figs. 6.8, 6.9). It is thus not surprising that Lynch and Sabol (2004b) have estimated that 46 percent of the prison population are currently divorced, compared to 17 percent of nonimprisoned adults.

The reduction in the rate of marriage is important in several respects. Families formed by marriage have more longevity than those defined by cohabitation, on average. Mothers in marriages expect and receive more support from their male partners than those in cohabitation relationships (Gibson, Edin, and McLanahan 2003, cited in Western, Lopoo and McLanahan 2004). With increases in family disruption and reduced male involvement in the home there are increased risks of poor school performance by children, of domestic violence, and of contact with the juvenile justice system (Western 2006, esp. figs. 6.10, 6.11).

For the men, there are also consequences of incarceration on marriage. Laub, Nagin, and Sampson (1998) have shown that stable marriages promote lifestyle changes in adults who were previously criminally active; marriage can thus serve as a turning point in their criminal careers (see also Sampson and Laub 1993). Men who do not get married tend to find it harder to form pro-social relationships and identify the positive social bonds that promote an end to criminal activity. It follows that reduced marriage prospects resulting from a term in prison are a risk factor in recidivism.

*Parenting*

While they are locked up, many men maintain contact with their children; about half receive mail and/or phone calls, and one-fifth receive visits while in prison (U.S. Department of Justice 1997, cited in Western, Pattillo and Weiman 2004: table 1.5). But the rate at which mothers dissolve their relationships with their children's father during the latter's imprisonment is very high, even for fathers who were active in their children's lives prior to being arrested (Edin, Nelson, and Paranal 2004). In general, incarceration has "a deleterious effect on relationships between former inmate fathers and their children" (Nurse 2004:90). In their longitudinal study of the Fragile Families Survey and Child Well-Being Study data, Western, Lopoo, and McLanahan show that "men who have been incarcerated are much less likely to be married to or cohabiting with the mother of their children twelve months after the birth of their children than men who have not been incarcerated" (2004:39–40). There are several reasons for this. For women who live in poor communities, "the decision to marry or remarry depends in part on the economic prospects, social respectability and trustworthiness of their potential partners" (Western, Lopoo, and McLanahan 2004:23). Against these criteria, many (or most) ex-prisoners do not fare well.

Even when mothers retain their relationships with the incarcerated father of their children, incarceration diminishes the capacity for effective parent-child relationships. Edin, Nelson, and Paranal point out that "incarceration often means that fathers miss out on . . . key events that serve to build parental bonds and to signal . . . that they intend to support their children both financially and emotionally. . . . The father's absence at these crucial moments . . . can weaken his commitment to the child years later, and the child's own commitment to his or her father" (2004:57).

Researchers point out that this general pattern has to be understood in the context of two caveats. First, as a group, young fathers who are poor and have marginal human capital typically struggle to maintain good relationships with their children and their young mothers, and incarceration may not be a cause of further difficulties so much as a correlate of the personality and situational factors that produce these difficulties. Under the best of circumstances, the bonds between criminally active fathers and their children are often quite fragile. As a result, sometimes young mothers who made progress when their male partners went to prison suffer setbacks when they return (Cohen 1992). Second, for some fathers who have had little contact with their children before imprisonment, the descent into prison is a life-changing moment that opens a door to renewal of those bonds in ways that are not only beneficial for the child but for the father as well (Edin, Nelson, and Paranal 2004).

There are, after all, over 600,000 men who enter prison in a year, and the range of parental interests and patterns for such a group must run the gamut. On the average, however, having one's parent go to prison is not a positive life experience. It disrupts the family and damages parenting capacity.

### Family Functioning

Lynch and Sabol (2004b) have estimated that between one-fourth and one-half of all prisoners disrupt a family when they are removed for incarceration. Joseph Murray's (2005) excellent review lists a dozen studies of the way incarceration of a male parent/spouse (or partner) affects the functioning of the family unit he left behind. The most prominent impact is economic—spouses and partners report various forms of financial hardship, sometimes extreme, that result from the loss of income after the male partner's incarceration. This "loss of income is compounded by additional expenses of prison visits, mail, telephone calls . . . and sending money to [the person] imprisoned" (2005:445). Because most families of prisoners start out with limited financial prospects, even a small financial impact can be devastating. Phillips et al. (2006) longitudinal study of poor, rural children in North Carolina found that having a parent get arrested led to family break-up and family economic strain, both of which, they point out, are risk factors of later delinquency.

After the male's imprisonment, the family responds to his incarceration in a variety of ways. In order to deal with changed financial circumstances, prisoners' families often move, leading to family disruptions that may include the arrival of replacement males in the family, reduced time for maternal parenting owing to secondary employment, and so on (Edin, Nelson, and Paranal 2004). Moves may also result in more crowded living conditions (especially when the prisoner's family moves in with relatives) and changes in educational districts that may produce disruptions in schooling.

There are also relationship problems. Female partners who find a male replacement for the man who has gone to prison often face the psychological strains that accompany the arrival of a new male in the household. Prisoners' spouses and partners report strains in relationships with other family members and neighbors. Carlson and Carvera (1992) showed that women often have to rely on family and friends to fill the hole left by the incarcerated husband, providing money, companionship, and babysitting and generally straining those ties. Strains in the relationships with children are also reported, often resulting from emotional and functional difficulties that spouses and partners encounter when a male partner goes to prison.

Residents of high-incarceration communities see imprisonment as one cause of weakened family functioning. St. Jean calls this "amputation without repair" (personal communication, 2006); in his ethnographic study of crime and neighborhood life in Buffalo, New York, he quotes one of the respondents as saying, "I say amputate, because when you take a son from his mother or from his father, you have amputated.... It is like someone cutting off your arm or cutting off your head. It is an unnatural extraction, that puts you in an unnatural place." St. Jean concludes:

> I observed through 4.5 years of intense ethnography that incarceration was the major strategy used to address high crime problems in Wentworth (a poor neighborhood of Buffalo) and when men and women went to jail or prison, they often ... became more angry and desperate than [when] they entered ... had more hopelessness ... and they were less employable. They also became part of a cultural attitude which seemed to treat incarceration as a right of passage.

## Child Functioning

Incarceration has an effect on the child that is both direct and indirect (Murray 2005). The mother's incarceration has been shown to produce "a significant worsening of both reading scores and behavioral problems" (Moore and Shierholz 2005:2). Likewise, male parent incarceration has been shown to lead to later antisocial behavior by children in an English sample (Murray and Farrington 2005). This latter study compared children whose parents were incarcerated during their early childhoods to children without parental separation, children for whom parental separation was due to other factors (i.e., death), and children whose parents went to prison and returned before they were born. Outcomes included delinquency, antisocial personality measures, and life successes. The children of incarcerated parents were between 2 and 13 times more likely to have had various negative outcomes than any of the comparison groups. These effects appear to be direct, in part because they survive in the face of statistical controls for social class and other family demographics.

Indirect effects stem from the way incarceration undermines family stability. Changes in parental working conditions and family circumstances often a result from incarceration and are known to affect children's social adjustment and norm transmission across generations (Parcel and Menaghan, 1993). Among the problems suffered by children during a parent's incarceration are: "depression, hyperactivity, aggressive behavior, withdrawal, regression, clinging behavior, sleep problems, eating problems, running away, truancy and poor school grades" (Murray 2005:466). Studies have also shown that parental incarceration is a risk factor in delinquency (Gabel and Shindledecker 1993), emotional maladjustment (Kampfner 1995), and academic performance problems (Phillips and Bloom 1998). In her summary of the literature on childhood loss of a parent, including parental incarceration, Marcy Viboch (2005) points to a range of common reactions to the trauma, including depression, aggression, drug abuse, and running away. Murray and Farrington's (forthcoming) systematic review of studies of parental incarceration on children find evidence of both direct and mediated effects on anti-social behavior, school performance, mental health, drug abuse, and adult unemployment. They conclude that "parental imprisonment may cause adverse child outcomes because of traumatic separation, stigma, or social and economic strain." (1)

The potential negative impact of incarceration on school performance is particularly important. School success is linked to family structure, which has an effect independent of social class and parenting style in impoverished families (Vacha and McLaughlin 1992). Behavioral problems in school are also correlated with problems in parental relationships, including child abuse—an early family dynamic that contributes to later delinquency. Psychologist Cathy Spatz Widom (1989, 1994), following a cohort of children from early school years to adulthood, has observed that victims of early childhood abuse had earlier criminal activity, increased risk of an arrest during adolescence (by more than 50%), and, when they became adults, twice as many arrests as controls.

The impact of incarceration on children may become stronger with higher incarceration rates. A study of the impact of incarceration on a

Swedish sample of children (Murray, Janson, and Farrington 2005) found the same kind of higher rate of delinquency for those children, but unlike the other studies cited above, it washed out when statistical controls were introduced. The authors conclude that sparing use of prison stays in Sweden—almost always for very short terms—tends to ameliorate the negative effects of parental incarceration. If that is the case, then the U.S. effects would be even greater than those found in European studies.

## Community Dynamics

At a most basic level, the absence of males restricts the number of adults available to supervise young people in the neighborhood. The presence of large numbers of unsupervised youth is predictive of various aspects of community-level disorder, including serious crime (Sampson and Groves 1989). It is also known that the existence of "adverse neighborhood conditions" as rated by mothers, tended to be associated with a decrease in the self-control of youth who live in disadvantage (Pratt, Turner, and Piquero 2004). Under these conditions, the informal social control over youths that might have been exercised by family members or neighbors often fails to materialize. These attenuated informal social controls are the springboard for crime, and the effects can be felt in adjacent neighborhoods as well (Mears and Bhati 2006).

In the face of community disruptions, some families isolate themselves from neighbors. In a series of interviews in the South Bronx, Andres Rengifo (2006) has observed that many residents seek to withdraw from their impoverished surroundings. One housing project resident, a single mother with four children (one of whom was attending Yale University and two of whom were in the prestigious Bronx High School of Science public school) said that although she had lived in the projects for seven years, "this place is a dump. I don't talk to anyone, I don't know anyone. That's how we made it here."

While it is commonly assumed that criminally active adults are less capable or less willing guardians, there is no evidence to support this. In fact, Venkatesh (1997) reports that although many problems within the housing project he studied were gang related, gang members involved in criminal activity tended to be accepted because they contributed to the well-being of the community in a variety of ways. For instance, they acted as escorts or protectors, renovated basketball courts, and discouraged truancy. These factors eroded perceptions of them as social deviants, partly because their roles as sons and brothers helped residents view them as "only temporarily" bad, and partly because the gang helped the community in tangible ways.

## Intimate (Sexual) Relations

The incarceration of large numbers of parent-age males restricts the number of male partners available in the neighborhood. This means that mothers find more competition for intimate partners and to serve as parents for their children. In the context of more competition for male support, mothers may feel reluctant to end relationships that are unsuitable for children, partly because prospects for suitable replacements are perceived as poor. Thus, even when men who have been sent to prison were abusers, if they are replaced by men who are also abusive, the trade-off is negative. Likewise, men living with advantageous gender ratios may feel less incentive to remain committed in their parenting partnerships. When the remaining family unit is forced to choose from a thinning stock of males, the options may not be attractive. For those women who end abusive relationships and live alone, the neighborhood implications may also be problematic.

Citing these dynamics, epidemiologists James Thomas and Elizabeth Torrone (2006) investigated the role of high rates of incarceration on sexual behavior in poor neighborhoods. They argued that the pressures on men for safe sex and monogamy are reduced as the ratio of women to marriageable men gets very high. Analyzing North Carolina counties and communities, they found that incarceration rates in one year predicted later increases in rates of gonorrhea, syphilis, and chlamydia among women. They also found that a doubling of incarceration rates increased in the incidence of childbirth by teenage women by 71.61 births per 100,000 teenage women. They conclude that "high rates of incarceration can have the unintended consequence of destabilizing communities and contributing to adverse health outcomes: (2006:1).

This latter finding is notable because teenage births are associated with numerous problematic outcomes for both the mothers and their children. For mothers, teenage births are more likely to lead to a life plagued with lower wages, underemployment, reliance upon welfare, and single parenthood. For *all* children of mothers who have their first child at a very early age, there is an increased likelihood that those children will be arrested for delinquency and violent crime (Pogarsky, Lizotte, and Thornberry 2003). Not surprisingly, rates of out-of-wedlock births also predict higher levels of incarceration across time in the United States (Jacobs and Helms 1996).

Incarceration also seems to explain at least part of the higher rate of HIV among Africa-American men and women. Johnson and Raphael (2005) analyzed data on AIDS infection rates, provided by the U.S. Centers for Disease Control and Prevention, from 1982 to 2001, combined with national incarceration data for the same period. As did Thomas, they posit that "male incarceration lowers the sex ratio (male to female), abruptly disrupts the continuity of heterosexual relationships, and increases the exposure to homosexual activity for incarcerated males—all of which may have far-reaching implications for an individual or group's AIDS infection risk" (2005:2). What is important about their perspective is that they assume *both* removal and reentry as potential destabilizing factors in sexual relations. They find "very strong effects of male incarceration rates on both male and female AIDS infection rates [and] that the higher incarceration rates among black males over this period explain a large share of the racial disparity in AIDS between black women and women of other racial and ethnic groups" (3).

## Incarceration and Families: A Summary

Available studies, listed above, show that incarceration imposes a long list of costs on families and children. Children experience developmental and emotional strains, have less parental supervision, are at greater risk of parental abuse, and face an increased risk of having their own problems with the justice system. Mothers find it harder to sustain stable intimate relationships with men who have gone to prison, and they have an increased risk of contracting sexually transmitted diseases. Families are more likely to break up, and they encounter economic strains. Girls raised in these high-imprisonment places are more likely to become pregnant in their teen years; boys are more likely to become involved in delinquency. Residents feel less positively about their neighbors, and they may tend to isolate themselves from them. The descriptions of these challenges to family life in impoverished places are not surprising, as we have long known that poor neighborhoods are problem settings for family life.

What is new is to see, demonstrated in the data, the role incarceration plays in creating these challenges by disrupting social networks and distorting social relationships.

To be sure, incarceration is not the sole cause of these situations. Studies find that parental problems such as drug abuse and mental illness also contribute directly and separately to these situations (Phillips et al. 2006). Addressing the problem of incarceration alone will not be sufficient to ameliorate these problems. By the same token, trying to overcome the many family deficits experienced by these at-risk children without considering the effect of incarceration is not likely to work.

## The Economics of Community Life

Mrs. Anderson is a 60-year-old, retired Florida state worker with a decidedly tired demeanor. One of the reasons she is tired is that she has eight children living with her. Five are hers and three are her grandchildren, living with her because both the father (her son) and the mother are currently back in prison. Mrs. Anderson is keeping them until the son gets released, due in another six months. Her pension barely stretches to cover the cost of keeping this hungry, active crew fed and dressed. She explains that she cannot afford to take the kids to visit their father, send him money for the commissary, and pay for the collect long-distance phone calls he sometimes makes. Instead, she has to choose only one way to help, whatever she can afford and whatever seems most pressing at the time. Usually, she sends canteen money. The children rarely visit or talk to their parents. Mrs. Anderson also says she is beginning to delve into her savings and has no plan to turn to when that money is gone.

Wealth is created by the production of goods and services that people want to pay money to acquire. It is sustained through the value of property. Incarceration, when present in large concentration, affects both the markets for goods and services in a neighborhood and the value of its property.

When money changes hands multiple times in a neighborhood, it creates income for each person who receives it. Even impoverished places have this kind of economic activity. Often, it is a cash economy comprising of legal economic activity related to marginal—sometimes off-the-books—employment and state welfare. Sometimes the work takes place in illegal markets. Illegal markets, such as drug trade, are one of the main ways money is brought into the neighborhood. This money can be a substantial source of funds when it changes hands multiple times in the same neighborhood. Much more typically, in other forms of commerce, the meager funds that poor people have quickly leave their neighborhoods to pay for rent, food, health care, and other services.

Of course, impoverished places are poor because people there do not make much money, from work or otherwise. People who get into trouble with the law are characterized by poor work records before they get arrested. Only 42 percent of mothers and 55 percent of fathers who are incarcerated were working full time at the time of their arrest; 32 percent of mothers and 18 percent of fathers were unemployed and not even looking for work (Uggen, Wakefield, and Western 2005).

On top of this poor starting place, going to prison is not good for long-term employment prospects. There is some evidence that during their initial period of release from incarceration, both women and men are slightly *more* likely to be employed, perhaps because they are required to get jobs as a condition of many community supervision agencies (see LaLonde and George 2003 and Cho and LaLonde 2005 for women; Western, Kling, and Weiman 2001 for men). Yet these short-term effects rapidly wear off, as participation in the labor market by people who have been to prison diminishes over time. Regardless of *rates* of participation, various economists have documented how going to prison has a serious, long-term negative impact on lifetime earnings. Jeffrey Grogger (1995) demonstrates that merely being arrested has a short-term, negative impact on earnings, while Richard Freeman (1992) shows that suffering a conviction and imprisonment has a permanent impact on earning potential. Jeffrey Kling (1999) finds small effects on the earnings of people convicted of federal crimes, mostly concentrated among those convicted of white-collar crimes. Western (2005: fig. 5.1) estimates that going to prison reduces annual earnings by about one-third among people sent to state prison.

We know, then, that most of these former residents of a neighborhood do not return there from prison better prepared to participate in the labor force. Uggen and his colleagues (Uggen, Wakefield, and Western 2005) argue that incarceration impedes the capacity for work by stigmatizing people convicted of crimes, damaging the social networks they might use to find jobs, undermining job skills, exacerbating mental and physical illnesses that impede work, and teaching bad work habits. In short, prison takes ill-prepared labor-market participants and reduces their work prospects. Western's analysis of the National Longitudinal Survey of Youth offers "strong evidence that incarceration carries not just an economic penalty on the labor market; it also confines ex-prisoners to bad jobs that are characterized by high turnover and little chance of moving up the ladder" (2006:128). This economic marginality explains some of the problems families encounter in high-incarceration neighborhoods, since men who are "stuck in low-wage or unstable jobs [find] that their opportunities for marriage will be limited . . . [and] the stigma of incarceration makes single mothers reluctant to marry or live with the fathers of their children" (Uggen, Wakefield, and Western 2005:221), with the result that *both* work and marriage prospects are degraded (Huebner 2005).

### The Production of Local Labor Markets

The economic prospects of people who live in poor communities are linked. Family members earning money contribute to the welfare of their families, and this is true even when some of those earnings are from criminal activity such as drug sales. Edin and Lein (1997) show that, in an effort to sustain their families, mothers rely on regular, substantial financial help from people in their personal networks, because neither welfare nor low-paying jobs provide sufficient income to cover expenses. In their study, up to 91 percent of the respondents reported that they had received money from members in their networks; 55 percent had received cash from their families, 32 percent received cash from their boyfriends, 41 percent from their child's father. Incarceration removes from the neighborhood many of the men who provide support to these women.

The concentration of formerly incarcerated men in poor neighborhoods not only affects them but may also damage the labor-market prospects of others in the community. Roberts (2004) points out that "the spatial concentration of incarceration . . . impedes access to jobs for youth in those communities because it decreases the pool of men who can serve as their mentors and their links to the working world . . . generating employment discrimination against entire neighborhoods (1294). Sabol and Lynch (2003) have shown that, as county-level incarceration rates grow, so do unemployment rates for blacks who live in those counties.

To the extent that incarceration primarily removes young men from the neighborhood, it also increases the likelihood of single-parent families being headed by women, with welfare as a consequence. Browne (1997) has shown that long-term exposure to welfare, lack of work experience, and having never been married are factors that disconnect poor women from mainstream society, a condition contributing to earning differences between black and white women. Thus, large-scale incarceration of men may influence the earning power of the women they leave behind. Communities with strong concentrations of families on welfare do not support a vibrant private labor market.

Sullivan's work (1989) suggests that, in impoverished neighborhoods, a work-age male generates economic activity that translates into purchases at the local deli, child support, and so forth. This economic value is generated in a variety of endeavors, including off-the-books work, intermittent illicit drug trade, theft, welfare, and part-time employment. Fagan's (1997) review of legal and illegal work confirms that it is simplistic to view these workers as solely oriented toward illicit income (see also Fagan and Freeman 1999). Research shows that many, if not most, of those who engage in crime also have legal employment, so that their removal from the neighborhood removes a worker from the local economy. Fagan recognizes the argument that sending a single person who held a legal job to prison frees that position for another (potentially law-abiding) resident. However, in local areas where a high proportion of residents engage in both legal and illegal work, Fagan notes that removing many individuals may injure the local economy. Even if sending someone to prison does free the legitimate job for someone else, at best this simply shifts the economic benefit of the job from one community household to another, with no net benefit to the neighborhood. In large numbers, however, it raids supplies of local human capital and leaves a gap in employable residents. The result is that numerous household units suffer specific losses and the community suffers a net loss. Even families that reap the individual benefit of newly available employment suffer the indirect costs of depleted neighborhood economic strength.

The erosion of local labor markets is a precursor to higher rates of crime. Economic hardship is one of the strongest geographic predictors of crime rates. The socially imbedded nature of crime and unemployment suggests that those communities suffering deprivation experience greater criminal involvement among residents (Hagan 1993). Therefore, it is reasonable to assume that a neighborhood experiencing economic loss as a result of incarceration will experience an increase in crime (Wilson 1987). In fact, studies have documented the impact of a community's economic well-being on its level of criminality. Taylor and Covington (1988) show that shifts in the rate of community violent crimes are linked to changes in relative deprivation, and Block (1979) finds a link between a community's crime rate and its ratio of wealthy to impoverished residents. Crutchfield and Pitchford (1997) show that the level of community-wide labor-force participation may be even more important than an individual's employment in shaping individual criminality. These studies confirm that social processes damaging a neighborhood's economic viability may also tend to make it less safe.

## The Value of Property

When it comes to the value of real estate, the saying goes, three aspects matter: location, location, location. Of the many factors that go into determining the value of residential property (square footage, amenities, age, and the nature of nearby structures), generalized community safety is by far one of the most important. Economists David Rasmussen and Allen Lynch (2001) have shown that nearby crimes reported in well-functioning neighborhoods have virtually no impact on the value of property for residential use. High-crime areas are another matter; in such neighborhoods crime substantially lowers the value of residential property.

Extensions of this work have analyzed the impact of incarceration on housing values in Jacksonville, Florida. Rasmussen and his colleagues developed a "hedonic model," a statistical representation of the contribution of each of the main characteristics of property in relation to its sale price in the year 1995. This work shows that localized (neighborhood) incarceration rates are correlated with hedonic values of housing, but that the correlation disappears when crime rates are taken into account. Thus, crime has a direct impact on the value of a home, reducing its sale price in high-crime areas by at least 37 percent. Incarceration has no direct effect on the sale value of a residential property.

That is not to say that incarceration is irrelevant to the value of property. To the extent that incarceration reduces crime in high-crime areas, it tends to improve the value of private property for housing. But if the effect of incarceration rates at the high end do not reduce crime, but rather increase it, the net effect is to reduce housing values if increased crime is the result of incarceration's effect on neighborhood stability. Rasmussen concludes that "the worst neighborhoods are characterized by crime and social instability that has a devastating effect on house prices. To the extent that excessive incarceration exacerbates this instability, we can be sure that house prices will reflect the accompanying increase in crime" (2004).

## The Politics of Community Life

It has been estimated that nearly 1 million of Florida's citizens are banned from voting for life because of a previous felony conviction, 50 percent of them black. The Florida laws are so strict that their enforcement formed the basis for a campaign warning people in black neighborhoods that ineligible residents who tried to vote would be subject to imprisonment. At least one set of form letters, sent out to tell black people they were ineligible to vote, had hundreds of inaccuracies. There is no telling how many legal voters assumed they were ineligible and how many more were intimidated from voting. Ironically, had Florida's felony disenfranchisement laws enabled even just the nonimprisoned to vote, most people believe the 2000 presidential election would have resulted in an Al Gore presidency.

In minority communities where incarceration is concentrated, prison is a part of life. The overwhelming presence of the American criminal justice system in high-incarceration communities goes a long way toward defining the meaning of the state for this segment of society. The state is more likely to be encountered as a coercive agent of control than as a fair agent of justice. Research now reliably shows that when people think the law is unfair, they are less likely to conform their behavior to its requirements (Tyler 1990). They may also fear it less. A black 10-year-old living in an impoverished place is likely to have at least one (and likely more) ex-cons among his fathers, uncles, brothers, and neighbors. There are many potential lessons to be learned from this. One is that state power can be used to harm family members and family interests. Another is that prison is not an unusual experience—not awesome, easily survivable. Widespread use of imprisonment becomes a kind of reassurance that the experience is "normal." Thus, the politics of imprisonment may be a combination of increasing resentment and decreasing marginal gain. Turning dominant cultural symbols upside down, there is even a claim that inner-city residents accrue street status from surviving prison.

### Attitudes toward Authority and the State

In high-incarceration neighborhoods, many residents do not believe that the state's justice agencies work on their behalf. Most minority children can tell stories of racism in the criminal-justice system, and the validation of these tales is apparent to the eye. One in three African-American males in his twenties is under some form of formal justice-system control (Mauer and Huling 1995); in large cities, as many as half are subjects of the system (Miller 1992). Many are casualties of the war on drugs.

Peter St. Jean (2006) has gathered extensive crime and community data on Buffalo, New York's, neighborhoods, including interviews of "old heads" in poor, primarily black areas. He concludes that "preexisting socio-economic and other conditions [combined with] preexisting law enforcement factors—profiling, discrimination, different responses to crime committed by blacks and Hispanics as opposed to whites" has led to a pervasive sense of cynicism among those he has interviewed." They describe the conundrum they face, choosing between cooperation with the police and support for their family members—a "darned if you do and darned if you don't" situation. For some youth, it is perceived that incarceration has become "cool," and this counter-normativity makes the older residents distrust the prospects for many young men who come back, while at the same time distrusting the police presence in their communities.

The alienation of residents who no longer feel part of a society that is so hostile to the drug economy leaves them less likely to participate in local political organizations or to submit to the authority of more formal ones. Stewart and Simons (2006) analyzed two waves of data from the Family and Community Health Study and found that experiencing racial discrimination and living in an impoverished neighborhood, combined with poor family discipline, promoted the adoption by young black males of what Anderson (1999) has referred to as "the code of the street." High concentrations of youth who adopted "the code" was in turn associated with higher levels of crime and violence in the neighborhood.

Sociologist Robert Crutchfield has been interested in the way social conditions, such as labor markets, affect attitudes toward society and community, especially social cohesion and trust as building blocks for social capital (see Crutchfield and Pitchford 1997). Recently Crutchfield (2005) investigated the impact of concentrated levels of young men in reentry on the attitudes of neighbors who had not been to prison. In a survey of residents of Seattle, Washington, Crutchfield asked respondents a series of questions regarding their attitudes toward the legitimacy of the law and the belief in authority—questions tapping social cohesion and trust. He found that in neighborhoods where there are high rates of young men returning from prison, overall social cohesion and trust are affected: in "neighborhoods with relatively large concentrations of former prisoners and, by extension ... communities with more churning of people into and out of the prison system ... [the negative attitude] in those places that we ordinarily attribute to economic disadvantage is due in part to sentencing patterns and correctional policies" (2004). This disrespect of formal institutions portends badly for community safety, as earlier work has shown that individuals whose jobs hold no future have less of a stake in conformity and are more likely to engage in criminal activity (Crutchfield and Pitchford 1997). In similar research in New York City, Tyler and Fagan (2005) show that people in the neighborhoods where incarceration rates are highest tend to view the police as unfair and disrespectful, corroding their views of the legitimacy of policing and broader governmental authority, and in turn signaling their withdrawal from social regulation and political life.

## Voting

Alienation and negativity toward authority tend to suppress political participation, further alienating people in these areas from influence on law and policy. But the effects of intangible attitudes on the exercise of political power are augmented by laws that restrict voting by people with criminal records.

All states impose voting limitations on people who go to prison—some states impose very broad restrictions, others much less so. It has been estimated that more than 5.3 million people in the United States are prohibited from voting as a consequence of their criminal records (Uggen and Manza 2006). These disenfranchised Americans mirror the prison population in their socio-demographics: one in seven black males is disenfranchised (Mauer and Huling 1995). They also tend to concentrate in poor neighborhoods, as we would expect, so that mass incarceration "translates the denial of individual felon's voting rights into disenfranchisement of entire communities" (Roberts 2004). A study of voter disenfranchisement patterns in Atlanta (King and Mauer 2004), for example, finds an extremely high correlation between the portion of voters who are disenfranchised and the racial composition of the local area. Areas that are predominantly black have a voter disenfranchisement rate three to four times higher than the rate in areas that are predominantly white. They conclude:

> The disenfranchisement effect contributes to a vicious cycle ... that further disadvantages low-income communities of color. The first means by which this occurs is through decisions of resource allocation. ... At a state level, beleaguered communities are affected through a diminished impact on public policy. (15)

Places with residents who do not vote carry limited potential for influencing the politics of resource acquisition and dissemination. In poor places that have so many ex-prisoners, voting rates are very low in part because of the laws, but also because of generally low rates of voting. People with felony arrests who may legally vote are 18 percent less likely to vote than those who have not been arrested; people in prison who are allowed to vote are 27 percent less likely to do so than their non-incarcerated counterparts (Uggen and Manza 2005).

Do high incarceration rates in poor neighborhoods suppress *legal* voting in those places? Jeffrey Fagan (2006) and his colleagues studied the impact of rates of incarceration on voting practices in New York City neighborhoods from 1985 to 1996. They found that poor neighborhoods had very low rates of voter participation in elections, but that the nonparticipation was not directly affected by the rate of incarceration. Voter registration and participation rates were lower in neighborhoods with high rates of incarceration, and especially in neighborhoods where drug enforcement was the primary engine fueling the incarceration rate. They concluded that the same factors that produce elevated crime rates, invite close police surveillance, and promote drug-law enforcement also encourage lower voter participation. The withdrawal of citizens from this most basic function of civil society may be another way in which citizens signal a perception that laws are applied unfairly, disproportionately, and in a manner that is disrespectful of citizens' rights and dignity (see also Tyler and Fagan 2005).

The result is that, in these places, political clout is diminished and the people struggle to influence the policy decisions that affect their interests. Tax policy, social welfare practices, and political priorities do not reflect the interests of these (non)voters. The macroeconomics of crime policy also damage inner-city communities by shifting government funding away from those communities and toward penal institutions. The harsh budgetary politics of the 1990s have corresponded to equally harsh punitive politics in which correctional expenditures have grown by billions of dollars annually while money to support schools, supplement tuition, provide summer jobs for teens, and so forth were diminished. The latter funding provided meager supports for communities already hard hit by crime and justice, and the funding become even more meager. Whatever role these social programs play in propping up informal networks of social control is eliminated with the depletion of their funding.

## Collective Action

Communities vary in the means they use to deal with problems. While it is generally perceived that poor communities do not organize, some clearly do (Henig 1982). Researchers have found collective activity, covering a broad range of approaches, in all types of neighborhoods (Podolefsky and DuBow 1980). Variations in collective action can be attributed to several factors. For instance, the extent to which communities rely on authority structures or formal social controls varies according to differences in the racial and class composition of the community (Bennett 1995). The degree to which residents perceive that they receive inadequate police services is also related to their propensity to organize locally (Henig 1982). The political capacity of the community may be a critical factor, too, particularly for communities that have fewer internal resources and need to increase their external resources (Bennett 1995). In other words, communities vary in their desire and their capacity to organize. The extent to which a neighborhood has developed a network of political and social institutions prior to the occurrence of a specific threat helps to determine whether the community will be able to mobilize collective action against the threat (Henig 1982).

Podolefsky and DuBow (1980) found that residents who define the crime problem as stemming from within the neighborhood advocate different control tactics than do residents who see crime as coming from outside. To the extent that this is true, residents are inclined to develop a social-problems approach to crime reduction; to the extent that they define the problem as coming from outside the neighborhood, they are likely to ask for an approach that emphasizes victimization and calls for law enforcement. A social-problems approach focuses on improving social conditions thought to be the root of crime, such as youth behavior, lack of job opportunities, and neighborhood environmental hazards. Policy makers who may not understand that residents make this distinction often implement victimization-approach strategies when the community would prefer a social-problems approach.

*Collective efficacy* is the term coined by Robert Sampson and his colleagues to refer to the "social cohesion among neighbors combined with their willingness to intervene on behalf of the common good" (Sampson, Raudenbush, and Earls 1997:918). Places that are collectively effective are capable of coming together to attain their common good. People organize politically, form social groups that advance collective interests, and assist one another in exerting informal social control.

Lynch and Sabol (2004b) investigated the incarceration-affected community-level variables, including collective efficacy, in Baltimore neighborhoods. They explain their conceptualization as follows:

> If residents have expectations that norms will be observed, in-voking norms ... is likely to bring about compliance because the belief is shared..... Without the ... shared beliefs about norms (or community solidarity), invoking norms can be unproductive or even dangerous. (140)

They found that "incarceration reduces community solidarity and at-tachment to communities," though it improves the level of collective efficacy as measured by normative consensus (157). Their results are mixed—an issue to which we will turn our attention again in detail in chapter 7. But for our purposes here, they find that incarceration is associated with a reduction in "the social processes on which social controls depend "(157).

## Economics and Politics: A Summary

A string of studies show that workers face labor-market problems as a result of their imprisonment. When they go to prison, they put financial pressures on those who remain. When they come back out, they struggle to participate in legal labor markets. When their numbers are quite large, they make it difficult for a legitimate employment market to flourish in the places they live. Adding to these economic strains are the ways that high-incarceration rates impede a place's ability to exert influence on politics. Because people disenfranchised as a result of felony convictions are often concentrated in a small number of communities, the political influence of poor communities is diminished. Because many who live in these impoverished areas are alienated from participation in political life regardless of their legal records, these places can have a dominant ethic of distrust of authority and disrespect for the state.

## Discussion

The purpose of this chapter was to consider evidence on the impact of incarceration on various aspects of community life. A host of studies was considered. Table 5.1 summarizes the main results of this work.

As this table shows, this chapter has been a long listing of empirical studies suggesting that elevated incarceration rates, focused on poor communities that already struggle, exacerbates the problems those communities face. Some effects are direct, as in the way children's life chances are reduced by parental incarceration. Some are indirect, as how incarceration sours political altitudes leading to low levels of political participation.

This chapter uses the metaphor of death by a thousand little cuts. This is an apt metaphor. Communities that provide large numbers of prisoners to the state and federal prison system struggle in a variety of ways. They have limited human and social capital. Incarceration, because it further damages the men who go to prison, eats away at the meager human capital that exists and erodes the social networks that provide the small doses of social capital on which people can call. Because it removes supports on which those who do *not* go to prison rely for quality of life, it

**Table 5.1** Summary of Studies of the Collateral Impact of Incarceration

| Area, study, and year | Impact on individuals | Impact on communities |
|---|---|---|
| *Children* | | |
| Gabel and Shindledecker 1993 | Juvenile delinquency | |
| Kampfner 1995 | Emotional maladjustment | |
| Phillips and Bloom 1998 | Emotional maladjustment | |
| More and Shierholz 2005 | Reading, school behavior | |
| Widom 1994 | Risk of juvenile/adult arrest | |
| Western, Lopoo, and MacLanahan 2004 | School performance, domestic violence, juvenile arrest | |
| Hagan and Dinovitzer 1999 | Emotional maladjustment, behavior problems | |
| Murray and Farrington 2005 | Antisocial behavior | |
| St. Jean 2006 | | |
| *Families* | | |
| Darity and Myers 1994 | | Female-headed households |
| St. Jean 2006 | Family supports | Norms of incarceration |
| Sabol and Lynch 2003 | | Black female-headed households |
| | | Neighborhood divorce rates |
| Thomas 2005 | Ever getting married | |
| Western 2005 | Parent getting married | |
| Western, Lopoo, and McLanahan 2004 | Family disruption | |
| Nurse 2004 | Father-mother relations | |
| Edin, Nelson, and Paranal 2004 | Broken father-child relations | |

| | | |
|---|---|---|
| Murray 2005 | Family economic well-being | |
| Clear et al. 1971 | Going on welfare | |
| *Parenting* | | |
| Edin, Nelson, and Paranal 2004 | Contact time with child | |
| Carlson and Cervera 1992 | | Strain on social supports |
| *Community* | | |
| Lynch and Sabol 2004b | | Isolation, fear of crime |
| *Health* | | |
| Thomas and Torrone 2006 | | HIV, STDs, teenage births |
| Johnson and Raphael 2005 | | Black HIV |
| *Economics* | | |
| Sabol and Lynch 2003 | | Black unemployment |
| Freeman 1992 | Lifetime earnings | |
| Kling 1999 | Lifetime earnings | |
| Western 2005 | Lifetime earnings | |
| *Politics* | | |
| St. Jean 2006 | Support for police | Trust |
| Crutchfield 2005 | | Trust and cohesion |
| Uggen and Manza 2006 | Voter participation | Impact of voting |

makes their lives less capable of producing the benefits they seek. Prison is a constant and virtually omnipresent factor in poor communities. There is no question that sending men to prison from these places may relieve some of the strains that dominate those locations, but there is, equally, no question but that at its highest levels it also increases strains.

We will continue these themes in the next chapter. The message will be largely the same, but the method will differ dramatically. This chapter has been built around a review of a range of quantitative studies. The content has been primarily numerical. In the next chapter, we consider the thoughts of people who live in these places, as they express them in their own words. The subject matter is life, as it is for people who live in high-incarceration communities.

# In Their Own Voices

People in

High-Incarceration

Communities Talk about

the Impact of Incarceration

6

In this chapter, people who live in two high-incarceration neighborhoods of Tallahassee, Florida, describe how incarceration has affected their lives, their families, and their communities. Tallahassee is the state capital of Florida, located in the Florida panhandle 20 miles below Georgia's southern border.

The two neighborhoods, Frenchtown and South City, are predominantly African-American communities in a county that is two-thirds white. These neighborhoods have the highest incarceration rates among communities in Tallahassee; they are alike in some respects and different in others. Frenchtown is older and more established. It is often described as a famous black neighborhood, with its name recognized throughout Florida's African-American community. South City is less well known, less well established, and has a larger dose of public housing. Forty years ago, the area now called South City was a rural community near Tallahassee.

Despite their differences, the neighborhoods have several important characteristics in common. Much of their similarity derives from the fact that they are populated almost exclusively by African Americans. As a result, they share much of the recent history of Southern race relations and its heritage of segregation: discrimination, economic inequality, and political isolation. Both areas are poorer than most of the rest of Tallahassee, both have large enclaves of substandard housing, and both are home to large numbers of unemployed, single-parent households, with most families who live here struggling to survive on marginal incomes. Within each neighborhood, however, there are also well-kept properties, solid middle-class housing, intact families with deep roots in the area, and residents who are well-known community leaders. Whatever the liabilities and assets of each neighborhood, the people who live in these locations, only about a mile apart, share a common history in their larger town: entrenched post–Civil War segregation followed by a turbulent civil rights period, a recent history of fast-paced economic change and political conflict, and a reputation for higher-than-average rates of crime and disorder. Both neighborhoods are fairly close to Florida's state capitol building, yet they also have in common a relative isolation from that political society and its dominant powers.

Frenchtown today is a mix of single-family homes, two-story apartment buildings, and a smattering of small businesses, convenience stores, and social service facilities. The population is primarily elderly. There are about 4,000 residents, 99.5 percent of whom are African American. While there are sections filled with square wood-frame shotgun houses on cinder blocks, Frenchtown also has numerous large, wooden houses with verandas, though many are in disrepair.

Located a mile south of Frenchtown, South City is a rectangular area immediately south of the Capital City Country Club, surrounded by large homes owned primarily by whites, and east of Florida A & M University, a traditionally black university. Sections of the community appear rural and secluded with thick woods, open fields, and many one-way lanes. The population of South City is over 2,500, almost all black. Overall, South City is considered to have poor housing stock, with a few modest and neatly kept homes with yards and gardens, but also several housing projects adjacent to old wooden shotgun shacks on cinder blocks.

## The Sources of Data for This Chapter

In 2001, Dina Rose, Judith Ryder, and I interviewed over 100 people in Frenchtown and South City (Rose, Clear, and Ryder, 2001). We talked to them about incarceration in Florida and how it affected their neighborhoods. We said we were interested in hearing their opinions about both the good and the bad effects of incarceration. Twenty-six of our subjects agreed to later participate in a series of group interviews, which were was recorded and transcribed.

The twenty-six respondents whose views are reported here represent a microcosm of the neighborhoods' populations. In South City, for example, our group included an officer of the neighborhood association, a black woman in her forties who was active in the local church that provided space for our interview. Her neighbor also came to the meeting, even though it became evident they were not on the best of terms. We also interviewed a 60-year-old woman who lived with her five children and three grandchildren in a large, crumbling white house looking out onto the main street that runs through the area. The South City group also included, among others, a young male student at Florida A&M university; a single homeowner in his mid-twenties whose private business operated in the neighborhood; the female head of a family of four who lived in the neighborhood's main housing project (and whose husband was in prison at the time); and a career civil servant who had lived in the neighborhood all his life. One of our contacts brought her sister because they both wanted to talk on the subject.

Our Frenchtown group had two ministers, one from a large AME Baptist church, the other from a tiny storefront operation along a back street. Both had relatives who had been to prison. There was one young woman, a twin, who was about to finish her associate of arts degree at Tallahassee Community College. Two service-delivery professionals attended: a man in his thirties who supervised the short-term housing that operated across the street from the homeless shelter, and a woman in her fifties who managed a second-hand store that provided low-cost goods for poor residents living in the area. The owner of a large retail store—the only white member of the group—attended, joined by a man who owned a small hardware store and had a history of employing men with criminal records. There was a middle manager in the local Urban League office—a woman whose son was just about to be released from prison. There was also a married woman with a teenage daughter; the family owned a small house off a neat side street to the main drag. The wife spoke with us openly, but her husband would not.

We interviewed the respondents in group sessions lasting about three hours. The sessions were transcribed and analyzed thematically. A report of these themes was prepared, and all participants in the study were invited to attend a debriefing of the results. About 50 people came to the debriefing, and their comments enabled us to further clarify the themes of the interviews. Here is what we heard.

## The Ubiquity and Value of Incarceration

Everyone in these neighborhoods knows someone who has been to prison. Many residents report they know many people who have been incarcerated, and it is typical that at least one person in the extended family has been to prison. High-incarceration in these neighborhoods makes this otherwise abnormal event seem normal. Said a college student: "It's [incarceration is] a commonality. You have more and more people coming in and coming out of the process. It's common for families and common for neighborhoods."

The repeated experience of incarceration among these neighbors surely contributes to our second general observation: these residents hold complex—and sometimes contradictory—views about the impact of incarceration on their lives and on the lives of their neighbors. Their views contrast with popular opinion, which understands incarceration in simplistic terms and in a mostly positive light. Our respondents' viewpoints, informed by experience, turn out to be more intricate. They can describe positive results of incarceration for various aspects of community life, and yet at the same time they see—and can point to—various negative implications of incarceration. Incarceration is viewed most negatively with regard to the perceived racism against African Americans by the criminal justice system, and these sentiments moderate how residents judge the seriousness of many offenses. Yet, alternatively, as one South City resident said, "He may be one of those kind of people that you're kind of glad to get rid of for awhile." Other respondents expressed relief when drug dealers and prostitutes were arrested and the neighborhood was safer. One Frenchtown homeowner said:

> Well, for one thing, like on the street where I live, we've got the drugs, we've got the prostitution and all of that, and we have the police riding by, they ride, and when they get one off the street, they incarcerate them, that's good, they're off the street, I don't

have to look at them passing the house ... I don't have to look at them hopping in and out of cars.

In the same vein, they have mixed feelings about whether incarceration serves as a deterrent. Explained one man in his mid-fifties: "Sometimes when they go to prison one time is enough, and then, you know, they try to make amends when they come out, and then again you've got some that go in there and it makes them worse when they come out." One 54-year-old woman felt that, "If they're locked up at the jailhouse, they sit down and play cards and watch television, it's not happening." Despite this ambivalence about incarceration as a social policy for pubic safety, they agreed on several points. They thought, for example, that there is a need for better services for people with criminal records and their families, and that their neighborhoods suffer from the lack of services. Available programs were deemed too short-term or too limited in scope.

## The Impact of Removal and Return: Four Domains

Residents' comments about the impact of incarceration on themselves, their families, and their neighborhoods fall into four broad categories. They discussed stigma, the financial effects of incarceration, issues associated with identity, and problems in relationships. The four domains clearly are interrelated (stigma impacts identity and relationships, for instance). Respondents were asked to explain both the good and the bad effects of removing people from the community and then returning them. While there are positive outcomes associated with these processes of incarceration, in general residents seem to see them as harmful and damaging to the community.

### *Making It against the Odds: Incarceration and the Problem of Stigma*

It is clear that being convicted of a crime and sent to prison carries a stigma, and being a criminal can become a person's master status. This alters the way people think about themselves and the way they are treated by residents in the community and by the broader society. While community residents stress that they think people from outside the neighborhood are primarily responsible for stigmatizing people, it also affects the way they think about their neighbors who have criminal convictions. Participants used language such as, "that's what he is," "another one," "these people," and "he's still going to be a criminal" when talking about people who had been incarcerated. Stigma sometimes also gets transferred to family members of incarcerated individuals. When communities send large numbers of residents to prison, stigma can also become attached to the community-at-large. For instance, stigma is the primary reason residents think people with criminal records cannot get jobs, but it also affects the ability of law-abiding residents to get jobs when businesses do not locate in these neighborhoods because of that stigma of criminal activity attached to the area.

The irony, of course, is that the incarceration experience is so widespread in these communities that it is not entirely stigmatizing. Simply having been to prison is not a permanent disbar from neighborly acceptance. Depending on the nature of the crime and the person's subsequent behavior, the stigma of a criminal past can be overcome in these locations—perhaps more readily than elsewhere. Most of the residents talk about welcoming people who had been to prison back into the neighborhood. One active church woman said:

> I mean, I really don't think the stigma comes from the community gossip. If there is any, I think it comes from the society, the greater society, the dominant mixed societies, the society they have to go up to and get a job from, that's where the stigma comes from. When they come back to the community, I mean, it's bad to say, but it has been known that people come out of jail, there's a celebration, there's a party and that's characteristic in a black community. When someone is released, there's a party just because they haven't seen them. It's a homecoming.

One woman told how her son had held his wife at gunpoint, and yet when he returned from prison he was treated by the family, "like their brother," with no stigma at all.

Some crimes clearly carry more stigma, residents said, and those crimes about which the community has gossiped carry the most stigma. Emphasizing this, one resident said:

> If there's any stigma attached to it, then it would have to do with the crime, but the majority of people that are being released

regularly are either something minor, in domestic violence or something of that nature, even if it's petty theft, things of that nature and they've been gone a long time, the community has not even—we have not sat around and talked about it.

How residents respond to community members with criminal convictions is complicated. On one hand, they keep in mind the individual's status as someone convicted of a crime, and on the other hand, they try to treat him better than residents believe people outside the community do. Illustrating this another participant said, "it's always going to be in the back of my mind that that's what he is," but qualified this statement by adding, "but I'm still going to treat him like a real human being."

The feeling that stigma comes primarily from outside is widespread and is emphasized particularly when discussing the inability of people with criminal records to get jobs. A woman whose son is in prison told us: "A lot of them change once they go into a penal institution. They go in, their minds are changed, their mind-set is changed. They come back to the community and they want to be productive citizens, but they don't get an equal chance, they don't get an opportunity, because there are so many strikes against them."

As one South City resident, a city employee for over 25 years, pointed out:

What the community wants to see is . . . an ex-offender come out and be productive, and that's not always going to happen because what they have is they have resentment towards the system, they have the environment to deal with. The same environment that was there that created them to do the wrong is still there when they get back and then you, it's coupled with lack of opportunity. You have the individual dealing with these emotions and these feelings, coming back into a society and against the efforts of the society that's saying, "look, what are you going to do? Are you going to be productive now? Are you going to do this?" So the pressure is on for that person to do well and it's not facilitated by anything that goes on in that environment, because they're coming back into the same thing they left.

But the shamefulness of going to prison is reinforced by the fact that it is not discussed openly. Neighbors do not talk about it with people who have a loved one in jail, and the silence reinforces the taboo of the experience. Thus, there is a collective stifling of conversation about prison. It is everywhere, and it is nowhere. The lack of openness about it helps keep its power as a disgrace. Even when neighbors offer assistance to families experiencing hardship owing to the incarceration of their family member, people are careful not to address the fact of incarceration directly. One respondent said she would say she knew the family had needs. She said, "If I know the situation, I wouldn't say it." Another respondent said she would offer assistance and that "nobody else would have to know about it."

The stigma of incarceration can transfer to both the family and the community. While respondents insisted they had not personally experienced the stigma attached to their own family members they had, however, seen it happen to others. Sometimes, they said, when a family member goes to prison, neighbors reconsider what they think of those who are left behind. Siblings often bear the brunt because there is an idea that if your sibling could be a criminal, then you could, too, and now "it was just a matter of time." This is particularly true if the crime committed was violent or unusually heinous. The whole family can suffer. One participant said: "And they [neighborhood residents] not only look at the specific offender but also the entire family, and if one has offended, you know, the neighborhood's reputation, then the entire family is looked upon as receiving. All of a sudden they're not the most respected, even from the church."

Locations with large numbers of people going to prison also become negatively stereotyped, and this affects how the area is perceived, thus transferring the stigma to the community. One person observed that when people leave the neighborhood because they are concerned about crime and the number of people with criminal records living there, they sell their house at a reduced value. Consequently, property values go down. Businesses find that some customers are reluctant to conduct their business in such a place. And police develop and spread a reputation about how bad these locations are. Whatever silence afflicts the family with stigmatic shame, open knowledge of the problem afflicts the community at large with ignominy. One technique for managing this stigma, then, is for residents to distinguish the community from the residents who have criminal records. As one South City resident said, "They ain't the neighborhood for what that one person did. It doesn't make it a bad neighborhood because a person came in and went back."

Communities that serve as "landing places" for large numbers of released prisoners also develop a reputation outside the community. In Frenchtown, for example, it is known that the walk from the bus stop to the inner city is a short one, and people who want to become anonymous feel they can do so in the community that has received large numbers of their predecessors. With public notification laws and criminal records posted on the Internet, it is perhaps most likely that, in those areas home to many people with criminal records, a person who has previously been to prison can arrive and assimilate. The people who live in these communities know that they have the reputation as a home for ex-convicts, and this is often a sore spot. Indeed, distinguishing between insiders and outsiders is one technique residents use for managing stigma. Residents in both neighborhoods were quick to point out that most crime that occurred in these parts of town was done by people living outside the neighborhood, and that it is the reputation of the locality that attracts them to the area. One respondent said of her neighbors with criminal records, "if you stopped them and asked them where they were from, they wouldn't say 'Tallahassee,' they would say, "Tampa, Miami, Chicago, New York.'" In the Frenchtown group interview there was consensus that crack was introduced into the area not by a local resident but by someone from Miami. As one resident said, "it's a whole lot of outside influence, because the people of Frenchtown love Frenchtown; they don't have any way to bring the stuff in. The stuff is brought in by other people."

The reputation of the community leads residents to feel they are stigmatized by members of the criminal justice system. This perception was true whether discussing attitudes of the police toward residents ("according to your address, you had to have done it") or commenting on the length of sentences ("sometimes persons from this particular area are incarcerated for longer stints for the crime that they have committed"). In the end, residents are torn between their conviction that discrimination and a downtrodden neighborhood are conducive to people committing crime, their concern that bias in the criminal justice system metes out unfair sentences, and their belief that individuals are responsible for their own lives. One way residents manage the stigma of neighborhood people coming from and going to prison is to vacillate between blaming individuals for not trying to change their lives and blaming the system for not giving them a chance to do so. Said one South City resident, "The community, they might put the blame on the system," but she also said, "At first, it's your life, you have to choose your life." When presented with this contradiction, this respondent concluded, "So actually, it's just the individuals. They have to be strong-minded."

### Economics: The Financial Impact of Incarceration

The most common answer residents gave regarding the impact of incarceration on their lives had to do with the way it affects them financially. Incarcerating a person who is actively criminal can provide financial relief to a family being stolen from or called upon to assist members with court fees and other costs associated with arrest, but respondents spoke more frequently about the financial cost of incarceration itself. The inability of people with prison records to get jobs, the loss of income for the family, and the lack of employment opportunities in the community were problems frequently cited by residents.

Residents told us that people who were engaged in crime nonetheless often provided material support (legal and illegal) for their families before they went to prison. Men who work "decent" jobs and provide for their children and support a home represent a severe loss for the family when they are incarcerated. This loss of support was almost never made up by the family. About incarceration, one 53-year-old man told us:

> Another way that it hurts the community is that once that individual is incarcerated, or upon incarceration, the family, the rest of the family of that individual, loses a productive member of the family. In a lot of cases, you know, he may be a construction worker when he leaves, but that's income that that family depends on and relies upon significantly, so once he's removed from the family, then that family is adversely affected from a financial standpoint.

Of course, not everyone who is incarcerated was previously working a legitimate job. Even those who were not, however, often provided income to their families. When asked if incarcerated family members had been contributing financially to their family, some participants responded, "Well, in a way," or "Well, not in the way you're saying." Families that suffer from the loss of an income sometimes have to rely upon local charities to survive, sometimes have younger kids who start to "follow in his footsteps," and sometimes reconfigure, as women who are left behind "find a boyfriend" to help make ends meet. Other families seem to fall apart from the weight of financial strain. One man explained that "they're so disorganized now and everybody is hustling and scuffling and trying to make it, you know, after he's been taken away from the family, that it's really difficult to pull that family back together or to recover from his incarceration."

There was agreement that the loss of income in the family negatively affects the children because the mother cannot support the family as well as the father could. One woman said, "so when that father is pulled away, that leaves him [the child] depending solely on the mother who cannot give him sufficient of what the father was giving him." An older woman who works in the neighborhood said she sees kids going hungry when the father goes to prison:

> So getting back to the kids, if they miss a day of school, I'm there, 'Why are you not in school?' 'I like to go to school because I like my breakfast, I don't have any breakfast or dinner now,' and I'll give them a little something to eat. I have maybe some cookies or candy or a soda. The kids are not getting food when that husband or boyfriend goes to jail.

In addition, the financial strain on families can force them onto public assistance and into public housing. A 26-year-old woman described the process:

> I feel that because of the fact, if they were taken away from that family, then that family had to go get on assistance, because if there was an income taken away, that they were directed to those areas. So when the offender comes back, he's going back to where his family is, and if that cycle begins, they never get out of public housing because they're never able to earn an income to pay for regular housing, so they have to stay in assisted housing.

This is not a simple picture, however. Many convicted of crime are not financially successful, and those who are not can be a drain on family resources, stealing family money and needing a constant flow of cash to deal with various troubles. Families experience financial relief when these family members are incarcerated. One family member told us that the financial burden on the family occurred when her nephew was "out doing whatever he was doing" because her sister lost time at work when she was called to help him out. Another family member told us that his mother experienced financial hardship due to "court fees, probation fees, time off of work because she has to go to court," when his brother was incarcerated and that she barely got by borrowing from other family members.

Yet for many families, a relative's stay in prison can simply shift the financial drain from maintaining the person on the streets to helping him cope in prison. Money spent to pay for collect telephone calls, reimburse an attorney, cover costs of transportation to the prison, or handle child care can amount to a significant loss of financial security for families without significant financial resources. One participant reported that it became harder and harder to visit a family member in prison because of the cost (they had to rent a car) and time involved. One woman in her sixties, telling how her family supported the incarcerated family member during his incarceration by rotating visits among members of the extended family, said: "We sent him money, we went to see him, we was just there for him. When he got out, we had him a house, we had his lights. We had him food. We bought him clothes, and now...when he got out, this is the whole eight years he was there, we was still trying to hold onto his job on the FSU campus for him and we did. He got it back."

Community members also try to help out family members of incarcerated individuals. Residents said they helped other families out with food and clothing and would provide cash to those in need. Family members end up absorbing more financial costs when someone returns to the community, needing new clothes for job interviews, church, and leisure; a place to stay; and assistance finding a job. Indeed, housing is a primary need of people returning to the community and their limited resources often means they end up living with family members. And, as one resident said, "They might not be on your lease, but they're going to be in your house," even if the public housing where the family lives might have rules barring them from the premises.

Owing to the stigma associated with incarceration, however, getting a job is difficult for most people released from prison. One man in his early fifties told us:

> I think primarily one of the ways that it's [incarceration] a problem for this community is once an individual is incarcerated, if and when they return to the community their life as a

productive citizen is pretty much over, because they're (quote) "unemployable." It's almost impossible for them to get a job. They are severely stigmatized, and that sort of goes along with the unemployability, their inability to fit into the mainstream of the community, into the active participatory portion of the community.

Another participant, a long-term neighborhood resident in her seventies, said:

When a person has a scandal or what have you, society puts a mark on them, and when they put that mark on them, you go put in an application for a job, oh, no, we cannot say you can't do this because you have been in jail but every time they look on there, prison, they keep putting it to the bottom, they keep putting it to the bottom. And their application had been in and been in for jobs, and they keep passing it to the bottom, and they never call because they look at that one record that they had been in jail, see. And society is a lot for the reason to fault. Like you say, they come out and they try to get a job and they go in and put in an application, they all, everybody says they're sorry, they don't want to work. Everybody that's been in jail is not sorry, and if they're not working it's not because they're sorry. Society has got it where they can go nowhere, they can't do anything.

Those who do get jobs have difficulty obtaining any degree of job stability. One participant relayed how a person with a criminal conviction is "not able to get a job, and then if he gets a job and somebody finds out that he's been incarcerated, 'Well, Johnny, you know, we're going to have to let you go, you know.'" In addition, many of the jobs are low paying and are less than 40 hours per week, so that there often isn't enough money to pay the bills, and people returning from prison have to take on multiple jobs. Others keep jobs until the background checks reveal their criminal records and they get fired. These people, we were told, "know they're going to get fired, but they take that job for a few weeks, four weeks, three weeks, two weeks, whatever, as long as they can get that one paycheck to help them out, they will go from job to job just to get that one paycheck, just because they know they're going to get fired."

As a result, residents thought, some turn to crime. As one respondent said, "You know, I mean, say this person was a drug dealer. He comes back in and it's either going to be selling drugs, getting $500, $600 a day to $200 a week working at a part-time, working part-time at the grocery store. You have to look at what the environment poses for that individual when he comes back out and when he goes in."

The situation is complicated further because there are so few businesses located in these high-incarceration communities and fewer still that are willing to take a chance on hiring an employee with a criminal record. One respondent thought that residents from a white community on the other side of town who go to prison had fewer problems finding employment when they returned from prison because residents in those communities have jobs to give out. Thus, there was the sentiment that the sheer dearth of businesses in these high-incarceration neighborhoods meant residents could not help people returning from prison solve their employment problems. Residents of the Frenchtown group interview said that, in a previous era, their neighborhood had been a vibrant community with black-owned businesses that had a stake in the community and whose owners knew the people who had been to prison and their families and would give them jobs. In contrast, today businesses owned by outsiders have no incentive to provide jobs. These employers should be pressured by the community to give out jobs, said a retired woman who was an active member of the South City neighborhood association:

> Just say, okay, what are you going to do for these individuals? You're in the community—we're giving our money to you to stay productive in our community. You're creating a service for us, but we're doing... our business is coming to you. We're the consumer. What are you going to do for these individuals that need these jobs?

On the other hand, one local businessman who had hired at least four people with prison records said his experiences had been, "overwhelmingly—well, maybe not overwhelmingly, maybe sixty-forty on the negative side." One employee he spoke of had stolen from him and another he mentioned had been unable to get along with customers. As a result of these and other bad experiences, he is now reluctant to hire people coming out of prison.

Other local businesses also suffer when people who cannot find employment hang out in front of area stores. One businessman noted that when people returning from prison, particularly those who are mentally impaired, loiter on the street, residents are reluctant to shop at those businesses: "The customers don't want to go in the business because these people hang around the business either begging, begging for money or food or drugs or whatever.... You're scared to go into the businesses because of those people."

Finally, the community suffers financially from incarceration in two additional ways. The area's bad reputation means that large corporations do not locate their businesses in these neighborhoods; and housing prices are diminished because, when residents flee, they sell their homes for whatever they can get, often at a reduced price. This, said one resident, reflects the value of the community. Thus, the overall housing market reflects a local economy and a local community, both of which are suffering. Indeed, this resident said "You say, how does it [incarceration] affect? That's how it affects; it affects every area, economic, education, politics, the whole mind-set."

Skills learned in prison are particularly important because they make people who return from there more competitive in the job market. One respondent said he knew of people who had benefited from getting off drugs and getting their GED and vocational training while incarcerated. Of these people he said, "It has been tough for them when they have come out to get a job and everything, but some of them have had positive outcomes, but not many." What frequently happens, others said, is that skills learned in prison are not translatable into jobs on the street.

### Incarceration and the Politics of Identity

The third way incarceration impacts the community is through the self-identity of residents and the expectations they have for their lives. Incarceration has a direct impact on the way people who experience prison view themselves. Just as important, however, incarceration impacts the identities of other community residents, too. Residents report that having been incarcerated impacts people's feelings of self-worth and self-esteem, primarily because it is tied to their inability to get a job. As one resident said, the number one thing people returning from prison need is "a job that they can be proud of, an income that they can be proud of... [because]

now, this guy, he's got on a decent pair of pants because he's got a job now where he's earning a decent income and he feels like somebody." Having a job "builds your spirit right up." Conversely, not being able to get a job and provide for their families makes people feel not "as worthy as someone else," and not being trusted by employers makes them feel bad. "[W]hen you go to jail and come back, people don't want to hire you even to cut their yard. If you're an ex-offender and they know that, they have to peek out, it makes them feel bad that you can't trust them." Thus, a job leaves an individual "feeling like somebody," which leads to a sense of self-worth and self-esteem. The pride that comes from a job can compete and overcome the stigma of incarceration; when someone has both the stigma of incarceration and the stigma of being unemployed, the result is a double blow to self-image. Not being employed is related to self-esteem in other ways. For instance, one respondent told us that she gets clothes for people with prison records who, because of unemployment, are not able to purchase their own, so that when they go to church they can look like the other people there and thus build their self-esteem.

When residents return to the community from prison, often they are filled with hope, but this soon suffers when they find the community in as bad shape as when they left, or perhaps, even worse, and they absorb the negativity of the environment. For example, a resident told of someone she knew who was not able to overcome his low self-esteem and low self-worth because he had internalized his "black sheep" status. This can be overcome, however, and people can change their self-image. Pointing out that there are success stories in the midst of a negative environment, one resident said "it's not where you are, it's how you live it." Confirming this sentiment, another resident told how he overcame his past of getting into trouble by changing his attitude.

The community as a whole benefits from people who feel good about themselves and suffers when individuals lack self-pride. People, we were told, who feel good about themselves make friends in the neighborhood and help other people; and those who don't, lack pride in their surroundings, which can translate into a lack of concern for their neighbors. One man explained:

> We are going to give these guys a job and we're going to give them a decent job so that they can feel proud of themselves. Now, once they feel that pride, but let's say that they don't feel

that pride, what is the result? How does that affect Frenchtown? If I don't feel pride in my own self I'm not going to feel pride in my surroundings, so I'm not going to keep up my yard, I'm not going to keep up my car, I'm not going to keep up my house. I'm not going to care about the young boys that are walking down the street slugging [sic] drugs, because I've got enough to deal with in my own psyche.... So it sort of spills over into the community, because when you get people back in the community and give them a sense of worth, then they come back feeling proud of themselves and being able to say, hey, look, man, don't do that, because see, man, I've been where you're at and I'm telling you it's not worth it.... And the other thing is, if I'm so depressed when I come out of prison that I can't help myself, I'm not going to help my community, I'm just not going to be able to do it. And it's not so much that I don't want to do it, you know. We're all human beings and we've got to feel good about ourselves, and when we feel good about ourselves we take into consideration other people's pain and other people's conditions.

One ramification of this for the neighborhood is the lack of role models, a deficit that sometimes discourages children from a belief in their future. Respondents reported that without positive role models, kids come to believe prison is their future. Said one young woman:

It [incarceration] affects the whole family, because we have young black males in the Frenchtown area, their fathers, it's a cycle, they're in and out. There are no positive role models in the community other than a lot of the offenders that have children, and it's just basically being passed down from generation to generation because they're getting right into the same system, the criminal justice system.

Another participant added, "You will find the average little child, now I would say seven out of ten, their goal is, [when you ask] 'What are you going to do when you grow up, what are you going to do?' 'I'm going to jail.' They have no role model." Even children who do not believe incarceration is their future suffer from a belief that they have no meaningful future. One respondent recounted a conversation he had with an area youth who was waiting to pick up a date:

> I said, "You need to go clean yourself up and then come back and talk to the young lady." He said, "Do you see where I live? Why do I need to clean myself up? I can't get no job, I'm out here hustling, nobody wants to hire me. Do you see who I am?" See, that attitude is pervasive throughout the young men in the community.

Family members also suffer when they begin to feel incarceration is inevitable and part of the experience of those living in the neighborhood. While many in the community seem inured to the experience of incarceration, some residents discussed a sense of hopelessness and depression. Speaking about his mother who lives in another area of Florida, one respondent said she was depressed when his brother was incarcerated because she was Panamanian, saying:

> [S]o she's not African American, and she deals with her culture being a bit different, and it's just harder on her because she wasn't brought up that way and her family wasn't brought up that way, and it's just harder for her. Kids just weren't going to jail in Panama. Kids aren't going to jail in Panama.

The community also is affected because residents begin to feel there is nothing they can do to effect change. Apathy is exacerbated because the residents are low-income and live among drugs. There is a feeling that things can't change, either on the individual level or the community level: "That's just the way it is," some say. This is compounded with a sense of discrimination in the criminal justice system and, "the life occurrences . . . of an African American in a white-dominated society," where the police focus their attention on youths in certain neighborhoods. One respondent said this results in people feeling demeaned, with less incentive to "lift [themselves] up." Continuing, this respondent said "If you treat me more like a human being, I will act more like a human being. If you treat me more like an animal, I'm going to act more like an animal." The cumulative effect on the community can be drastic.

### Incarceration, Family, and Community Relationships

One of the primary ways in which incarceration impacts the community is the way it changes relationships. When someone from the family is incarcerated, remaining members report feeling bad and experiencing anxiety and a sense of loss. About having someone go to prison, residents said, "it's hard." Sometimes this results in a physical illness of a family member; sometimes other conditions such as depression occur. Residents also talked about feeling disappointed and guilty when someone was incarcerated, feeling that family members might have been able to prevent it had they been able to do more. A woman in her late forties revealed the following:

> I think for me, in terms of the family, no matter what the behavior was like, for the family members perhaps they still suffer a sense of loss, because that's a relative or that's someone that maybe was important to them, whether they were being mischievous, misbehaving or whatever the situation was, so maybe experiencing a sense of loss that they're not there for them to contact.

Relationships among family members suffer when someone is incarcerated, simply from the incarcerated person's absence. If the spouse is incarcerated, this may affect the marriage, which grows distant from the separation. As one resident pointed out, "Of course, when he returns, it's going to be different because that relationship between the mother and father has been damaged by that separation." Residents report, too, that children can lose respect for both parents—mom because she is a single-parent; dad because he has been to prison. The lost respect (and the loss of a caretaker) often translates into behavior problems with children. Thus, these children are at risk for delinquency and for repeating the cycle of their parents. Explained one man:

> By him being gone for that period of time, by the time he comes back the kid has no respect. He loses respect for the mother who is a single parent and when he comes back he has no respect for his daddy, because now he knows where the daddy has been, that makes it even worse. Like you say, that makes it a vicious cycle. That kid goes out and gets into trouble and he goes through the cycle. Then it goes on to the siblings.

When one parent is gone, it is often difficult for parents to supervise children. One respondent said that when the father was incarcerated, the children stopped going to school and, in one case, "the younger boy started carrying a gun." One participant noted that sometimes when one parent is incarcerated, there is no one left to supervise the children, particularly if the mother has a problem with drugs: "[W]hen the boyfriend or the husband leaves, if the lady is on drugs, then the children don't have anybody to control them. Those kids go in and out the door, in the door, out the door, across the street, across town. They don't know where they are."

Alternatively, some residents report that the relationship between family members improves when someone was incarcerated. This occurs because, while committing crimes, the individual usually drains the family both emotionally and financially, leaving little for other family members. Thus, incarceration provides a sense of relief for the family (sometimes simply because they now know where the relation is residing) and time for them to improve their relationship in a calmer and less stressful environment. One participant said that when her family member went to prison, the other children in the family became closer, "because when he was out, he was more like wanting attention and with his mom working and going to school, I guess he was one of those kids that just needed more attention than the other child, so he acted out in a different way." Following the incarceration, the family member learned to express himself, so the respondent saw his incarceration as positive for family dynamics.

The relationship between neighbors also is affected when someone goes to prison. Neighbors navigate a difficult relationship as they reach out to the family members of someone who has been sent to prison. While some of the empathy expressed by residents for families dealing with incarceration comes from the sense that "what happened to them could happen to you," most people are more altruistic, expressing concern for the family, particularly their financial well-being and the well-being of their children. Upon seeing the family with an incarcerated loved one, one woman said she would give them a big smile, "[l]et them know that if they need you, you will be there, also." A resident described trying to reach out to these families, saying she would, "let them know that the church is a family, their family, and when one is hurting, when one is going through something, the whole church family is going through it."

Yet there is also a sense that people convicted of crime get what they deserved, and that their families often get shamed and experience a loss of respect in the community. When this happens, families sometimes isolate themselves from the citizenry. One participant said, "If something happens in your family it's like they will be ashamed of the whole family, and you know, you're going to kind of avoid going around people, you know."

Upon return from prison, people rely heavily on the support of family members to transition successfully back into the community. The support is typically described as emotional (believing the person has changed, giving him a chance), and people coming home from prison are described as fearful and in need of nurturing. Support also is defined in the form of tangible help, like financial assistance, providing a place to live, giving them clothes, and offering assistance getting a job. In fact, without someone providing this type of support, respondents believe that people returning from prison will recidivate. Speaking about offenders, one resident said, "They are demoralized while incarcerated, and so they need a real strong support system. When they get back to that community, they need a real strong support system to help raise them above that level of demoralization."

In addition to recognizing that formerly incarcerated people need support, residents express a variety of reactions to releasees returning to the neighborhood. First and foremost, they discuss the event as one of celebration, a day when a homecoming party would be held. For those who did not know the individual before he was incarcerated, they said they would be welcoming and nonjudgmental. They respected the individual's privacy and "did not get in anyone's business." On the other hand, residents said they look for signs that the person is trying to change his life around, and attending church or looking for a job are two ways to accomplish that. One woman said she wonders, "What is he going to do, after he's out what is he planning to do? ... What steps is he going to take to ... make a change or keep himself from going back in?" And that there was a tendency to trust he'll be different, "until I see him going to make that mistake again." One South City respondent said, however, that it was the commonality of the experience that makes him less likely to be compassionate and more likely to wonder how the individual is going to act now. "It's not uncommon, so being that it's not uncommon ... I'm not thinking more along the lines of, 'Wow, you know, this is hard.' I'm thinking, "Okay, what's going to happen now?' "One man said, "I know he's probably going to do something wrong, but I'm just going to pray for him and that's basically all I can do."

While the respondents generally see themselves as being supportive of someone returning from prison, they report that others are less welcoming. One participant said that others would gossip. These people, the respondents said, make comments like "he won't be out long, he'll be going back directly." Some other people, they said, can be blaming, shaming, and generally distrustful. Some people are met with suspicion and fear. A resident in South City said:

> I think as far as fearing or thinking it, is the fact that they're right next to you, and say, for instance, if you may be a single parent. You're working every day. Your child is in school and that child comes home and you're saying, "Oh, my child is home now and that person is next door." You know, you're going to have these negative thoughts running in your mind now.

Clearly there are conflicting responses to people returning to their neighborhoods from prison. On one hand, residents purport to welcome them back, nonjudgmentally, and on the other hand, they report some degree of suspicion, cynicism, and fear. One resident said that if someone with a criminal record moved in next door to her home, she might "do a background check." Another said he was "going to watch him." One resident in Frenchtown said she had found out about a neighbor's crime because she "happened to run by it on the Internet." At the same time she said "I never get into anybody's personal business, I never ask. He probably don't even know I know." Respondents are more likely to attribute negative reactions to others than to themselves. When we asked group interview participants to respond to a formerly incarcerated person's statement to us that their neighbors thought they were evil, residents denied this was true, saying that this sentiment reflected the person's own self-perception. One South City resident said, "In other words, if it were me and I was them, that's what I would feel."

Noting the difficulty of accepting residents back into the community once they have been to prison, one South City respondent said that acceptance is difficult to obtain because a bond of trust has been broken between the resident and the community, and mistrust is hard to overcome. Another said he had known about families being stigmatized to the point where they left their churches "because people didn't treat the families the same no more."

Frequently, what determines how someone is treated upon return to the community depends on the gravity of the crime, the degree to which the community has gossiped about the crime in his absence, and signs from the individual that he is trying to make a change (the same conditions related to stigma). While residents called for harsher sentences for (hypothetical) drug dealers, when asked how they would treat a drug dealer returning to their community, one resident said he would welcome him back. This resident drew the line at sex offenses. There is consensus that those who have committed especially egregious crimes, particularly against the community, would not be welcomed back. Speaking hypothetically about how the community would deal with someone returning from prison after having murdered a child, one participant said the community would "plan a lynch party." Another respondent acknowledged that there was a difference between the public and private ways in which residents respond to people returning to the neighborhood. In public, residents are welcoming and supportive. In private, however, they are stigmatizing and blaming.

> They come together at church. They say, "Oh, we're there for you, we want to do all these things for you," but then behind your back they're like, "He deserves it." . . . So it's hard. It's real hard. It would be silly for us to deny the fact that there's a stigmatism that's put on you and we facilitate it.

In general, respondents report that one of the effects of incarceration is that individuals are more likely to be isolated. Isolation also is heightened by residents' decreased willingness to "hang out" with friends on the street. Respondents report that having numerous people around who have been to prison means that the police were more likely to question anyone. The manager of a small second-hand store told us:

> [Y]ou can take five or six boys walking up in front of the store going to the park, they're going to stop on the corner and talk. The police rides by, they're going to stop, they're going to run all six of those boys in just to see what is going on. Naturally, they're going to take somebody to jail because they've got something on them.

Not wanting to be stopped by the police, one respondent said, "you have to be careful what you do. We better not gather here." Another said some people are wary of their own response were they to be stopped (anger, possibly resulting in arrest), and that this served as a disincentive for socializing in public. "I mean, if I'm hanging out on the corner with my friends and one of them happens to be an ex-offender, if the police come by and he's rousting me, it's going to make me very, very angry and I may do something that's stupid, yes, but it gets me into trouble."

Overall, relationships in the community are changed by incarceration as residents are called upon to support people sent to prison and their families. The tension of being welcoming and nonjudgmental versus being cautious and self-protective while waiting for signs of change means that neighbors are reluctant to know each other in more than a superficial way. These are communities where people respect each other's privacy, but try to find out what they need to know to assess their own risk. What develops is a culture of taking care of yourself and trying to help out neighbors (when you know them) as best you can without putting yourself at risk. As one resident noted, it takes the community to send the message that troublemaking will not be tolerated, and for that to happen, residents have to be willing to act. In this environment, however, where those returning from prison are related to neighbors and people stay out of other people's business, it does not happen frequently.

> So the people that live here now, when a troublemaker comes to the neighborhood, you turn your back on them. If drug dealers don't have anybody to sell dope to, they're out of business. If the dope users don't have anybody to buy from, they're out of business. So it's got to be all about the people. You can create any programs you like, but it's got to have some participants that are willing to say, "That's wrong," and pick up your phone and let somebody know that you don't like it instead of just block-ading your own yard, because it's not only about your own yard because the trouble is spilling over from the neighbor next door's house to my house.

When this is added to feelings about the criminal justice system, the community is in a bind, where calling the police can be viewed as an act of disloyalty, getting involved in neighbors' affairs is seen as being intrusive and judgmental, and where limited resources require family units to coalesce around their own needs and overlook the needs of the neighborhood. The result is disrupted networks and isolation, and as one respondent said, "no community, there's no community."

## Discussion

These residents were animated in their comments on incarceration, and their various comments pointed to a complex relationship between incarceration and community life in their neighborhoods. In some ways, they saw incarceration as a positive force in community life. Arrests that removed prostitutes and drug dealers were seen as a positive contribution to public space, and seeing people convicted of crime receive their just punishment was seen as appropriate and socially positive. Residents also told stories of ways in which some of the people they knew posed trouble for their families and friends, and when they were removed, things improved for everyone. Nobody objected to the existence of prison, and there were frequent enough calls for stiff sentences for people engaged in drug crime and harsh penalties for those convicted of sex crimes and crimes of violence against children.

Yet, as Meares (1997) has observed about inner-city residents and the police, these people were troubled about crime but also about criminal justice. By far, our participants reserved their most spirited comments for voicing objection to the way incarceration sometimes damaged their communities. In their experiences and their perspectives, they repeatedly pointed to the problems that stem from high incarceration rates. We can divide their observations into two arenas of theoretical importance to the concept of social disorganization: human capital and social networks.

### *Human Capital*

In general, they saw those who experienced incarceration as having suffered damage to their life chances: reduced opportunities for gainful employment, lost trust of their neighbors, and lessened support from their families. This is not a unidimensional argument. Because incarceration is anything but abnormal, the residents' feelings about neighbors who had been to prison were characterized by the sentiment—"it depends." It depends on the crime committed since most people who came from prison had, they thought, made "mistakes" or committed minor crimes for which they were being punished too harshly by a biased criminal justice system. It depends on the willingness of the person to change when he returns. Most residents claim a certain empathy for people coming home from prison and a willingness to give them a chance to "turn things around," and even a little help along the way. But for each appeal to hope, they voiced numerous complaints about how the decks are stacked against them: problems getting and keeping good jobs, strains in resuming roles of spouse and parent, financial struggles, and a wary public all make for a convergence of difficulties.

Nor is that incarcerated person the only one affected. Our participants described unparented children, unsupervised young people, and struggling single mothers as symptoms of incarceration, and these problems existed in abundance in their neighborhoods. The human capital of anyone who was dependent on a person headed to prison is damaged by their removal, and this damage was seen as systemic, especially in family life. The women and children who remain behind face uphill battles in sustaining a decent quality of life, and the syndromes of welfare and undesirable housing were endemic to the problem of incarceration. The lack of a positive self-image, and hopes for the future, unmanageable children who stopped going to school resulting in intergenerational trouble with the law, was seen as a product of missing fathers and weak parental control. There was a sense in which our participants saw their whole neighborhood as marginally poorer, directly as a result of the large number of men who were occupying prison cells instead of living productive lives.

### Networks and Social Capital

In social disorganization theory, mobility is thought to contribute to increased chances of crime through the way it produces anonymity and lack of social integration among community residents. Neighbors who are transitory know each other less and are more reluctant to call upon one another for support. Thus, the informal social-control capacity of those areas of high mobility is attenuated.

We see how coercive mobility works in similar ways to reinforce anonymity and lack of integration. We were struck by the degree to which the neighbors we canvassed in their homes tended to stay indoors and reported that they did not know their neighbors. This seemed particularly true in the project housing areas, where families with members in prison concentrated. While our participants told us that they wanted to help their neighbors, they also reported that the knowing of someone's criminal past made people wary of one another and that when a family member goes to prison, the remaining family members often withdraw from social life. The existence of a large number of people in the community with criminal records builds stigma, and becomes a part of their story that is "not to be talked about." This reinforces a detachment about the hardships that may come to those with a loved one in prison.

In addition, families may move to new neighborhoods so that, upon release, the returning family member can begin living in a new environment, maximizing the chance of staying out of prison. Thus, while incarceration produces mobility owing to removing the individual, it may also produce mobility when families relocate for the benefit of the person when he returns. This mechanism of staying clear of trouble produces the very anonymity and disintegration that were originally observed by the social disorganization theorists. We must also recognize the way in which stigma makes high-incarceration neighborhoods more isolated from other locations. People are reluctant to venture into these locations, businesses are loath to open, and social groups are difficult to get started.

The narratives reported above closely parallel the stories told by anthropologist Donald Braman (2004) in his study of families of the incarcerated in Washington, D.C. He spent three years interviewing families who lived in one of the area's most impoverished neighborhoods, a place where many young men end up going to prison or jail. He followed families as they dealt with loved ones being arrested, going to prison, and returning. While his book has a richness and depth that only a long-term ethnography can provide, the story he tells through the voices and lives of the subjects is remarkably consistent with that told by our respondents in a few short interviews. The financial, emotional, and interpersonal hardships he describes for those whose loved ones go to prison are documented by the events he himself observed in the lives of his subjects. If the insights of our respondents are the conclusions we might draw about the neighborhood impacts of high rates of concentrated incarceration, Braman's study offers the data that give face validity to what we were told in Tallahassee. Braman sees the array of difficulties encountered by the people in his study, and he concludes with an observation that would receive much support from the people in our own study:

> By employing incarceration—the bluntest of instruments—as the primary response to social disorder, policy makers have significantly missed the mark. The very laws intended to punish selfish behavior and to further common social interests have, in practice, strained and eroded the personal relationships vital to family and community life. Crime cannot go unpunished. But by draining the resources of families, by frustrating the norm of reciprocity that inheres in family life, and by stigmatizing poor and minority families, our current regime of criminal sanctions has crated a set of second-order problems that furthers social detachment. (2004:221)

Like Braman, we find support for the idea that incarceration offers both positive and negative consequences for neighborhoods' life. We also find a plethora of evidence, in the experience and perspectives of our participants, that in their neighborhoods—heavy hit by high rates of incarceration—the net result of imprisonment policy has not been solely (or even predominantly) positive. The participants in our study see the incursion of imprisonment policy in their neighborhoods as double-edged. Their stories help us understand the human dimension of the studies cited in chapter 5 regarding the negative effects of incarceration.

# The Impact of Incarceration on Community Safety

7

The coercive mobility hypothesis holds that high rates of incarceration, concentrated in poor communities, will destabilize social networks in those communities, thereby undermining informal social control and leading to more crime. A conceptual model of this hypothesis, derived from figure 4.1 and table 5.1, is provided by figure 7.1, below.

This figure posits that incarceration will tend to suppress crime through incapacitation and deterrence. Given what we know about the impact of incarceration on crime, we would expect these effects to be small. We would also expect that, as levels of incarceration grow in impoverished communities, there will be a negative effect on the community's economic structure, family stability, parental capacity, and pro-social beliefs. Each of these effects would also be small. There will also be crimes committed by those now in reentry from prison. It is easy to see how these latter effects, even if small, might in the aggregate outweigh the impact of deterrence and incapacitation. This is the coercive mobility hypothesis, sometimes also called the Rose-Clear hypothesis (after Rose and Clear 1998): after a certain point, high incarceration rates concentrated in impoverished communities will cause crime to increase rather than decrease.

There have not been very many attempts to test, directly and empirically, the coercive mobility hypothesis. The few empirical studies

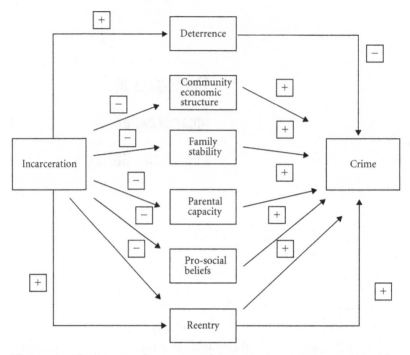

**Figure 7.1** The impact of concentrated incarceration on poor communities and crime. The figure shows coercive mobility—the impact of incarceration on communities.

Source: Clear, Rose, Waring, and Scully 2003.

that exist provide results that are in some ways consistent and in some ways problematic. This chapter provides a discussion of the various studies of coercive mobility.

## Social Disorganization as a Theoretical Context

The context of this work is the long tradition of research on neighborhood factors that cause crime, various aspects of which have been mentioned in earlier chapters in this book, especially in chapters 4 and 5. The most important early work on communities and crime was done by Robert Shaw and Clifford McKay in 1942, looking at Chicago. These two ground-breaking sociologists argued that the stable way in which certain neighborhoods of Chicago produced high rates of delinquency across the years was a consequence of social factors that produced "disorganization" in those locations. Their conclusion has come to be known as social disorganization theory. The social factors they described as most important were poverty, normative heterogeneity (seen through the lens of ethnic heterogeneity), and mobility.

This idea has remained prominent in criminological research, though it has been hotly debated and, in a few instances, carefully reworked. What has sustained the idea is the repeated finding that certain inner-city locations remain high crime places over lengthy periods, even when the composition of those places changes substantially. A dominant characteristic of these places is the extreme social and economic disadvantage that their residents experience. The persistence of neighborhood-level crime in these disadvantaged communities has focused the attention of criminologists on identifying what makes these criminogenic communities stay that way.

Most of the debates about this line of research are devoted to disputes about the actual processes at work. Much of the dispute focuses on theories of crime. Sociologists who believe that inequities in the social structure cause crime argue that unfair distribution of social resources is at the heart of persistently high levels of crime. They say that what makes communities safe is the stake the residents have in the dominant social arrangements and the benefits they receive from them. To the degree that racial exclusion and economic deprivation relegate members of these communities to second-class status, unable to compete within the prominent social sphere for goods and services, crime will result, because conforming to the law does not offer the same benefits as breaking it does. Prominent arguments that take this point of view have been made by Wilson (1987) and Braithwaite (1979). Wilson argues that a few inner-city places have become so extraordinarily alienated from mainstream economic and social processes that they become an area of the permanent underclass. Braithwaite, using international data, shows a strong correlation between the degree of inequality in a society and its amount of crime. He offers several explanations for this result, but primarily that social inequality moves large segments of people from formal commerce, gives them reason to envy the wealthy, and provides symbolic and practical endorsement for the development of illicit economies.

An alternative to this view is that, in the face of extreme disadvantage, social controls break down. This view holds that most very poor neighborhoods do not produce patterns of high criminality in *reaction* to the disadvantages they experience; rather, one of those disadvantages is that the usual mechanisms that suppress crime are lacking or deteriorated. The original work by Shaw and McKay emphasized the destabilizing effects of social disorganization. This is the view taken by *disorder theorists*. Skogan (1990) has argued that disorderly communities chip away at voluntary social participation and other aspects of social interaction that produce informal social control. Wilson and Kelling (1982) have offered a popular thesis they call *broken windows*, in which the pervasiveness of disorder in poor places leads everyone there to expect that deviance will be tolerated, especially among those who are inclined to be deviant.

These two contrasting viewpoints are important because they suggest different remedies. If the problem is inequality, then the remedy is to improve the allocation of resources. People who argue that inequality causes crime advocate for programs that strengthen labor markets and improve other forms of opportunity in the poorest locations of our inner cities. Those who see the problem as weakened social control argue for bolstering formal and informal social controls in these areas, often through police or school-related programs.

Like most simple classifications, this debate between theorists of inequality and those of social control is easily overstated. Some of the evidence cuts both ways, and the distinctions are often subtle. Just as important, the ubiquity of heavy-crime areas has spawned various ways of reworking the original Shaw and McKay trilogy of heterogeneity, poverty, and mobility. Ethnologists have noted that racial and ethnic heterogeneity no longer occurs in the nation's poorest places. Anderson (1999), for example, argues that the normative dissensus Shaw and McKay saw as a product of ethnic heterogeneity is still present in poor communities, but exists in racially homogenous communities. These all-black neighborhoods are homes to people of divergent views about conventional norms, and those who share a conventional view regarding conduct struggle with people who are disorderly and disruptive. Wilson points out that the disappearance of labor markets in these areas has eroded residents' ties to conventional social systems. The rift between the old-fashioned value groups and those who are out of the social mainstream is one of the problems these places face. Thus, important observers of the current urban scene see that poverty has become an extreme hardship, creating a structure of inequality that impedes informal social control. The fact that cities are extremely segregated racially means that the normative heterogeneity exists for a community of people who are racially alike.

Mobility has a similar story. In the world that Shaw and McKay described, mobility meant that people acquired sufficient financial resources to move out of the neighborhood. This also had a normative effect: people who could move—those with prospects for a better future— did not see a reason to become connected to the neighborhood. They instead remained aloof from their neighbors and sought ways to establish connections to other places. The result was a neighborhood where the interpersonal connections were weak and collective action was rare. These same problems apply, but mobility is not the same kind of culprit, mostly because for the residents of these places there is very little real prospect for upward (or outward) mobility. The same interpersonal alienation exists in these places, but it derives from lack of trust and a failure to see interests as common. The damage is done by deteriorating economic conditions that interfere with effective interpersonal relations and impede the normal way that informal networks exert social control, especially on young people (Wilson 1987, 1996).

There have been three notable attempts to update social disorganization theory. These studies show the resilience of the belief that crime-prone places are an important criminological problem, and they also show how the major concepts of social disorganization have been molded to incorporate new theories and evidence about crime.

## Collective Efficacy

Robert Sampson and his colleagues conducted a long-term study of Chicago neighborhoods (Earles et al. 1994) to investigate the social and interpersonal sources of differences in neighborhood circumstances. Of particular interest to them was the fact that some neighborhoods that looked similar in terms if poverty and other characteristics had quite different crime rates. They hypothesized that the difference could be explained by processes of informal social control they termed *collective efficacy*. As was pointed out in chapter 5, collective efficacy is "social cohesion among neighbors combined with their willingness to intervene on behalf of the common good" (Sampson, Raudenbush, and Earls 1997:918).

This view of neighborhoods sees them as having capacity for collective action. The foundation is a sense of shared normative expectations about how people will behave. To this is added an understanding of what people will do when it appears these expectations are being violated. Survey questions used to test for collective efficacy ask respondents if neighbors are likely to intervene in each other's behalf in the face of suspicious activity around a neighbor's property, disruptive groups of youth, and disorderly activity. Tapping a longstanding body of research coming out of the Chicago School of sociological empiricism, Sampson et al. argue that what makes neighborhoods safe is precisely this shared expectation that people who live there will have action-oriented concern about each other's well being—not just a concern, but a willingness to do something on a neighbor's behalf.

What makes neighborhoods safe, in this view, is a particular kind of informal social control—the kind that develops when people take an interest in one another's well-being. Neighbors know each other and are willing to provide tangible support for one another. This has obvious relevance for the original ideas of social disorganization theory, because it is the interaction of normative conflict that stems from heterogeneity and the poor neighborhood attachments that result from mobility (see Sampson and Groves 1989) that undermine collective capacity.

Proponents of the idea of collective efficacy have been quick to point out that theirs is not just an elaborate "disorder" argument. Disorder is an important aspect of crime, in their view, but what matters is not the degree of disorder but what people, in their private lives, are willing to do about preventing it (or cleaning it up). Their work gathered direct observational data about disorder, driving around the streets of Chicago and systematically recording what they saw, so that they could test this question. In a later paper (Sampson, Raudenbush, and Earles 1997), they show evidence that disorder variables alone relate to rates of robbery, but for other types of crime, collective efficacy provides a superior explanation. The findings regarding various measures of collective efficacy have been robust, receiving at least some support in virtually every study that has employed them as measures and demonstrating the importance of community-level concerns in crime (Sampson 2002).

## Systemic Theory

Robert Bursik and Harold Grasmick (1993) sought to rework the underlying concepts of social disorganization theory to incorporate recent criminological perspectives and findings. They begin with Wilson's work on the isolated poor (1987) and his follow-up study (1996) of the impact of the decimation of labor markets on the areas where isolated poor live. One of the main effects demonstrated by Wilson is that social networks become weakened and are incapable of providing the social capital that people need for a minimal quality of life. Bursik and Grasmick theorize that these weakened primary and secondary relational networks undercut the mechanisms of social control. Using Hunter's (1985) classification of social controls, they show that poor secondary relational networks make it difficult for residents to call upon public social controls. People's networks lack the ties that can influence policies about formal controls provided by the state—schools, police, and law enforcement. Weakened primary networks damage the way parents socialize their children and undermine the formation and maintenance of parochial social controls through which neighborhoods exert informal social control.

It is a useful oversimplification to say that Bursik and Grasmick view neighborhoods as elaborate socialization mechanisms. Their focus is on the way a neighborhood serves as a context for the choices its residents make to refrain from or engage in crime. They marshal a broad array of studies to show that factors associated with social disorganization cause problems in social (they refer to these as relational) networks and thus in informal social control. They also show how these factors damage the capacity of the neighborhood to generate public forms of social control by securing public goods and services from outside the neighborhood.

Central to the story that Bursik and Grasmick tell is the problem of residential instability. They argue that unstable neighborhoods cannot sustain the relational networks upon which people rely for solving the problems of everyday life. When residents stream in and out of neighborhoods, strong, long-term relationships do not develop. People do not tend to interact in social relationships outside their intimate household relations, and day-to-day public interaction does not provide the surveillance and control of public space. Under conditions of weak public control, thin interpersonal relationships, and limited public surveillance of space, deviance can flourish.

## The ESIOM Paradigm

In their book *Delinquent Prone Communities* (2001) Australian criminologists Don Weatherburn and Bronwyn Lind noted that most English-speaking countries experienced a growth in income inequality in the 1980s accompanied by "large increases in spatial concentration of unemployment in large metropolitan areas" (2001:1). Their thesis was that this should situation contribute to increases in crime for those societies. To explain this, they develop a revision of the thesis that unemployment causes crime. Their revision, which they refer to as the ESIOM paradigm, is then tested using data on urban areas of New South Wales.

ESIOM stands for *economic stress-induced offender motivation*. It holds that crime is linked to economic stress—low incomes, inadequate work, and sustained financial hardship. Places that have large concentrations of people who face repeated and sustained economic hardship are prone to delinquency. Evidence provides at best weak and inconsistent support for the direct connection between unemployment and crime, but there is consistent evidence to support the indirect impact of labor-related problems on criminality. The researchers empirically test a model in which economic stress leads to problems in parenting that include abuse, neglect, and inadequate disciplinary practices. Poor parenting, in turn, leads to crime.

Two aspects of this work are interesting. First, their description of the way economic stress works to promote delinquency at the individual level gives a picture of how traditional factors of interest to social disorganization theorists play a role in the overall dynamic. Summarizing their evidence, they say:

> Other things being equal, parents with dependent children who experience higher levels if economic stress are more likely to neglect or abuse their children or engage in disciplinary practices which are harsh erratic or inconsistent. This ... increases the chances that children ... will gravitate to or affiliate more strongly with their peers. To the extent these peers are involved in crime, this association increases the likelihood that susceptible

juveniles will become involved in crime. These effects are attenuated when parents...are enmeshed in a strong social support networks but they are exacerbated...when parents face added parenting burdens, such as absence of a partner...(2001:102)

Figure 7.2 shows their model. It portrays economic stress as an overarching effect that is mediated by supports and social stress. What this work adds to our discussion of social disorganization is that some of what they call "social supports" falls within the idea of collective efficacy as developed by Sampson and his colleagues. Many of the studies of

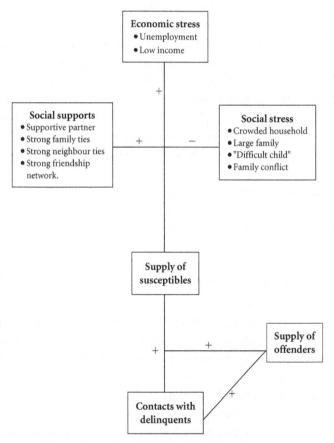

**Figure 7.2**   An epidemic model of offender population growth.

Source: Weatherburn and Lind 2001.

incarceration's effects on families and job markets, reviewed in chapter 5, fall within the category of social stress. This theory of delinquency-prone communities is closely linked to social disorganization processes and theories.

A second interesting point is the aspect of Weatherburn and Lind's work (2001) that considers how delinquency is caused by the relative supply of delinquents and susceptibles, as shaped by the nature of peer influence. Drawing upon Crane (1991) they posit an epidemic model of delinquency transmission. In this model, rates of social problems rise in a linear fashion as the number of high-social-status residents declines, until the latter reach a certain low point (5 percent of residents) at which the growth rate of the social problem shifts sharply upward in an exponential fashion. Crane modeled school dropouts and teenage pregnancy; Weatherburn and Lind model delinquency.

The connections between their work on delinquency-prone communities and our interest in concentrated incarceration are twofold. On the one hand, high rates of coercive mobility should aggravate the social stresses they have shown to help bring about the type of parenting that causes delinquency. Of equal salience is the epidemic model, which suggests that the effects of socially disorganizing factors will be nonlinear and will have a tipping point at which they become extremely mutually reinforcing and ever-more prevalent. This aspect of their work places the theory distinctly in the social disorganization tradition, for it makes a community-level argument about crime. It also serves as a useful lead-in to our discussion of coercive mobility.


## Coercive Mobility

The concept of coercive mobility can be understood as a theoretical argument in the tradition of social disorganization and its progeny. It posits an effect of incarceration that is consistent with this line of studies and arguments. The central process is the removal and return of young residents, by far mostly men but also women, from and to exceedingly poor places. There are two effects on crime.

First, removal of young residents for imprisonment is a mobility process that affects crime. It changes the density and spread of what Bursik and Grasmick have called secondary relational networks. This reduces the capacity of those networks to link to resources outside the neighborhood and bring them to bear on problems of people in the neighborhood. It weakens attachment to the neighborhood and ties to neighbors, and thereby erodes the collective efficacy that Sampson and others have argued serves as a foundation for informal social control. The social stresses identified by Weatherburn and Lind are increased by parental disruptions that lead to changes in the home and increased stresses on the home. Since these occur in the context of low social supports in high economically stressed communities, it generates the parental dysfunctions that lead to delinquency. In short, high rates of removal of parent-aged residents from poor communities sets off a series of effects that destabilize the capacity of those communities to provide informal social control.

Key to this idea is that the setting is already impoverished and the numbers of persons being removed from it are high. Low incarceration rates would be expected to have limited overall effects—potentially even a slight reduction in crime through an incapacitation effect during the period of incarceration. Or, if the high incarceration rate occurs in a neighborhood with strong resources, then the social supports might exist to counteract the destabilizing effects of removal.

The second effect occurs in reentry. This is a much more straightforward effect. Poor communities absorb large numbers of people returning from prison. These high-need residents become the very stressors for families that Weatherburn and Lind have described. They tie up the limited interpersonal and social resources of their families and networks, weakening their ability to import resources from outside the neighborhood—a problem Bursik and Grasmick have discussed. Their presence promotes attitudes inimical to the formation of collective efficacy; instead, they influence their peers and networks to isolate and insulate themselves from mainstream social processes. They also increase the supply of motivated offenders.

In this way, coercive mobility can be theorized as a mechanism that contributes to crime by sending large numbers of people from impoverished places to prison, and then returning them. The particular model it suggests would have a tipping point: the most deleterious effects of coercive mobility would take effect after a certain large number of people are caught up in the removal and return cycle. There would also be separable effects of removal and return.

## Testing the Coercive Mobility Hypothesis

The first attempt to test the coercive mobility hypothesis on its own terms was published in 2003 (Clear et al.). This study built a statistical model of the impact of 1995 incarceration rates on 1996 crime rates in Tallahassee neighborhoods. Address at the time of arrest for Tallahassee residents sent to prison in 1995 was geo-coded to Tallahassee neighborhoods. Crime rates in 1996 were also coded for those neighborhoods. Using U.S census data, other demographics for Tallahassee neighborhoods were measured. The coercive mobility model assessed the impact of 1995 incarceration on 1996 crime, controlling for neighborhood-level measures of social disorganization (concentrated disadvantage) reentry rates in 1996 and violent crime in 1995. A negative binomial regression, modeled as a quadratic, was built (see Osgood. 2000).

The logic of this modeling strategy is straightforward. Using a quadratic for neighborhood incarceration rates means that the effect of the number of people sent to prison is entered into the regression equation simultaneously as a raw number, the square of that number, and the cube of that number. Thus, if a neighborhood had 2 people removed for incarceration in 1995, three numbers would be modeled: 2, 4, and 8. A somewhat higher number of people going to prison, such as 5, would yield a much greater spread in the numbers entered into the equation: 5 (raw), 25 (squared), and 125 (cubed). Thus, quadratics are useful ways to test the idea that the effect of a variable is not constant across all of its levels. If the idea is that the *way* a factor has an effect changes when that factor gets very high or very low, then a quadratic term will find that the squared and cubed terms will *each* have a separable, significant effect. This is exactly the theorized effect of the coercive mobility hypothesis. It is argued that at low levels, removing residents for incarceration will have little impact on crime—at best, a small effect in reducing crime. But after a certain point is reached, a tipping point, those incarceration rates will begin to have a substantial effect on crime in the other direction, increasing it. If this is true, we would expect that the coefficients for each of the quadratic terms would be different and that the *direction* of the effect would potentially change as well.

The model employed then controls for social disorganization characteristics of the neighborhoods (because the coercive mobility argument derives from this theory). The rate of violent crime in 1995 is also controlled, as a way of controlling for other factors that may be causing crime rates to fluctuate. The result provides a robust, though partial, test of the coercive mobility model.

Because of extreme neighborhood effects, several models were tested, with different extreme observation deleted in each model (see Clear et al. 2002 for a discussion of the models). Multiple models were tested to investigate the robustness of the results. Figures 7.3 and 7.4 show the curves these results suggest and the 95 percent confidence intervals around the estimated coefficients. These resulting models are similar, whether extreme observations are left in or removed, and the confidence intervals show that even though the sample size is very small (80 neighborhoods),

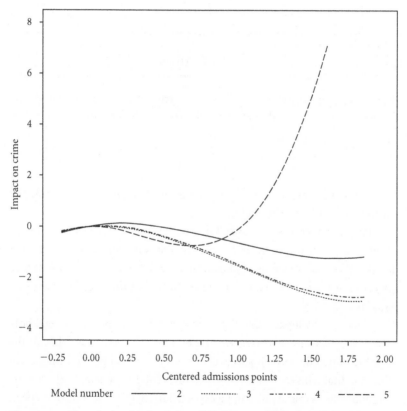

**Figure 7.3**   The relationship between a Tallahassee neighborhood's incarceration rate in one year and its crime rate the following year, controlled for neighborhood characteristics and prior crime rates.

Source: Clear, Rose, Waring, and Scully 2003.

The Impact of Incarceration on Community Safety

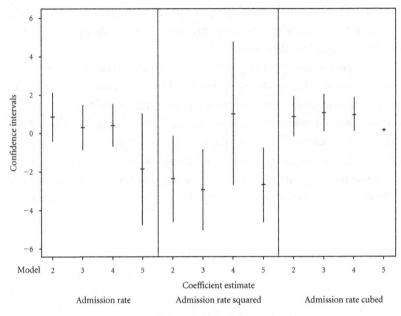

**Figure 7.4** Confidence intervals (95%) in the relationship between incarceration in one year and crime in the next, for Tallahassee neighborhoods.

Source: Clear, Rose, Waring, and Scully 2003.

results remain consistent with the coercive mobility hypothesis across the various models that were tested.

Figure 7.3 shows the curvilinearity of the relationships between incarceration in one year and crime in the following year, controlling for the effects of social disorganization variables. Figure 7.4 shows the 90 percent confidence intervals for the coefficients to the curves, for those same models.

Their results suggest that there are two different impacts of neighborhoods' incarceration experiences on their rates of crime. One is linear: the number of people returning to prison has a direct and positive impact on crime, so that with each additional person reentering a neighborhood, the neighborhood's crime rate can be expected to increase. The second effect, shown here, is curvilinear. At low levels, incarceration is unrelated to crime or has a small impact on it. At higher levels of incarceration, crime tends to go up as the number of people removed for prison increases. The researchers observe "that increasing admissions to prison in one year has a negligible effect on crime at low levels, a negative effect on crime the following year when the rate is relatively low, but, after a certain concentration of residents is removed from the community through incarceration, the effect of additional admissions is to increase, not decrease, crime" (Clear, Rose, Waring, and Scully 2003: 55). This finding tends to confirm the coercive mobility hypothesis.

The Tallahassee coercive mobility model has been replicated in six locations. Table 7.1 shows the results from those locations.

The first replication occurred in Tallahassee itself (Waring, Scully, and Clear 2005) in which data from additional years were added to the original sample, allowing analysis of effects of concentrated incarceration across a nine-year period, from 1994 to 2002. Coercive mobility models equivalent to those originally published in 2002 were estimated. The results were virtually identical to the earlier paper (Clear, Rose, Waring, and Scully 2003). When these results are desegregated for type of crime, there is curvilinearity for burglary, drug crime, and auto theft, but not for robbery (Waring, Scully, and Clear 2004).

Renauer and his colleagues (2006) employed the Tallahassee coercive mobility model on Portland (Oregon) neighborhoods, testing the impact of prison-sentence removals in 2000 on crime in the following year. They found that while coercive mobility variables were not significantly predictive of property crime (although the correlations were generally in the right direction), they were predictive for violent crime, in the same curvilinear way as occurred in Tallahassee. In Columbus, Ohio, a similar direct replication was attempted (Powell et al. 2004). A curvilinear

Table 7.1 Results of Tests of Coercive Mobility Hypothesis: Curvilinear Pattern Found Consistent with "Coercive Mobility" Hypothesis

| Site and years | All crime | Property crime | Violent crime | Drug crime |
|---|---|---|---|---|
| Tallahassee 1994–1995 | Yes | Not tested | Not tested | Not tested |
| Tallahassee 1994–2002 | Yes | Yes | Some | Not tested |
| Portland 2000–2001 | Not tested | No | Yes | Not tested |
| Columbus 1999–2002 | Not tested | Partial | Yes | Not tested |
| Chicago 2000–2001 | Not tested | Not tested | Not tested | Yes |
| Cleveland/Baltimore 1996–1998 | Partial | Not tested | Not tested | Not tested |

pattern is again found. The curves for violent crime are similar to those found in Tallahassee. For property crime, it is at the middle level that concentrated incarceration tends to lead to an increase in crime, and this effect is quite pronounced. Levels of crime begin dropping at the highest levels of incarceration.

In Chicago, Susan George and her colleagues (George, LaLonde, and Schuble 2005) tested the impact of *female* incarceration in 1999 on drug crime in 2000. Studying female incarceration is an important extension of the Rose-Clear coercive mobility hypothesis. While the aggregate number of women who go through the incarceration process is much smaller than men (about one-tenth), George and her colleagues argue that poor women are central to the community functioning of their neighborhoods in ways that men are not, and the ripple effects of locking up a woman are far more significant than those for a man. They test a coercive mobility model and find that drug crime is associated with incarceration of women in the same pattern elicited between total incarceration and total crime in Tallahassee.

Results in Baltimore and Cleveland generally replicate the Tallahassee results, though less closely than Portland, and with some nonsignificant coefficients that are in the correct direction. (There are additional issues in the Baltimore and Cleveland data, discussed below.)

The Columbus pattern, and the weak confirmation in the Baltimore and Cleveland data, indicates that the coercive mobility hypothesis is only partly affirmed by these data. There are, however, two reasons not to discard the model on the basis of these results. First, there are important numerical limitations in the way this particular model is built. These samples are small, and so coefficients that are in the right direction may fail to rise to statistical significance, mostly as a consequence of sample size. The model is an extremely conservative one. Controlling for the previous year's crime rate removes a great deal of variance in crime rate and places a substantial statistical burden on the capacity of other variables in the model to explain the much reduced variance that is left. Moreover, the effects being modeled here are theorized to occur only in a few of the neighborhoods: two in Portland and three in Tallahassee. This is, after all, a test of extreme cases. It is not surprising that small samples would only partially support the coercive mobility hypothesis, for mathematical reasons alone.

Two recent studies give additional credence to the tipping point idea. Fagan and his colleagues (Fagan, West, and Holland 2003) investigated the impact of incarceration on crime rates at the neighborhood level in New York City, from 1985 to 1996. They find that:

> [O]ver a relatively long time period . . . incarceration tends first to unfold as closely related to crime, and then, over the interval, become somewhat independent of crime. As this cycle spirals forward, incarceration threatens to become endogenous in these neighborhoods . . . permanently staining the social and psychological fabric of neighborhood life in poor neighborhoods of New York. . . . Over time, incarceration creates more incarceration in a spiraling dynamic. (23)

While their model does not expressly posit a tipping point, their results are interpreted within that light. They suggest that "the spatial concentration of incarceration distorts neighborhood social ecology and attenuates the neighborhoods economic fortunes" (23), and it is this damage that leads to higher crime for those places with sustained high rates of incarceration over time.

In a neighborhood study not involving incarceration, Robert J. Kane (2006) investigated the effect of "arrest rigor" (arrests for violent crime per officer) on rates of burglary and robbery in New York City precincts.

> [T]he study found a curvilinear relationship between arrests per officer and subsequent burglary and robbery rates; as arrests per officer increased, robbery and burglary decreased to a point; but when a threshold of arrest vigor was reached, robbery and burglary began to increase. (208)

He interpreted these results within a structural-deterrence framework, making assumptions about the way potential lawbreakers in those precincts calculate their chances of being caught. But because arrests are so closely linked to incarceration rates, these results are consistent with the predictions of the coercive mobility hypothesis.

Seen from this frame of reference, the findings across these several sites, with independent datasets and using different lenses, do not "prove" the coercive mobility hypothesis. But they do find evidence that substantially comports with the predictions the theory would make. Said another way, these data *do not* provide support for an alternative conceptualization of the impact of incarceration. The data are *not* consistent with a belief that incarceration is *helpful* to crime rates in the poorest neighborhoods. Clearly, there is good reason for concern that as incarceration rates grow past a certain point, crime will start to rise.

## The Problem of Measurement

The general theme of this analysis is to propose that incarceration "causes" various social problems when it is concentrated in poor communities, and through them, crime. In the social sciences, to say that some social factor "causes" another is to bear a heavy statistical burden of proof. Many things are correlated without a causal connection: in presidential elections since the Civil War, for example, winners tend to have longer names, but nobody would suggest that their name length causes them to win. There is, then, the weighty problem regarding incarceration as a cause of a community-level effect, particularly public safety. In statistical terms, this is known as the problem of simultaneity, or endogeniety. There are related issues of statistical significance, and the role of extreme cases.

### *Simultaneity*

A concern that is immediately apparent, *simultaneity* is the idea is that crime rates "cause" incarceration rates, while simultaneously incarceration rates also "cause" crime rates. The conceptual problem is that while the theory posits that incarceration causes crime, it is far more straightforward to assume that crime causes incarceration. If these different effects are not separated, then they will tend to cancel each other out.

Indeed, Rose and Clear (1998) originally proposed coercive mobility as a nonrecursive model of incarceration and crime, in which higher crime rates lead to higher rates of incarceration, which at the upper level cause higher crime rates. To fully test this effect, researchers would need to create what is referred to as a "nonrecursive path model," that is, an approach that separates out the way crime leads to incarceration in one period, then later leads to more crime. Time-ordered data are needed to produce such a model: changes in incarceration rates and crime rates over time are used to show the way the crime rate goes up as a *consequence* of the earlier high level of incarceration. Path models tend to be a favorite choice of sociologists.

There are two additional methods for dealing with simultaneity that use other variables to resolve the problem. One is to avoid it altogether by selecting a proxy-dependent variable. This approach models the impact of incarceration on an outcome that is not likely to be a simultaneous "cause" of adult criminality. For example, juvenile crime rates, housing prices, sexually transmitted diseases, voter participation rates, and so forth may be affected by adult incarceration, but it is unlikely that any of them cause adult crime. A final option, one favored by economists, is to employ an instrumental variable. An instrumental variable is one that "works" to isolate the portion of the variance in crime that can be explained by incarceration, by removing the portion of the covariance in crime and incarceration that derives from the way crime leads to incarceration. Instrumentation is used to eliminate the correlation between crime and incarceration that is a result of the way crime "causes" incarceration, leaving only the part that results from the way incarceration causes crime.

Each of these solutions has weaknesses. Nonrecursive path models require sufficient data to array relationships across time. When the idea is to test effects that occur in *places*, as the theory suggests, then place-specific changes in an array of characteristics across time are needed. It is rare to have such data. Using alternative-outcome variables can be unpersuasive when it is thought that these variables themselves are consequences of other, nonmeasured causes (we discuss this more in the section on endogeniety, below).

## Endogeneity

The problem of *endogeneity* (a statistical modeling challenge similar to that posed by simultaneity) arises when the relationship being displayed is spurious, because both crime and incarceration are caused by a third (unmodeled) variable. It is plausible, for example, that both crime and incarceration result from external processes, such as concentrated disadvantage, economic marginality, and so forth. The usual way to address this problem is to include more variables in the study as statistical controls, making sure that the causal relationship between incarceration and crime is not eliminated when other factors are taken into account. This kind of strategy is not foolproof, however. Under the best of circumstances, the way the relationship between incarceration and crime is measured, even when many statistical controls are included, leaves a lot of variation in crime unexplained. Since crime is hardly random, this leads us to think that some of what is causing crime rates to be different in one place (or time) from another has not been taken into account. We must worry that if those factors were added to the equation, the relationship between crime and incarceration might change—or even disappear.

### Other Problems in Measurement

The problem of *statistical significance* is a simple one. Most localities have a small number of neighborhoods, and this means that degrees of freedom in statistical models rapidly diminish. It is entirely conceivable that meaningful relationships could exist but are not found "significantly" present owing primarily to sample size. *Extreme cases* are also of concern. There is no obvious solution to the fact that a handful of neighborhoods (sometimes only one or two) produce the vast bulk of the crime and incarceration. When these neighborhoods are dropped, of course, significance disappears largely because the remaining neighborhoods look very much alike—they have little variation. But basing an entire model on results that stem from the pattern of a few cases raises a problem of interpretation. Some of this problem is ameliorated by the fact that the coercive mobility theory itself holds that the effects result from what happens in the extreme cases of incarceration and crime.

## A Competition of Models

For these reasons, an empirical test of the coercive mobility thesis is conceptually complicated. Crime rates are thought to be both a *result* of incarceration and a *cause* of incarceration. That means that the theory holds that there is a simultaneity to the crime-incarceration relationship. It is beyond dispute that crime *causes* incarceration—there cannot be an imprisonment without a crime, and the more the crime, the more likely the imprisonment. Yet the coercive mobility thesis holds that (at least at the high end) more incarceration *causes* more crime. Thus, argue Bhati and his colleagues (Bhati, Lynch, and Sabol 2005; see also Lynch and Sabol 2004b), it could be misleading to interpret a positive correlation between incarceration and crime as affirming the coercive mobility thesis. Instead, all that might be going on is that the model is picking up the entirely expected positive relationship that results from crime leading to incarceration. This is the problem of endogeniety—incarceration is *both* a result and a cause—and since crime rates at the neighborhood level are highly correlated across short time intervals (say, year-to-year), they worry that the use of violent crime as a covariate does not fully control for this type of auto-correlation. Their concern is that the model needs to find a way to parcel out the portion of the correlation between incarceration and crime that is a result of the way crime leads to imprisonment, and then study how the remaining correlation affects later crime rates.

Proponents of the time-ordered model argue that their method deals with these issues. When they test for spatial auto-correlation, they find no need to adjust their models due to this problem (Clear et al. 2003; Renauer et al. 2006). The problem they want to investigate, they say, is not that crime and incarceration are correlated, but that changes in crime rates come in part from changes in incarceration rates. They then point out that the use of a quadratic in time-ordered data is a powerful way to pick up the direction of changes in data across time, which is the central equation of coercive mobility. If there is no underlying relationship other than one in which crime leads to incarceration, then there is no reason to expect a quadratic to work better than a simple regression. And the fact that there are sign changes in the terms of the quadratic further supports the coercive mobility thesis and is not consistent with a purely crime-driven process.

The critics of time-ordered models have not been satisfied with that reply. Their case that incarceration is endogenous to crime is a strong one. A typical solution to the problem of endogeniety—one preferred by economists—is to employ instrumental variables to identify the causal relationship between incarceration at one time and later crime. This is an exercise that is both conceptual and empirical. What is needed is a variable that is correlated with the independent variable (incarceration) but not with the dependent variable (crime). The instrument is then used to "remove" all the covariation between incarceration and crime that can be thought of as the way crime leads to incarceration. The remaining variance is then seen as "clean" of the endogeniety of incarceration, and therefore can be modeled as a consequence of crime.

The way this modeling strategy works has been demonstrated in a couple of recent papers (Bhati, Lynch, and Sabol 2005; Lynch and Sabol

2004b). They employ drug arrests as an instrumental variable. Drug arrests are useful, they argue, because the number of drug arrests is directly related to the number of people going to prison, but drug arrests are elastic in the sense that there is a nearly inexhaustible supply of potential arrestees, and so there need not be any relationship between crime and the rate of drug arrests. To further cleanse the simultaneity problem, they

> [t]ake the residual of the regression of the change in drug arrest rates between 1987 and 1992 on the change in index crime rate over the same period and then regressing the change in the prison admission rate on this residual. The instrument satisfies the conceptual and empirical requisites of and instrument: it was correlated with the incarceration rate and independent of the crime rate. (Lynch and Sabol 2004b: 150)

Their resulting analysis not only fails to confirm the results from the coercive mobility models described above; it also finds evidence of the opposite effect. When the instrument is included in their model, the relationship between incarceration and crime changes, with higher incarceration rates predicting *lower* crime rates. They compare this result to a two-stage least-squares model, without the instrument, in which the effect of changes in incarceration rates are modeled on changes in crime rates, and they again find evidence of a negative, though not significant, relationship between incarceration and crime. (They also find that incarceration has negative impacts on some underlying processes of informal social control, a result described in chapter 5.) They conclude that their work provides "some support for both those who argue that high levels of incarceration undermine the ability of neighborhoods to perform their social functions and for those who allege that incarceration is beneficial for communities" (158).

The results of instrumented models pose a profound challenge to the coercive mobility thesis, but they do not, by themselves, refute it. There are reasons to think that an instrumental approach will provide a problematic test of the coercive mobility thesis. The choice of an instrument is crucial. By using drug arrests, Lynch and Sabol have a plausible candidate, but one that is potentially contaminated by the fact that the "discretionary portion" of the supply of potential arrests is linked to the very neighborhoods that have high rates of incarceration. Indeed, in Chicago

(George, LaLonde, and Schuble 2005), drug crime rates are associated with incarceration rates for women in exactly the manner predicted by the coercive mobility hypothesis. It is not clear whether using this variable as an instrument will elucidate the relationship or tend to eliminate the way the coercive mobility process is at work in these neighborhoods. If the latter is the case, then the very places of interest—high-incarceration places—are controlled out of the model. A particular strength of the coercive mobility models tested above may be that they focus attention on the effects at the extreme levels, while instrumentation may tend to weaken the detectability of those effects.

An ingenious way of avoiding the problems inherent in trying to model the relationship between adult incarcerations and adult crime is to incorporate a dependent variable that is clean of the simultaneity problems of adult crime. This would occur, for example, if we were to model the effect of adult incarcerations on juvenile crime. There are good theoretical reasons that these effects would be substantial. Yet this strategy completely avoids the predicament of simultaneity. It can be argued that high rates of adult incarcerations, concentrated in the poorest communities, would lead to weakened supervision by parental or adult supervisory figures, and this would ultimately translate into more juvenile crime. A relationship in the other direction is not plausible unless a jurisdiction has a phenomenally high rate of transfers of juveniles to adult courts. That is, for a span of just a couple of years, there is no plausible reason to think that increases in juvenile delinquency rates would increase the chances of adult incarcerations in a given neighborhood. Thus, using juvenile delinquency rates as a dependent variable resolves some of the more difficult modeling problems in the coercive mobility hypotheses.

This strategy has been taken by Ralph Taylor and his colleagues (2006). They analyze the impact of adult arrest rates in Philadelphia police districts on later rates of serious juvenile delinquency, between 1994 and 2004. Two of their findings are important. First, they find the familiar pattern, as have others who modeled coercive mobility directly, that higher rates of adult incarceration predict higher rates of lawbreaking in later periods. But because their measure of lawbreaking is serious juvenile delinquency, the problematic link between adult imprisonment and adult crime does not arise. Second, they find that the impact of adult arrest rates on juvenile delinquency becomes more intensely associated with the neighborhood itself if more time is allowed to pass between the period of adult arrest and the rate of delinquency. Stated differently, if more time is allowed to pass between the adults getting arrested (and presumably some fraction of them getting removed for some period) and the delinquents' coming to the attention of family court, the link between the two is more clearly located within the neighborhood. Both results are consistent with the coercive mobility hypothesis—places that have higher rates of adults going to prison are more likely to be places that have serious juvenile delinquency in later months or years. This result is consistent with Murray and Farrington's forthcoming finding that "parental imprisonment predicts at least double the risk for antisocial-delinquent behavior of children".

### Discussion: The Level of Evidence and the Burden of Proof

This chapter has reviewed a series of theoretical and empirical studies that sought to test empirically the coercive mobility hypothesis. That idea, briefly stated, is that high rates of incarceration, concentrated in poor communities, will lead to more crime. There has not been much work that directly considers this question, and all of the studies have significant methodological limitations. Every study to date that examines the effect of high rates of incarceration on neighborhoods finds evidence of various problems resulting from incarceration. Studies that assess outcomes that serve as a foundation for informal social control find, as well, that incarceration has deleterious effects on informal social controls. Incarceration has problem-inducing effects on family structure, family formation, and parenting in ways that would suggest a grater propensity for crime.

The few studies that attempt to assess the impact of high rates of incarceration at the community level provide findings that are dependent on the modeling strategy selected. To date, there is no definitive answer to the question. What is to be made of this?

One way to think about this is to use an adversarial metaphor. Incarceration stands accused of contributing to the problem of social disorganization and crime in our poorest neighborhoods. There is a great deal of evidence that links the two, though no study provides a smoking gun, and at least one line of studies offers a potential alibi. The verdict we reach may well rest on the test of the level of proof required.

Perhaps we ought to require that proof of the problems of incarceration be given that is "beyond a reasonable doubt." That is a stringent standard—so stringent that it is unlikely that any single study will ever be conclusive. As Shawn Bushway and David McDowell (2006) put it in a different context:

> A reasonable solution...is to conduct rigorous statistical analysis...using multiple sources of data and different research designs. If these analyses begin to repeatedly find the same answer, we can have more confidence in the result, despite the absence of any one research design that proves the fact beyond a reasonable doubt. (467)

Despite the absence of a single, definitive study, it is hard to see how incarceration cannot be implicated as a problem for poor communities. As Bushway and McDowell might point out, there are simply too many studies that point to the problem for the connection to be ignored. Incarceration is, after all, an intervention directed at its highest level at the poorest communities, and it has as one of its aims imposing long-term negative consequences on the people who experience it—and who return, eventually, to those communities. There is good evidence that high rates of incarceration destabilize families, increase rates of delinquency, increase rates of teenage births, foster alienation of youth from pro-social norms, damage frail social networks, and weaken labor markets. It requires a stretch of logic to think that concentrated incarceration contributes to all of these problems, each of which tends to weaken informal social control, but somehow incarceration does *not* lead to less public safety. It would be special, indeed, for incarceration to be a source of *all* of these problematic neighborhood dynamics without affecting crime. Taken as a whole, it is hard to not to see a preponderance of evidence in favor of the coercive mobility thesis. There is, after all, a great deal at stake. The consequences of being wrong do not fall equally in both directions.

If we approach incarceration as a problem that needs to be confronted, we will look for imaginative solutions that will have as their aim the reduction of a host of community problems stemming from mass confinement of community residents. If we are successful, we will strengthen families, reduce delinquency, decrease health problems, and establish a basis for a more vibrant labor market. If the coercive mobility thesis turns out to have been wrong, we will not, however have reduced crime. As a package, this seems like a net improvement on the current situation in these impoverished places.

We might, on the other hand, choose not to address the problems of incarceration in poor communities, because we think the way incarceration damages public safety has not been sufficiently demonstrated. What if we are wrong? Then we will unwittingly contribute not only to the damage wreaked by mass imprisonment but also to the victimization resulting from crime rates that are kept high by it.

Given these stakes, there seems a clear moral requirement that we do something about mass incarceration of people from impoverished places. The following chapter provides a glimpse of the strategies this requirement entails.

# Dealing with Concentrated Incarceration

## The Case for Community Justice

8

The basic facts are these: U.S. prison populations have grown every year for over 30 years, and we have had for some time the highest incarceration rate in the world. Imprisonment in America is concentrated among young, poor—dominantly minority—men and (to a lesser extend) women who come from impoverished communities. The way these young people cycle through our system of prisons and jails, then back into the community, leaves considerable collateral damage in its wake. Families are disrupted, social networks and other forms of social support are weakened, health is endangered, labor markets are thinned, and—more important than anything else—children are put at risk of the depleted human and social capital that promotes delinquency. After a certain point, the collateral effects of these high rates of incarceration seem to contribute to *more* crime in those places. Crime fuels a public call for ever-tougher responses to crime. The increasing way in which the face of criminality is the face of a person of color contributes to an unarticulated public sense that race and crime are closely linked. The politics of race and justice coexist malignantly, sustaining an ever-growing policy base that guarantees new supplies of penal subjects in a self-sustaining and self-justifying manner.

It is, as I said in chapter 1, like a perfect storm. What is to be done? How do we steer our way out of this penal mess? In this concluding chapter I think strategically about the courses of action we must take if we are to address the problem of mass incarceration that concentrates in poor places. We begin by considering some of the reasons this problem is so hard to confront. At one level, it is a very simple problem: too many people go to prison, and too many of them stay there too long. But if only it were this simple, we would have found our way out of the mess a long time ago. So I consider why this problem is so hard to confront.

The lesson is that the problem of mass incarceration transcends policy and extends to U.S. culture and politics. I then identify three policy agendas that, however popular among penal reformers today (and however valuable in their own right), will *not* help. It is important to start here, because we need to understand why the usual penal reform agendas, so hotly debated in the field, are, sadly, simply irrelevant. I then suggest what we *must* do: sentencing reform.

The difficulty of achieving meaningful sentencing reform in the current policy environment is a good reason for pessimism about the prospects of doing anything. This suggests that, in the end, if we are to make headway on this problem, we must reconsider the very values that undergird penal policy. In this regard, I offer a conceptualization of community justice as an alternative that promises a set of new values that might lead us to new ways of justice. But, as mentioned above, the line of analysis begins with frankness about why we find it so hard to attain penal reform.

## Why Is This Problem So Hard to Confront?

The idea that out-of-scale use of imprisonment in the United States is a serious problem is not a new thought. That huge prison populations are a policy error is a point that has been made repeatedly and consistently for years by critics of prison ideology—critics ranging from social theorists such as David Garland (2001) and Loic Wacquant (2007) to activists like James Austin and John Irwin (2006). Even scholars whose own work linked falling crime rates to growing imprisonment no longer suggest that more prisons will result in less crime. From fire-breathers such as John DiIulio (1999) to sociologists known for their cautious methodology (Liedka, Useem and Piehl, 2006), there appears to be a consensus developing that continued prison growth will no longer pay off as public policy. To this short list of prominent names could be added a dozen or more public policy scholars who have expressed doubts about the value of prison. It seems that only the fringe remain proponents for making our prisons continue to grow.

Evidence about the diminished value of incarceration for crime control surely plays a role in this development. Just as surely, social scientists who at one time may have been friendly to the value of prisons in society have grown troubled by the increasingly apparent collateral consequences of our reliance on prisons as the main strategy for social control. As evidence grows of the inescapable harm that mass imprisonment does to young people of color, their children, and their communities, even those who give a friendly reading to the prison's contribution to public safety cannot avoid being concerned about the damage imprisonment causes to the lives of the innocent, not just the guilty.

Given all this disquiet, one would think that we would be on the cusp of a new direction. Perhaps we are, but the signs are not very promising. A couple of years ago, it looked as though prison growth would slow, dragged down finally by a seemingly precipitous national drop in crime. But the figures of the Bureau of Justice Statistics say otherwise: since 2003, the prison population has grown by about 5 percent, even while crime dropped about 9 percent. Prison growth has become a structural component of the justice system, self-sustaining in the face of declining confidence in imprisonment by informed observers; growing despite a drop in crime. For these reasons, the nation's prison population has been projected to grow another 6% over the next five years, even though crime has been dropping for a decade (Austin, Naro, and Fabelo 2007).

In the United States, prison populations are kept high and growing by two policy problems: an unexamined commitment to the punitive theory of criminal justice and the lack of alternative strategies that can be demonstrated as effective. These policy problems reinforce each other. The punitive ideology means that when we look for alternative strategies, we first ask that they satisfy our foundational need for punitiveness. For example, proponents of nonprison alternatives such as intensive probation supervision, public shaming, boot camps, electronic monitoring, and the like often begin by pointing out that these alternatives are as onerous as prison. Yet once these alternatives are evaluated, we see they do not (and probably cannot) achieve their aims; this leads to a false conclusion that we have no options other than prison. Our commitment to punitiveness restricts the options we will consider, and the restricted range of options we are willing to entertain guarantees, in the end, that we will discover few realistic options to prison. Prison reformers often find themselves in what computer programmers used to call a "do-loop": they try to find a nonprison strategy that satisfies the punitive instinct without the collateral damage, but when the dust settles they find they are back where they started.

It is clear that the criminal justice system today feeds upon itself. There are many ways this is true. Increased police presence in a "troubled" neighborhood increases the probability of detecting violations of the law and subjecting people in those places to criminal justice. When concentrations of arrests get to a certain point, crime begins to rise rather than fall, creating more eligibility for detection and arrest (Kane 2006). In places with more police presence and (thus) more arrests, more adults go to prison. Then, the chances of a child becoming involved in delinquency are increased by having a parent go to prison, in part because of the way loss of the parent affects socialization and adjustment (Hawkins et al. 2000). Being exposed to neighborhood violence and being victimized as a child increase the chances of adult criminality (Kaufman 2005). Similarly, a child who becomes involved in the formal juvenile justice system as an adolescent is at greater risk of criminal activity in early adulthood, owing to "the negative effect of intervention on education attainment and employment" (Bernburg and Krohn 2003:1287). People who are convicted of crimes as juveniles are targeted for prison terms as recidivists; people who go to prison are more likely to recidivate (Spohn and Holleran 2002). As crime grows, pressure grows for more aggressive policing in problem places, and pressure for more stringent penalties does as well. And so the cycle begins again.

Because the criminal justice system feeds on itself, it is irrational to think that we can reduce the need for criminal justice by growing the system. This is, paradoxically, the often unstated claim of proponents of criminal justice as a means of crime control. They say that the only way to fight crime is to strengthen the criminal justice system; by implication, they say a stronger criminal justice system will make crime drop, that reductions in crime will eventually make less pressing our need to strengthen the system. This is a logically problematic idea if the criminal justice system actually does fight crime, but it is a downright mistaken one if, as I have shown so far, the justice system produces, at least in part, its own business.

There are caveats to this conclusion, of course. Major social forces, from changes in the economy to shifts in culture, influence rates of crime as well. The growth of criminal justice is not an oscillating system tending toward instability; it is subject to constraints both social and practical. But the major point is true enough: the need for prisons comes in part from a growing criminal justice apparatus that creates, at least in part, the unquestioned need for prisons. Therefore, the first order of business is to be clear about what will *not* work.

## Three Distractions from the Agenda of Penal Reform

Our ability to confront the problem of increasing incarceration is made more difficult by the interference of three distractions. I call them distractions because they are immediately apparent ideas that stand out in the arena of penal reform, and when they appear, they exert an almost deafening call for our attention. They are self-deceptions, though, because no matter how cogently we turn our attention to these issues, their resolution will not help us address the problem of prison growth. Experience shows that these are an appealing set of ideas, but ultimately a red herring in the agenda of penal reform. They are (1) penal philosophy (or ideology), (2) penal programs, and (3) the problem of the "extreme case."

### *In Search of a Penal Philosophy*

There is no discernible, principled foundation for U.S. prison policy. In place of what might be thought of as a political philosophy of punishment, we have what my colleague, political scientist Diana Gordon, has described as the "justice juggernaut" (1990): "being tough" on crime, regardless of evidence or experience in the matter. Faced with disgracefully crowded prisons, local and state budget crises, a seemingly endless stream of program failures, and recidivism rates that stay high no matter what we do, we clothe every "new" policy option in rhetorical and programmatic "toughness," or else it stands little chance of being enacted.

For a nation that prizes freedom as a cultural and political organizing principle, this lack of a coherent frame of reference regarding punishment is a paradox. We are used to a fairly sophisticated public conversation about other matters in the polity, such as the allocation of responsibilities between the federal and state governments, the role of the private sector in providing state services, the legal and social status of differences in sexual preferences, the relationship between church and state. Each of these thick topics is the subject of considerable public discussion, private conversation, and media coverage. Yet there is little in the way of public consideration or discussion when it comes to carrying out the criminal law.

The absence of a considered and principled conceptualization of criminal law has meant that thin ideology reigns. Bedrock ideas such as the presumption of innocence, the prohibition of cruel punishments, dignity in the criminal justice process, and the requirement that guilt must be proven before punishments may be imposed fall prey to a barely articulated ideology of "public safety." In recent years in the United States we have seen the return of chain gangs, an increase in routine returns of parolees to prison for failure to follow rules, expulsion of people convicted of drug crimes from their homes at the same time they are made ineligible for college loans, development of registration systems for people who have completed their sentences for sex crimes, and creation of inner-city ghettoes as the only places people convicted of these crimes are able to live. People placed on probation and parole are made to pay part of the cost of their surveillance. Some people with three felony convictions are placed in confinement for decades, regardless of the limited seriousness of their crimes. In today's atmosphere, these disproportionate penalties and the indifference to infringements on liberty are enacted with astoundingly little debate and almost no objection. We live in a time when considered reflection on the merits of our justice system is rare, but somatic reactions are typical. Though we have a national self-conception that we distrust governance by coercion, in the area of crime control, this self-image is patently false.

The lack of a viable, dominant philosophy of criminal justice means that there are few brakes to be exerted on the juggernaut. New ideas do not have to meet the criterion of a widely held public sense of fairness because such a sense of fairness does not exist. When a new, always more onerous proposal arises, the question is not, Will this work? Rather, the question is, Does this sound like it might work? Balanced against that standard, almost every suggestion that sharpens the law's cutting edge or makes its demands more weighty is seen as a good thing. The uncritical thinking we give to penal toughness operates like a penal Gresham's law, in which bad ideas drive out good ones. Until we change the lens under which we consider penal options, we will have trouble choosing useful ones. That reality is illustrated by the weak potential of the current policy agenda to do much about concentrated mass incarceration.

## Good Ideas and Valuable Programs That Will Not Solve the Problem

Three strategies—rehabilitation programs, alternatives to incarceration, and reentry programs—are often suggested as ways to deal with the problem of growing incarceration rates. These strategies cannot succeed in stemming the growth of imprisonment, and today's advocates for reducing imprisonment waste resources describing, evaluating, and defending these programs as part of their agenda. Here is why they cannot help very much with the larger cause of penal reform.

### Rehabilitation Programs

The common debate, punishment versus treatment, is unwarranted. Both punishment and treatment are coercive penal strategies, and they are not opposite; they are merely different. The opposite of punishment is reward; the opposite of treatment is neglect. Nobody, confronted with people who have broken the law, argues for either reward or neglect. Duff (2001), for example, in advocating for a liberal (as in "liberty") penal theory, calls for "hard treatment" as the appropriate way to communicate censure for illegal conduct. Restorative-justice advocates call for offender "accountability" and restorative "sanctions." On the other hand, those who believe in the punitive ethic are by no means required to neglect the needs of the person who has violated the law—far from it. In fact, it is quite possible (and quite usual) for penal reformers of all persuasions to say that a wider array of treatment programs ought to either be required or be made voluntary for people who are being punished in prison.

This limitation of rehabilitation programs is worth emphasizing, because when many people hear complaints about mass imprisonment, they often automatically assume, quite wrongly, that opposition to prison means favoring rehabilitation. Prison rehabilitation may be a good thing, but opposing prison does not mean favoring rehabilitation. Indeed, some judges will say that they send people *to* prison *in order* to get rehabilitated. People who oppose mass imprisonment and the concentrated level of incarceration felt by poor communities need not embrace rehabilitation as the option of choice, and many do not.

There may, of course, be a role for rehabilitation programming in penal-code reform. In recent years, there has been a growing body of work showing, quite persuasively, that certain kinds of programs reduce recidivism rates more than trivially (Andrews 2001; Lipsey 1999). Evaluation studies done over a generation now show that some treatment strategies for people who have broken the law will reduce their propensity to commit new crimes (Sherman et al. 1997). If our aim is to help those who have broken the law become restored to their communities as pro-social citizens, we would be unwise to ignore this work. It is worth noting, too, that programs are more likely to work to the degree to which they (1) focus on people considered to be higher risk, (2) maximize the use of the community as a program setting, and (3) give preference to therapeutic care when using confinement settings. Tough, prison-oriented, and threat-based programs simply do not work.

Still, a 15 to 20 percent reduction in rearrests, while welcome, hardly constitutes a new penal regime. To emphasize, rehabilitation programming may soften the prison experience, but it attacks the problem of high incarceration rates by reducing, only marginally, the rate at which those who were once locked up return.

We should, undoubtedly, offer rehabilitation programs whenever and wherever we can. If we expect people who have broken the law to become reformed, it is both senseless and cruel to deny them proven means to do so. And if we make a concerted commitment to rehabilitation, we will tend to rely on programs in community settings and more humane institutional regimes. But a wholesale adoption of rehabilitation as an ideal is not likely to reduce mass incarceration by itself. Psychologist Richard Tremblay (2006) has pointed out that, when programs are directed toward youth in their teens, the programs are already too late. He advocates instead that prevention programs be focused on children in their kindergarten years. A recent substantial review of the literature on the effectiveness of prevention programs reaches the same conclusion (Farrington and Welsh 2007). Yet such programs, targeted at the very young, cannot legally or morally be done coercively or in confinement settings without violating basic ideas of justice.

*Alternatives to Incarceration*

By now, we should know that programs sold as alternatives to incarceration rarely replace incarceration. There are two reasons. First, to be politically feasible, most alternatives have to come with the promise to be tough and uncompromising. Second, they typically state that they will not put the public at risk, so they forgo dealing with serious law violators. These two promises make most alternatives irrelevant as potential solutions to mass incarceration.

The most famous illustration of the "toughness" problem was demonstrated in the California Intensive Supervision (ISP) field experiment (Petersilia and Turner 1990). California probation departments developed intensive supervision caseloads for felony probationers and programmed them with stringent conduct requirements, close surveillance, and strict probation officer accountability. The result of the tough requirements and close surveillance was that those who were diverted from prison to ISP violated the rules of supervision at higher rates and ended up doing more prison time overall than those who were sentenced as usual. The commitment to being "tough" meant that prison became *more* likely as a backup sanction when probationers had trouble abiding by the more stringent requirements.

The problem with promising not to put the public at risk is that this promise is usually carried out by limiting the prison alternative to people considered low-risk—for example, people convicted only once of a property crime. But these people rarely end up in prison, anyway. So the programs that take this strategy divert few from prison; instead, they expose a less serious group to expanded levels of social control. They widen the net (Cohen 1985).

Alternatives to incarceration may be good programs, but they do not hold the promise of controlling mass incarceration. There are exceptions to this rule, of course—isolated studies find that prison alternatives *actually* divert some of their clients from prison (Kurlychek and Kempinen 2006) or reduce rates of community failure and return to prison (Gebelin 2000). Such findings suggest that traditional alternatives to incarceration, well designed and well managed, are useful. But even these exceptions to the rule do not offer effects that are *large* enough, or spread across a sufficient number of people, to have a significant impact on the size of the prison population.

*Reentry Programs*

Interest in reentry programs has been intense ever since the National Institute of Justice announced that over 600,000 people would reenter communities from prison (Travis 2005). The National Council of State Governments (NCSG 2005) has built a model legislative and programmatic package for reentry; at least one influential foundation has called the problem of reentry a "crisis" (Good and Sherrid 2005). Researchers and policy makers have focused on this issue. This interest is welcome, because people who leave prison face daunting problems that have led to high failure rates.

The potential for improving the prospects of people in reentry from prison is significant, but there is at least at least an equal chance that this new attention will backfire. Studies of both traditional parole (Solomon, Kachnowski and Bhati 2005) and "new generation" reentry services (Wilson and Davis 2006) have cast doubt on their value. But the potential for failing programs is not the main reason for concern. We should be wary that the increased attention to reentry will promote the usual changes: closer surveillance, more restrictions, and greater emphasis on being "tough." This leads to a problem of "back-end sentencing," as the prison term a person serves becomes lengthened by community supervision requirements that result in revocation (Travis and Christiansen 2006).

The central problem is even more basic. Unless reentry programs are wildly successful—and there is no reason to think they will be—they cannot solve the problem of mass incarceration. The inescapable fact is that reentry comes *after* the person has gone to prison. We have 600,000 people in reentry each year because we removed them in prior years. Our concern about reentry cannot solve the problem of mass imprisonment because it is, itself, a consequence of mass imprisonment.

Reentry programs deserve support, of course. It is clear that there are ways to design parole supervision programs to increase the odds of successful reentry (Burke and Tonry 2006). The point is not that reentry programs are *wrong*, just that they come too late to have much impact on mass incarceration.

*The Issue of the Extreme Case*

Before we can usefully consider options for reducing the problem of mass incarceration and its implications for poor communities, we must be sanguine about the way community justice is vulnerable to extreme cases. Any set of reforms that have as a core aim to reduce the overall prison population will, of necessity, put more people who have been convicted of crimes in community settings instead of institutional settings. Some of those people will commit crimes; some of those crimes will be violent. Every violent crime will raise questions about the wisdom of the overall strategy.

Of course, no orientation to criminal justice is perfect; all criminal justice strategies make mistakes. Traditional thought about criminal justice tries to avoid errors that result directly in crime. An emphasis is placed on putting young men and women in prison, in part to avoid taking the risk that, if left in the community, they will commit a new crime. In having a low risk threshold for these kinds of crimes, traditional criminal justice accepts as a cost of doing business all the consequences we have described in this book—consequences visited upon the families, children, and neighborhoods of the incarcerated. These consequences are treated as collateral damage, and rarely do the proponents of traditional criminal justice mention them as costs of their policies. But if this book has anything to say on the matter, it is that these consequences clearly are costs, and substantial one at that. A recent paper by Thomas Lengyel (2006) estimated that the total costs of incarcerating the parents of children in New York State (including collateral damage he calls "social costs") outweighs the benefits by a factor of up to 7:1. These costs are rarely included in studies of the cost benefits of incarceration.

Ironically, the prison is never held accountable for the violent crimes that its former clients commit. We have large numbers of people returning to our communities from prison, not as a natural law, but because we decided to send them to prison in the first place. Without a doubt, many who go to prison have exhibited a reprehensible indifference to the well-being of others. When they leave prison, they often do so with the same indifference to the suffering of their victims, but with a new dose of embitterment about their lives because the prison experience did not ameliorate the original sentiments. Indeed, as we have seen, it may even have exacerbated them (Veiraitis, Kovandsic and Marvell 2007). More than two-thirds of today's prisoner releases are rearrested within three years, and the rates of both probation and parole failures are slightly higher today than they were ten years ago. A generation of growing prison populations has left us ever-more vulnerable to extreme cases, yet curiously this has never been seen as a failure of the prison. If a rehabilitation program had two-thirds of its graduates commit new crimes, we would say that it did not work. The same conclusion applies to prisons as a change program.

A shift to another paradigm will entail costs. Some people who are not placed in prisons will perform poorly, they will commit crimes or relapse into drug abuse. These problems need to be reduced as much as possible. But we should not lose sight of the fact that, even though new programs will have their failures, these failures will be no different in kind (and will be no more frequent in level) than the failures already occurring under current policies. Human beings will fail no matter what we take as our philosophy of justice, and no system exists in theory or practice that can avoid this fact. We have to accept that, in a system that handles millions of cases every year, extreme cases will occur no matter *what* our policies are. Our aim cannot be to eliminate these cases, because we cannot do so. The better strategy is to focus on public safety, more generally, by emphasizing strategies that can be adopted without increasing the overall crime rate.

### The Obvious Need: Sentencing Reform

Any solution begins with a recognition of two threshold points: First, programmatic tinkering has not reduced the prison population to date, and it will never have much effect, even under the most optimistic assumptions. Second, to overcome mass incarceration requires that we incarcerate fewer people. There is no getting around it. If the problem is mass imprisonment, then the solution is to change the laws that send people to prison and sometimes keep them there for lengthy terms. Thus, we need to consider the points discussed below.

#### *The Number of Entries and Their Length of Stay Fully Determine the Prison Population*

There are two points of leverage for controlling the size of the prison population. This conclusion follows from the simple fact that two variables fully determine the number of prisoners in any prison system: the number of people who go in, and how long they stay (Frost 2006). It follows that the best way to influence the prison population on a major scale is to change either, or both, of these numbers. The choices are not subtle.

## Mandatory Sentencing

The main reason for the growth in the prison population in the United States during the 1980s was a reduction in the use of probation as a sentence for people convicted of felonies, a move that began in the 1970s. Before the first round of sentencing reform in the 1970s, most received probation sentences. But a wave of sentencing-code revisions had as its core purpose restricting the use of probation for people convicted of felonies, and over time these laws changed the face of penal codes in the United States. Probation sentences are still common, but they are not the majority of sentences as they once were, nor are they seen as generally appropriate sanctions for people who have prior records or whose crimes threatened physical harm to a victim.

The U.S. penal policy was changed nationwide in the late 1980s and early 1990s, with the enactment across the country of mandatory sentences for drug crimes, starting with federal laws and later extending into the states. Before these laws came into effect, people with drug convictions were a small fraction of the U.S. prison population—about 6 percent. Today they are nearly one-third of prison admissions and about one-fourth of the population. People convicted of drug offenses are churned through the prison system. They serve relatively short sentences, come out in large numbers, and fail at high rates, and often quickly return to prison. The amount of drug crime prevented by their incarceration is negligible, because their arrests create drug-distribution job openings that are quickly filled by replacement dealers.

Eliminating mandatory prison terms across the board would have a substantial impact on the prison population. Much of this impact would involve having fewer people serving time for drug-related crime. There is substantial public support for our dealing differently with drug crime. For instance, a large minority favors decriminalization of some drugs. A clear majority of California voters supported Proposition 36, which replaced prison terms with mandatory drug treatment for people convicted of certain drug felonies. The infamous Rockefeller drug laws that set long terms for possession in New York State are under sustained criticism, and some initial reforms were made in the laws in 2004. But it is the early days of the drug-law reform movement, and it's too soon to say where these reform efforts will lead. Yet a sustained willingness to eliminate mandatory prison terms for those with felony drug convictions at the state and federal levels would substantially reduce prison populations with little impact on crime.

There will be less of an impact when it comes to mandatory penalties for other kinds of felonies. Federal judges have complained that mandatory penalties constrain their hand unreasonably in some idiosyncratic cases, but these judges seem the exception rather than the rule. Enabling judges to choose nonprison penalties for other kinds of felonies will have an effect on the size of the prison population, but because many of these felonies are serious enough to warrant some loss of freedom—and often the prison sentence results from the person's prior felony record—the overall impact of eliminating the mandatory penalties for nondrug offenses will likely be small.

### Sentence Length

In the last 30 years, the average time served by people going to prison has almost doubled, and the amount of time they are under parole supervision has also increased. This has meant that the system maintains a growing prison population through length-of-stay decisions and post-release failure rates. Criminologists James Austin and John Irwin (2006) have pointed out:

> Not only are sentences significantly longer than they were in earlier periods in our penal history, they are many times longer than ... in most modern nations. For the same crimes, American prisoners receive sentences twice as long as English, four times [the] Dutch, ... five times [the] Swedish, ... *five to ten times* as long as similarly situated French ones; and almost certainly even longer by comparison to German convicts. (Citing Farrington, Langan, and Tonry 2004; Whitman 2003)

Length of stay in the United States could be rolled back considerably and leave the country with a smaller prison population and a punitive policy more in line with other Western democracies. Because decreased length of stay does *not* lead to increased chance of failure (if anything, the relationship is the opposite), and almost everyone going to prison gets out anyway, we can reduce sentence lengths substantially without increasing crime rates. For example, if the average length of stay, which today is 30 months for new court commitments, were instead 20 months or even 24 months, the prison population would drop as a consequence, with little long-term crime increase.

Some reduction of the prison population could be achieved merely be reducing the length of post-release supervision, thereby decreasing the possibility that former prisoners would return because they failed to follow the rules of supervision. But a more focused effort to eliminate technical revocations is also warranted. One-third of all prison admissions are parolees or probationers who have not been accused of a new crime, but instead have failed to abide by the conditions of their supervision (for example, reporting to parole agents and treatment programs, passing drug tests, maintaining approved living situations; Jacobson 2005). Parole violators serve an average of 18 months for their offenses, an amount of time that used to be the average *entire* sentence in the 1970s. Some officials say that as many as 20 percent of these technical violations have been pursued in lieu of criminal processing (see Petersilia, in press) following an arrest. This is a questionable practice at best, especially since new convictions do not always result in revocation, and there is no evidence that technical revocations prevent crime. Technical revocations of parole could be reduced or eliminated without meaningful public safety implications. (see also Jacobson 2005)

A final target is extremely long sentences. They used to be rare in the United States, but they are becoming more common: at most recent count 132,000 are serving life terms (28 percent without possibility of parole); one-fifth of all prisoners serve sentences with a minimum term of 25 years or longer. People who receive sentences of this magnitude nearly always have committed atrocious acts that shock the conscience (the exception is the more extreme versions of three-strikes legislation, such as occurs in California), and the sentence was imposed at a time of heightened public outrage. Yet with little exception, the outer years of these terms have almost no public-safety value—most people who serve long sentences and reach the ages of late forties or even fifties pose little threat to the public. Placing an upper limit on sentences, and making release more readily available to people in their fifties, would help reduce incarceration with few implications of risk to the public.

These targets—mandatory penalties (especially for drug crime), long sentences, and technical revocations—offer fertile opportunities to reduce the size of the prison populations. Austin and Irwin (2006) have estimated that a concerted effort to reform prison policy by making these changes could reduce the U.S. incarceration rate to 170, or about what it was in the early 1980s (Austin and Irwin 2006: table 12). These estimates may be overly optimistic, but they illustrate the power of focusing, not on programs, but on who goes into prison and how long they stay.

## Toward a New Philosophy of Penal Justice: The Idea of Community Justice

Community justice is an emerging paradigm that proposes a rethinking of the aims of the criminal justice system. It sets as a central criterion that the justice system contribute to the quality of life in communities—to help make the places where people work, live, and raise their families, *good* places to do these things.

Under the community-justice rationale, crime is an obvious element of quality of life, even a major aspect of it. But it is only one element, because crime is only an aspect of a broader interest in public safety. Michael Smith (2001) describes this idea when he points out that crime has to do with the amount of lawbreaking, but that public safety encompasses how people feel about their homes and streets, their neighbors, and even the police. When there is public safety, people feel welcome to partake of community life, and they feel a sense of commitment to one another and to in the place where they live. We can easily imagine places where crime rates are low but people feel little confidence in public activity, citizenship institutions, or government services such as the police—places like those collections of white people's houses hidden behind walls in Johannesburg, South Africa, for example, as Michael Smith has pointed out. These places may be safe, but they provide little in the way of what we broadly conceive of as public safety.

Community justice shares many themes with traditional conceptions of justice, and yet in embraces other considerations as well. Traditional conceptions hold that justice has occurred for individuals when the innocent are acquitted and the guilty are convicted. Justice requires that laws be applied under the principles of equal protection, and justice is made possible when its operations are sufficiently funded to carry out its mandates. Community justice embraces these values, but also holds that the rationale for them lies in the way they contribute to the quality of life in a community. Who would want to live in a place indifferent to innocence and guilt, or that was discriminatory in the application of the law? These are ends that have value within a community justice framework, but their value comes from how *central* they are to good community life. Over and above procedural and substantive justice, community justice gives high value to social and economic equality, racial and ethnic tolerance, and the strength of structures of opportunity.

There is no single, comprehensive statement of community justice, and space here is not sufficient to fully explore the idea. Various writers have developed ideas that lie easily within the community justice framework, without ever using the term. A few years ago, David Karp and I developed the following definition of community justice:

> Community justice broadly refers to all variants of crime prevention and justice activities that explicitly include the community in their processes and set the enhancement of community quality of life as an explicit goal. Community justice is rooted in the actions that citizens, community organizations, and the criminal justice system can take to control crime and social disorder. Its central focus is community-level outcomes, shifting the emphasis from individual incidents to systemic patterns, from individual conscience to social mores, and from individual goods to the common good. Typically, community justice is conceived as a partnership between the formal criminal justice system and the community, but often communities autonomously engage in activities that directly or indirectly address crime. (Clear and Karp 2000:6)

## Community Justice Philosophies

One of the best philosophical explorations of community-justice principles is R. A. Duff's *Punishment, Communication and Community* (2001). I summarize his argument in some detail, not because it is the only plausible version of community justice, but because it is a particularly eloquent statement illustrating community justice values.

Duff describes, in detail, the principles of punishment that would apply within a "liberal political community"—that is, a community of people who seek maximum liberty and autonomy within a sense of mutual citizenship. The basic principle underlying his ideas is Kantian in its roots: "I *should* care about the extent to which *all* citizens achieve the goods of autonomy, freedom, and privacy, and value my own autonomy, freedom, and privacy only insofar as others, too, can achieve those goods" (Duff 2001:55; emphasis in the original). Crimes stand opposed to the pursuit of these goods. From this view, crimes are

> [n]ot wrongs against "the public," but wrongs in which "the public," the community as a whole, is properly interested. . . . [These are] matters on which the community as a whole can and should take a stand, through the authoritative voice of the law, . . [and which] merit a public, communal response. Those who commit them should be called to account and censured by the community. (55)

Punishment is thus primarily a communicative function, in which the state imposes upon the individual a burden "through which the moral implications of her crime can be communicated to her, and she can communicate her apologetic repentance to the community" (155). Duff recognizes that *what* gets communicated and *how* it is communicated matters crucially. Punishment, he says, is "a species of secular penance. It is a burden imposed on an offender for his crime, through which, it is hoped, he will come to repent his crime, to begin to reform himself, and thus reconcile himself with those he has wronged" (106). For this ideal to become real in practice, Duff proposes a set of obligations shared among the state, the victim, and the criminal. Under the heading *Who Owes What to Whom*, he says:

> [C]riminal punishment is not just a source of *goods* such as repentance, reform, and reconciliation, but . . . it is something that is *owed*—something the liberal state has a *duty* to do. . . . We can begin with the obvious point that the state owes it to its citizens to protect them from crime. . . . But the state owes something too to its citizens as potential *criminals* . . . what it owes them is to treat and address them as members of the normative political community. . . . What the offender owes the

victim is an apology that recognizes the nature and seriousness of the wrong done. This is owed to the direct victim of the crime, if there is one, but also to the wider community... for the wrongs done to the individual victim is also a wrong against the community.... The community certainly owes it to the victims to recognize the wrongs they have suffered... [and] various kinds of "victim support," not just aimed at remedying whatever material harm was caused by the crime,... but offering moral support and reassurance to those who have been wronged.... [The victim] owes it to her fellow citizens to assist in the offender's detection and prosecution... [and] also owes it both to them and to the offender to be ready to be reconciled with the offender through his punishment: to treat him, as a fellow citizen who has paid his penitential debt. (112–114, emphasis in the original)

I give detailed attention to Duff because he writes so persuasively and with such clarity and perception. He is answering critics from two opposing sides—the punitive tradition of just deserts, and the consequentialist positions of incapacitation and deterrence. He carves out, not a middle ground between them, but instead suggests a different approach entirely, one that has as the aim the production of liberal political community. Such communities are properly understood as normative collections of autonomous and free citizens whose destinies are particularly connected in the case of criminal wrongdoing, because crime undermines the capacity for members of a liberal community to pursue and enjoy their goods. Under the version of justice proposed by Duff, victims and the people who victimize them are treated equally as responsible members of the liberal political community, and the state is seen as both obligated to them and acting upon them in the pursuit of community. This is a community justice account, and a notable one.

There are other quite useful accounts that deserve mention. For example, Pettit and Braithwaite (1993) have developed a "republican" theory of justice that differs in several respects from Duff's described above. They propose a criterion for justice that is housed not solely in rights and liberties, but rather in the capacity of people to act autonomously in their own self-interest. This leads them to a similar proposal for the way the justice system should operate. As a matter of simple justice, their "republican" theory requires that *before* people can justly be punished, they must have had the reasonable capacity to attain their preferred ends within the law. What the state owes to those whom it would punish is a reasonable chance at a good life as that person might describe it (within the limits of law). There are two implications we might draw from this argument. First, when choosing among punishments, there is a preference for penalties that tend to expand legitimate capacity rather than destroy it. Second, punishments are automatically suspect when they have, as an unintended consequence, the expansion of inequality. These two limitations would, taken together, promote the sanctions that build community, for people who are being punished are considered part of the community.

Ideas from which community justice concepts can be derived have, thus, different potential orienting frameworks. Said another way, there is no single version of community justice. What the versions have in common, however, is the goal of promoting community life as a central value. Most putative community justice models are expansive, in that they include both the victims and those who broke the law in the equation. Others, such as Weed & Seed programs, use community justice rhetoric, but have one or another problematic aspect (such as a policy of exclusion) that raises questions about how fully they express values of community justice. Some versions of community justice make community variables explicit targets, such as community service sentencing programs. For others, such as many restorative justice programs, the community justice orientation is implicit rather than explicit.

Because community justice is an idea with a variety of expressions, it is, necessarily, a broad concept that cannot be covered under a single umbrella statement. There are three core elements of all versions of community justice, however. First, there is an emphasis on restoration. Victims' losses are restored, those who are convicted of crime likewise may expect to be able to be restored if they take appropriate action, and the community peace that was fractured by the crime is, for want of a better term, restored. Second, there is an emphasis on maintaining those who are convicted of crimes within their communities. This enables both them and their loved ones to keep their community ties, and it eases post-penalty restoration to community life. Third, purely punitive sanctions, such as solitary confinement, are deemphasized in favor of ameliorative sanctions such as community service. For these reasons, community justice, in whatever form it takes, is an idea that proposes minimal use of imprisonment. It is a philosophy that provides a philosophical pathway out of the current morass.

How would it work? What would our community justice strategies entail?

## Community Justice Strategies

Community justice initiatives could thrive under a regime of reduced imprisonment. They could also contribute to reductions in imprisonment. They will have three elements: (1) a focus on high-incarceration places; (2) attention to norms and values in those places; and (3) attempts to improve schools, jobs, and housing as targets.

### High-Incarceration Places

Concentrated incarceration is not a problem in most places where people live or work. While every community contributes at least some people to the prison system, urban areas have but a handful of high-incarceration neighborhoods. Research reported in chapter 7 identifies never more than a half-dozen each in Baltimore, Chicago, Cleveland, Columbus, Philadelphia, Portland, and Tallahassee. Every urban area has such places, but not many of them. These are the places where incarceration has become part of the fabric of the place, a community-level dynamic as significant as poor housing or inadequate schools.

The small number of places at stake is an advantage for community justice, because it means we do not need community justice initiatives everywhere. We can make do with a few targeted and strategic initiatives targeting a handful of places. This was a lesson learned in the days of Weed & Seed. The places where incarceration is concentrated are well known, and while it is always a good idea to verify our beliefs about crime and justice geography by mapping it, any police chief, probation administrator, or mayor can specify where a community justice strategy needs to be started. These will be places where there are plenty of problems to worry about: widespread unemployment, a predominance of single-parent families, active drug markets, youth gangs, a high rate of school dropout, homelessness, and substandard housing. Prison is a fellow traveler with these social problems (Cadora, Swartz, and Gordon 2002).

The irony is that these places—the homes of a permanent underclass that William Julius Wilson (1987) has called "the truly disadvantaged"—often are the target of social programs. Welfare workers are there, drug- and alcohol-abuse programs proliferate, and private-sector philanthropic initiatives may even be common. These are not places where few investments are made. The big investment, of course, is in criminal justice: the police and courts, and especially corrections. Eric Cadora and his colleagues have mapped the comorbidity of welfare participation with prison and jail expenditures in Brooklyn. Their analysis shows the close spatial association between TANF (temporary aid to needy families) and incarceration. Remarkably, they have identified more than a dozen blocks in which *one year's* expenditures on prison exceeded $1 million. These are special places in two important respects: they contribute a large number of people to New York's prison system, and they are the target of substantial public investment in the form of welfare, police, and prisons. The current strategy of investment does not change these places or their problems very much. They are ripe for community justice.

*Norms and Values*

Community justice can be described as a series of programs, but that description fails to capture the central ethic. Community justice tries to restore these places' informal social-control mechanisms so that they may perform functions that have been taken over by formal social control agencies in the face of their breakdown. This entails strengthening the social-control capacity of families and neighborhood groups, as well as improving the effectiveness of schools and increasing the vibrancy of the private sector's presence. One aspect of this work is to strengthen the impact of norms and values that already exist but are not being effectively marshaled for public safety.

My colleague David Kennedy has been thinking, writing, and designing projects that address the issues of norms and values in problem communities. His initial efforts in this area gave rise to Boston's well-known Ceasefire project, and his writing emphasizes the idea of "pulling levers" (1997). His initial thinking sought to align the strategic capacities of law enforcement, corrections, and private (family members) and parochial (religious institutions) sources of social control into a single message: hurt someone with a gun and you will go to prison for a long time. The "pulling levers" aspect of Ceasefire was to get everybody "on message"—to align the voices of informal social controls in delivering and supporting the message, and to coordinate the actions of formal social-control agents to deliver on the promise, publicly and irrefutably using every available lever to attack gun violence.

This strategy was credited with a dramatic reduction in gun-related violence and homicide in Boston. Replications of the Ceasefire project in numerous places throughout the country have led Kennedy to elaborate on the "pulling levers" strategy for a more formal theory of deterrence in problem-stricken urban environments (Kennedy 2006). This version of deterrence takes account of the real-world lives of young men who live in impoverished places and who encounter economic and racial discrimination as a regular aspect of their lives. For these young men, mere threats are not effective. What is needed, Kennedy argues, is a normative foundation with which young men can identify ("your criminal activity hurts your community") and a mechanism for communicating it (family members and community leaders). In this reformulation, sanctions matter, but the normative message and the relational messengers are central engines of deterrence. As this work evolves (2007), Kennedy places even more importance on the normative component. The point is not to impose sanctions per se, but to activate the power of community norms as expressed through the concerted actions of members of the community (in contrast to representatives of the state) and to provide concrete ways that the public commitment to those norms can be affirmed.

There are several points to make here. First, there is recognition of the futility of penalties, no matter how harsh, that are disconnected from normative content as understood by the target of those penalties. In places where racism and economic disadvantage are central aspects of life, penal interventions can easily be understood as just another aspect of ever-present "bad luck," or worse, another manifestation of oppression. Connected in this way to what the subject sees as illegitimate, the customary sanctions do not shape conduct. But when the sanctions are connected to values that the subject holds dear (community, family, and racial solidarity), and the message is communicated through channels that matter (loved ones and peers), they *can* shape conduct. People whose opinions carry weight say to the young man something like this:

"Police harassment is what we all have to suffer *because* you are not doing your part. If you would help stop the violence, the police would leave us all alone." The *police* do not create safety, the community does.

Kennedy's work is not the final word on this topic, of course, but it is instructive. Safety comes about not as a consequence merely of enforcing the law, but by creating a grounded sense of the community's norms and its willingness to enforce them. Community justice seeks to strengthen the power of norms to shape behavior, and it treats potential law violators as *members* of a community whose conduct should be shaped by those norms; and who, when they understand the impact of their conduct on their community, will change. (See also Rojek, Coverdill and Fors 2003.)

### Targets: Schools, Jobs, and Housing

A third aspect of community justice is the desire to strengthen the social support provided by informal social controls. The thesis is that, in strong communities, these institutions of informal social control are a main source of public safety, but in high-incarceration communities, they do not perform that function effectively.

Inner-city schools in impoverished neighborhoods are notoriously poor at educating, socializing, and preparing young people for adult roles. One in five adult African Americans lacks a high school degree—twice the rate of white youths—and in impoverished neighborhoods, the picture is worse. As was shown in chapter 5, lack of a high school diploma is one of the factors that most distinguishes the prison population from nonprisoners. Poor inner-city schools are so problem-stricken that they have trouble retaining their youth. The result is high rates of truancy and school dropout—factors that serve as "a pipeline to prison" (Losen and Wald 2003).

The failure of schools in poor, mostly minority inner-city neighborhoods is a precursor to a lifetime of troubles in the labor market for most residents. Unemployment among men in poor neighborhoods is a double negative for the places they live: first, these men fail to bring the economic and network resources to their intimates—assets that most other young men provide through bridging to work; second, they are a drain on the already thin financial and personal resources of those around them, as these men seek support for their own lives.

Public housing is a staple of these high-incarceration neighborhoods. Public housing need not be problem housing, but it often is. All of the so-called million-dollar blocks in Brooklyn—places where over a million dollars was being spent annually in incarcerating residents of that block—are public housing blocks (Cadora, Swartz, and Gordon 2002). When there are problems in public housing, they often take the form of gangs, drug markets, and violence. These problems persist, even though people with criminal records are prohibited from living in some types of public housing, and getting arrested can subject a public-housing resident to immediate eviction.

These are the problems. And there is plenty of evidence of the benefits of overcoming these problems. Children who finish school, even in poor neighborhoods, compared to those who do not finish, are less likely to become involved in *both* juvenile and adult crime (Hawkins et al. 2000). Despite having juvenile records or criminal records as youth, young men in their late twenties and older who are provided with job opportunities, even if marginal, become involved in crime less frequently in adulthood (Uggen 2000). People who leave inadequate public housing in impoverished urban areas to live in places with higher quality housing and better schools achieve more positive school and economic outcomes (Polikoff 2004). Men who survive crime-free for seven years past their most recent criminal conviction no longer look more likely to commit a crime than do other adult males their age (Kurlychek, Brame, and Bushway 2006).

Community justice initiatives typically take these problems head-on. An example is provided by the Safer Foundation's Safer Return project (Williams et al. 2006). Tellingly, they refer to the project as a "community empowerment reentry initiative." It earns its name by offering to "comprehensively address the transitional needs of both the returning prisoners and their communities...[with the] premise...that an entire community must be addressed" (3). The project engages multiple stakeholders in the community: faith-based organizations, the business community, community-based services, and criminal justice agencies. To do its work, the Safer Foundation creates an intermediary along the lines of the Local Initiatives Support Corporations (LISC) to broker relationships among various partners in the project and to serve as contact point to the community. The intermediary creates a Community Advisory Council that advises in the development of job placements, family supports, housing, substance-abuse treatment, and community service assignments. The Safer Foundation sees high levels of offender reentry in a community as both a symptom of larger community disadvantage and an opportunity for community development in several areas of need. This approach takes advantage of what has been learned about comprehensive approaches in workforce preparation for disadvantaged young men (Holzer, Edelman, and Offner 2006; Kotloff 2005). These lessons are extended to problems of education, housing, and reconnecting men to their families.

### Funding Community Justice: A Justice Reinvestment

Criminal justice reformers have argued that no new monies are necessary for community justice to be accomplished. What is needed instead is to "reinvest" existing commitments on crime and justice so that they pursue community justice ends. This philosophy is called *justice reinvestment,* and it is a basic proposition: sufficient money is being spent on crime, but it is being spent in unproductive ways. Tucker and Cadora (2003) describe the problem in this way:

> We advocate taking a geographic approach to public safety that targets money for programs in education, health, job creation, and job training in low income communities. This includes making parole officers responsible for particular neighborhoods rather than dispersing their caseloads across a wide span. It means that reentry from prison becomes a shared responsibility involving the community, government institutions, and the individual and his or her family.... Under this proposal, local government could reclaim responsibility for dealing with residents who break the law and redeploy the funds that the state would have spent for their incarceration. The localities would have the freedom to spend justice dollars to decrease the risks of crime in the community. They could choose to spend these dollars for job training, drug treatment programs, and preschool programs, as well as incarceration for the dangerous few, in which case the state would levy a charge back for imprisonment costs. The key is making the locality accountable for solving its

public safety problems and allowing local governments to reclaim resources. The redirected penal funds could be blended with other government funding streams to focus on local community restoration projects and could be leveraged to attract other public or private investment in housing, employment, or education. ... Other investments might include a locally run community loan pool to make micro-loans to create jobs or family development loans for education, debt consolidation, or home ownership and rehabilitation, transportation micro-enterprises for residents commuting outside the neighborhood, a one-stop shop for job counseling and placement services, or geographically targeted hiring incentives for employers. (Tucker and Cadora 2003:3–4)

In this way, the funds needed for the agenda of community justice, strengthening the informal social-control capacities of poor communities, already exist. They are tied up in the inefficiencies of prison and therefore are unavailable for other priorities. But by shifting these funds to community justice initiatives, two goals are accomplished. First, the community-development programs receive the resources they need to strengthen poor communities. Second, and just as important, money spent in the community prevents the collateral damage that otherwise comes from locking up so many residents. Community justice can be a solution that does not require new funds.

## What Can Law Enforcement Do?

It is tempting to say that law enforcement cannot do much about the problem of concentrated imprisonment—it *is* the problem. There is some truth to this idea. When the criminal justice system gets involved in the problem of incarceration, the problem seems to get worse. But it is too easy merely to say that the nation's law enforcers should simply "get out of the way." More can be done than that. The components of the traditional criminal justice system that enforce the law can also take important steps toward community justice (see Clear and Cadora 2001). Let's consider each of these components.

*Policing*

Much has been made of two versions of community justice that are part of policing: "broken-windows" policing and community policing. These have very different implications for the practice of community justice.

"Broken windows" theory, originally developed by James Q. Wilson and George Kelling (1982), is an argument that public disorder, when unchecked by public authorities, promotes crime. The broken-windows image was salient because it helped people visualize city streets made ugly by broken windows and thugs emboldened to break more of them. The mere statement of the theory gives an impression that it would be friendly to notions of community justice, suggesting as it does the repair of urban decay as a way to fight crime. Indeed, when William Bratton was head of the New York City transit system, that is what he did: he fought graffiti on the subway trains by immediately cleaning the trains as soon as they were spray-painted. Trains were more pleasant, and graffiti artists were no longer emboldened by seeing graffiti on the subway cars. Perhaps the disorder of broken windows and other kinds of urban decay that lead to crime could be similarly eradicated by policies of reclamation.

Not so. In their book about policing the problem of disorder, fetchingly entitled *Fixing Broken Windows*, George Kelling and Catherine B. Coles (1998) describe the need to arrest and prosecute homeless people, vagrants, and the drunk and disorderly. They do not mention repairing a single broken window. Such a prescription was bound to stir loud support and equally loud antagonism. While numerous essays have been written about the concept, there have been few empirical studies. Some of those studies have found support for the idea of policing misdemeanor crime (see, for example, Worral 2006), but others tend to find, with Harcourt and Ludwig (2006) "that there appears to be no good evidence that broken windows policing reduces crime" (316).

Community policing, especially the "problem-oriented" variety, gets a better grade in reducing crime. Studies consistently find that a policing strategy that is problem-focused and carefully executed reduces the problem (see, for example, Braga et al 1999). Problem-oriented policing can also be friendly to community interests, as police enlist members of the community to help in identifying high-priority problems. The key seems to be the degree to which citizens perceive the police as legitimate in their use of authority. When citizens see the police as fair in the way they enforce the law, they are more inclined to cooperate (Tyler and Fagan 2006), even in high-crime communities (Pattavina, Byrne, and Garcia 2006).

What kind of policing strategies do people who live in high-incarceration communities want? We know that many people in these communities do not trust the police, and they see the police presence as an invasion. We know, as well, that the public desire for police activity in these locations is complex. Citizens want the police to intervene with problem people and in problem situations. But they do not want wholesale arrests. Drug crime is a great example. People want drug markets cleaned up, especially open-air markets. But they distrust street sweeps and aggressive strategies. And in the end, if policies are little more than arrest-focused, they are orthogonal to the problems that arise from concentrated incarceration.

Under an ethic of community justice, police would make arrests, of course, but that is not all the police would do. Traditional community-oriented policing links the police to local leadership through community advisory groups that help develop the priorities for police work in that location. This cooperative effort also means that the *methods* of police work are discussed with the community. The community policing agenda has long held that police have a role in community-development activities, providing support for citizens' needs, working with troubled youth, and taking seriously the priorities citizens feel apply to their neighborhoods. They do this for several reasons. Listening to local people opens the door for their cooperation and support for policing efforts. Providing support for people dealing with problems, especially young people, gives the police a human face that improves their credibility with people who might otherwise distrust them. Setting police priorities in cooperation with citizen leadership makes sure that the problems addressed by policing will match the concerns those people feel (see Bayley 1997).

*Adjudication*

The specialized court movement, with its drug courts and mental health courts, includes community courts that are designed to meet the needs of the particular neighborhoods in which they operate (Berman and Feinblatt 2005). The first community court was designed to deal with the disorder in midtown Manhattan, with its unique set of problems in an area that houses two of New York City's major tourist attractions, the theater industry and the bright lights of Times Square. The second high-profile community court opened in Red Hook, a section of Brooklyn with long-term problems of poverty and crime-ridden housing projects along-side gentrification by an emergent artistic community.

The Red Hook model combines some of the elements of traditional community-oriented policing with the broken-windows model, in part because it was developed in New York City at a time when support for broken-windows policing was at its apex. There is a citizen advisory group and regular community meetings for open discussions of the problems the court is trying to address. Judges in the community court deal with minor crimes: drug possession, public order offenses, and so forth. They do so with an array of social services that offer counseling, job training and placement, case management, and other assistance. Judges take a personal interest in cases, making it a priority to let defendants know they genuinely care about the person's progress in dealing with problems—usually drug abuse and unemployment. As the case-based approach solidifies, the community court has entertained broader involvement, such as in landlord-tenant issues, school problems, and the like.

Studies of special-problem courts hold that they have had positive results (Berman and Feinblatt 2005), but there have been no broad-based studies of community courts. In Red Hook, there is good anecdotal evidence that the court enjoys wide support from the community and the justice system alike. There is also a sense that the court is still in its early days, and it is working to broaden its interests as it gains further confidence in the community-based approach.

Community courts are opening up in other New York City neighbor-hoods and around the country. Like their predecessors, these courts are designed to focus on misdemeanor crimes, public disorder, and incivility as community problems. They process the cases of local residents who are accused of these (mostly petty) crimes, put them into treatment pro-grams, and provide them with counseling and other services and training. The courts will lock these persons up when they do not take advantage of what is being offered, however.

There is considerable pride in the way these courts respond to community problems. Yet it is instructive to consider the community problems these courts will *not* confront. For instance, they will not prosecute absentee landlords whose apartments violate housing codes and represent health and safety risks for the residents. There will be no "perp walks" for schoolboard members whose policies perpetuate inadequate education in substandard classrooms with outdated books and unstocked laboratories. Absentee owners of vacant and run-down properties will not be held in contempt of court for maintaining a public nuisance, even though their properties are community eyesores and may even contribute to crime. Individuals who live in the community are held accountable for their behavior, but external forces whose neglect or exploitation victimize the community will be left alone.

So when asking what adjudication processes may offer to the community justice agenda, theorists can provide a nice, but short, list of successes for the community-court movement. There is a longer list of what has yet to be tried.

### Appraising the Community Movement in Criminal Justice

The community policing movement was a bellwether for what has become a community-oriented ethic in criminal justice. There are signs that this new ethic may be softening some of the harder edges of contemporary criminal justice. When district attorneys set up community-based prosecution offices, they learn that citizens want enforcement of laws that relate directly to their quality of life, such as landlord regulations and financial codes (Coles, Carney, and Johnson 2000). When community-based public defender services were established, they learned some of those same lessons, but they also learned that defendants want not just to "beat the charges" but also to get the help they need to change their lives—to overcome addiction, get better jobs, resolve marital and family conflicts, and so on.

It is as though the community movement in criminal justice has given simultaneous voice to two stories that do not go together well, but coexist nonetheless. One story is the dominant crime-fighting idea that we are so used to hearing and thinking about. In this story, communities are ravaged by hardened and remorseless criminals. The criminal justice system, a lumbering bureaucracy, cannot seem to focus on these problems. Predators who victimize their neighbors may get arrested, but revolving-door justice means that they will be back on the streets within hours. Until the justice system is brought face to face with outraged citizens tired of being victims, nothing will get done. But once the system is forced to *listen* to the public, the point gets through and sincere justice officials will reorient and refocus their work to address the criminal element making community life so difficult. In this story, the community orientation helps a reinvigorated justice system stand tall on behalf of a beleaguered citizenry.

In the second story, the criminal justice system suffers not so much from the ossification of bureaucracy but from an obsession with "serious" crime. Of course, everyone wants murderers and rapists to be caught, prosecuted, and punished. But even in the highest crime areas, these events are uncommon. What really makes daily life hard for the poorer neighborhoods are not the crimes that movies are made of, but the incivilities of life: open-air drug and prostitution markets, loitering gangs, and other kinds of disorder. When the justice system begins to ask what citizens want, these are the problems they bring up. In this story, like everyone else, poor people want to be able to walk down the streets without being hassled and without feeling unsafe; they want their children to be able to walk to school without being approached by drug dealers and harassed by bullies. As the justice system listens to citizens tell this story, it begins to reorient its efforts to police the people whose behavior makes poor neighborhoods so uncivil. It arrests drug dealers, beggars, vagrants, gang bullies, and other idlers.

Like all caricatures, these two stories have some basis in reality. Any politician, any justice-system official who has attended a community meeting in a poor neighborhood will say that both versions can be heard. Given a podium, the citizens of poor places will complain about the failure to take crime seriously at the same time as they fret about the disorder that dominates their streets. If a person wants to hear a request for tougher laws, there will be plenty said to that effect; if a person wants to hear about cleaning up the streets, that, too, will be mentioned. What makes these stories realistic is that they have some basis in reality.

Yet these two versions of the world simplify reality. When the topic is the police or the courts, citizens talk about crime and disorder. But when they are asked what they need without regard to the specific agenda of criminal justice, a different set of priorities arises. People who live in poor places want good, local job markets that can provide a strong economic infrastructure for their lives. They want schools for their children that teach them and prepare them for adult lives. They want places to live that are comfortable. Yes, they would also say that they want safe streets. They want what everyone wants: aspirations for the foundation of a good quality of life.

So here is the question: Is there nothing the criminal justice system can do about these larger aspirations? Some would say that to ask the justice system to consider these aspirations is to ask too much; that the justice system is equipped only to provide safe streets, and that everything else has to be left to others, including citizens as private citizens. Perhaps this is so. But the difficulty is that in pursuing the aim of safe streets, the criminal justice system has contributed to the very problems it has promised to solve by exacerbating some of the forces that erode quality-of-life. The justice system can instead do better. It can evolve into a mechanism for community justice. It can have as its agenda the well-being of communities—the infrastructure for a reasonable life free from crime, but also free from dominance by a penal system.


## Concluding Comment

At the beginning of chapter 1, I described our current penal policy as a perfect storm, a kind of self-generating disaster for which there is no obvious remedy. The metaphor works because a confluence of policies has created the problems we face with our prisons, and no plausible solution has yet become apparent. I have suggested three ideas in this chapter. First, the common debates in penal reform about rehabilitation, diversion, and reentry offer little hope to meaningfully address the situation. Second, sentencing reforms that eliminate mandatory sentences, reduce sentence length, and restrict technical revocation could have substantial impact on the problem. Third, we could go a long way toward overcoming the impediments to change if we would embrace a new vision of community justice. I then described what a community justice agenda entails.

We now reach the end of the book. A big, optimistic ending would be nice, but what would it be based on? There is plenty of reason to be pessimistic. During the year I spent writing this book, the prison population grew by 2.6 percent; the Supreme Court has held that in pursuit of drug crime, police can make searches of private dwellings without knocking first (*Hudson* v. *Michigan* 2005); and new, more punitive laws have been passed with little meaningful debate about their potential for collateral damage. A pessimist would conclude that this storm is far from waning.

What would the optimist say? He or she would begin with the observation that we now know and cannot deny that the enormous growth in the U.S. penal system has carried with it a burgeoning list of problems. Almost nobody of any importance on the scene today—political leader, scholar, or community advocate—believes that the racial and economic inequality spurred on by a rousing incarceration rate is something we should be proud of. Almost all thinking persons would prefer to have a different reality, if we could. In addition, some states facing severe budget shortfalls are cutting back on their corrections apparatus, as a matter of practical fiscal imperative (Wool and Stemen 2004).

A realist would say that the punitive apparatus of criminal justice, with its guarantee of continuing collateral damage, continues unabated. The glimmers of hope we have for a different reality are just that—mere glimmers. Yet at the same time, we cannot afford to simply ride out this storm, even if we could manage to do so. Instead, we have to steer our way through the policy whirlwind to a new approach that will promise justice for our communities. We simply must, if we are to have the social justice that is the pride of our nation.

The change in direction will take single-mindedness and nerve. But a true realist would also say that we have no other choice.

# Appendix

## Imagining a Strategy of

## Community Justice

There are no obvious, proven strategies for community justice. What we need now, more than anything, are creative, nontraditional ways of promoting community justice. This addendum describes a few ideas about the form such innovations might take. These ideas are offered with two aims in mind: first, to illustrate the potential power of community justice; and second, to stimulate the reader's imagination of what might be possible. Here, then, is an idea to get the juices flowing.

### Imagining Community Justice on the Ground

David Karp and I have described a hypothetical community-justice initiative in an extremely poor community. I repeat it here at length because it goes a long way toward describing what a community-justice orientation might look like.

#### Community Justice in Tocqueville Heights

Tocqueville Heights is an old, inner-city neighborhood in the city of Megalopolis. Comprising roughly 100 square blocks, Tocqueville Heights has three multistory public housing complexes and a small business section, and it is served by a public school complex named Tocqueville Heights School. One-half of the residents have incomes under or just over the poverty line, and the area has high rates on all indicators of disorganization: single-parent families, many high school dropouts, high unemployment, vacant dwellings, and people on public assistance. The area also is among the highest in arrest rates for drug and street crimes.

The Tocqueville Heights Community Justice Center (CJC) is located in a renovated building across the street from the police precinct. What used to be a mom-and-pop deli now serves as an office for Miriam Bledsoe, Director of the Center, her staff of two, and a regular assortment of volunteers and interns. Bledsoe is a lawyer and community activist. Her staff includes Jethro McDowell, an MSW former probation officer, and Luke Wallace, a para-professional. The office has a $250,000 annual budget and is a nonprofit organization funded by fees.

The CJC runs a number of projects, but the most popular are:

- *Crimestop.* Working with the local police, the CJC convenes meetings of local residents to discuss crime problems in their areas. They then lead a "crime prevention" analysis of these problems, and develop mechanisms for reducing the incidence of targeted crimes.
- *Victims' Awareness.* Local residents who are victims of crime are brought together to talk about how victimization has affected their lives. The nature and extent of crime in Tocqueville Heights is discussed, as well as the programs in existence that try to reduce crime. Opportunities are given for mediation between those harmed by and those convicted of committing crime. Methods for preventing repeat victimization are described, and individuals are assisted in taking steps to secure their living areas from crime. The VA sessions help CJC funnel victims into appropriate services through referral to a range of services the CJC may purchase for clients or send them to.
- *Too Legit to Quit (TLQ).* This is a recreational club that meets two nights a week and on Sunday afternoons in the local school. It is open to teenage male children whose fathers or mothers are incarcerated; each child is paired with two adults and another child. Adults with criminal records under a community-justice sentence attend with one of their children, and they are teamed

with another adult who is a mentor for the child whose parent is in prison. The TLQ team attends workshops on parent-child relationships and engages in organized, supervised recreation with other teams. The structure is designed to strengthen ties between parents and their children and to establish supports between people with criminal convictions and other local adults.

- *Tocqueville Heights Habitat.* Squads of people under community justice sentences rehabilitate local buildings, which become available to the homeless or for small businesses at advantageous rates. Habitat workgroups employ local residents who are paid wages at near prevailing rates, as well as people with criminal records, who receive minimum wages. Private contractors for renovation projects must agree to employ local residents and be willing to supervise people with criminal records, who are required to abide by the same regulations as full-pay employees, as part of the crew.

- *Seniorcare.* People with criminal records are paired with elderly residents who are otherwise without services. Formally, each person pays weekly social visits on elder-care partners and keeps them company; but informally deeper relationships are encouraged, including accompanying the senior citizen to health appointments and community social clubs. In some cases, the TLQ teams spend regular time in visits with senior citizens.

- *After-School.* Local adults supervise a series of after-school activities for youngsters, ranging from recreation to creative arts. The activities are age-relevant, and those volunteers with criminal records are always paired with other residents in a supervisory capacity.

- *Resolve.* Citizens in this neighborhood who have a dispute are typically unable to afford legal assistance and certainly avoid the municipal civil justice system. Resolve is a dispute resolution program that provides mediation to local residents who have a conflict they cannot resolve on their own.

- *Circles.* CJC convenes sentencing circles with formerly incarcerated people and members of the community, especially the crime victims. The Circles have three objectives: to reaffirm local behavioral standards; to reintegrate people returning from prison; and to negotiate sentencing agreements that establish terms of community supervision and reparation for the harm caused by the offense.

These projects are all made possible through partnerships with existing organizations and citizen volunteers. The local probation department has assigned a unit of its staff to a special team caseload involving the approximately 1,000 probationers living in Tocqueville Heights. The state's Parole Department assigns two Parole Officers to the area as well, and they are housed in an office adjacent to the CJC. They both work in close partnership with the CJC, paying attention to clients they have in common. By "partnership" we mean not only cooperation and information sharing but also mutual goals involving community safety and client adjustment. The CJC shares the official agency goals and interests, and stays aware enough of client behavior to serve as another check on client adjustment. Indications of alcohol or drug abuse are immediately reported to the appropriate justice agencies, and there is a continual attentiveness for signals of new problems in an individual's circumstances, and these are immediately made known to authorities. The two correctional agencies have come to rely on the expertise and sympathetic involvement of the CJC in their clients' lives.

To support the work of the CJC, the court system has specialized its assignments. An Assistant District Attorney handles all but the capital cases against residents (the city DA office has a homicide division), and most criminal cases are heard by a judge whose jurisdiction is Tocqueville Heights. This geographic specialization is seen as an essential foundation for the cooperative working environment sought by the CJC, but cooperation is actively pursued by Bledsoe's regular formal and informal contact with stakeholders in the community and the justice system.

The CJC uses a network of volunteers, as well. Every participant in a CJC program must have a community sponsor, and finding and maintaining these sponsors require a substantial effort. The most common sponsorships come from three of the local churches and the local mosque, but the CJC has also received assistance from a few local businesses that have hired participants and/or sponsored them. The most important volunteers are the Program Associates, the citizens who participate in each of the three programs—teaching building-renovation skills, joining in the TLQ teams as foster mentors, or contacting and supporting seniors who participate in Seniorcare. CJC also maintains a community board made up of volunteers who provide oversight of CJC activities.

## How the Program Works

### Mission

On the wall facing the front door, a four-foot sign declares the mission of the CJC of Tocqueville Heights. It says:

> The Tocqueville Heights Community Justice Center seeks to strengthen the capacity of residents of our community to manage their own affairs, solve their own problems, and live effectively, safely together. This is best achieved by giving everyone a stake in the quality of community life. Our specific focus is on people who have violated the law. We seek to reestablish their community ties and reawaken their connection to community life. We recognize that our clients are among the most important to our community harmony, because they have disturbed it in the past. Therefore, we are dedicated to improving the quality of community life by addressing the harm directly. We believe in a basic truth: every member of our community—including people convicted of crime—has a stake in maintaining a safe neighborhood.
> Our commitment to the community is:
>
> • To ensure that people with criminal records coming into this community are offered an opportunity to compensate the community for the costs of their crimes.
> • To ensure that people with criminal records coming into this community receive interventions or controls that will guard against reoccurrence of their crimes.
>
> Our commitment to victims of crime is:
>
> • To ensure some compensation and reparation for the losses caused by crime, and to involve people convicted of crime in making that compensation.
> • To promise that no one with a criminal conviction will return to this community through the CJC without a complete evaluation of their risk and the establishment of programs to manage it.

- To include victims in every step of the community justice process.

Our commitment to people with criminal convictions is:

- To provide the best set of opportunities for making reparations to the community.
- To help create and strengthen ties to community life.

## Approach

The CJC thinks of itself as having three distinct client groups: community, victim, and person convicted of crime. It operates with a community advisory board, but it maintains numerous ties to influential members of the community. The Director, Bledsoe, is a dependable presence at local meetings, where she often speaks in support of a safer community and higher quality community life. As a steady voice for community justice, she sees herself not only as an advocate but also as an educator and conciliator. The facts, she believes, are on her side: while nearly every Tocqueville Heights resident convicted of a felony spends some time incarcerated—in jail awaiting trial and/or in prison terms averaging about two years—nearly all will return to live in Tocqueville Heights. The problem of community safety, she reminds her audience, is not dependent on the length of confinement nearly so much as it is on what happens upon return to the streets.

She sees victims of crime as her most important ally in this effort, for they are often the most neglected. Her staff, led by McDowell, tries to contact victims as soon after the offense as possible, to prepare them for what occurs after the crime. The focus of their efforts is on the various aspects of injury suffered by victims of crime—concrete losses as well as emotional damage. The CJC builds its efforts with victims to restore their faith in community life and in the potential for community safety.

With people convicted of crime, the foremost objective is to situate them in community activities and restrictions that control their risk, but this cannot be fully accomplished without the individual making reparation to the community and the victim. Thus the CJC concerns itself with risk by opening the community to stronger and more effective connection to the individual, and it brokers opportunities for him/her to compensate for the offense.

The CJC recognizes that it is not the only agency carrying these responsibilities. Elected leaders are responsible for community development, victims' services agencies assist victims of crime, and correctional agencies manage the risk people with prior convictions pose to the community. What makes the CJC unique is its concentrated focus on Tocqueville Heights—the neighborhood is its ultimate client. The CJC knows that it can use its strategic location in the community to strengthen the way existing agencies carry out their functions, but this is possible only if the CJC works in partnership with those agencies. By the same token, the existing agencies see the CJC as helpful to accomplishing their mission in this difficult neighborhood.

### Practicing Community Justice

There are four main elements of community justice practice for the CJC: risk assessment and control, victim restoration plan, community contract, and cost sharing.

#### Risk Assessment and Control

Because the CJC practices its correctional program within the environs of Tocqueville Heights, it can engage in risk management more holistically than office-bound correctional agencies. Most of traditional community correctional practice focuses on the problems people with criminal records face, and how those problems contribute to risk. The CJC also considers opportunities for crime and seeks to increase the environmental controls on opportunity for new crimes. By "opportunity" they mean the factors that are essential to crime, based on the "routine activities" concept. This model asserts that for a crime to occur, two factors must be present and two absent.

Here are the factors that must be present:

- A motivated individual—A crime is committed by a person, and that person must want to gain the benefits of the criminal act.
- A suitable target—There must be a place or person that is desirable as a target of the crime.

Here are the factors that must be absent:

- A capable guardian—Targets, no matter how suitable, can be made safe from crime by the presence of a person or system that guards them against crime.
- An intimate handler—A person with a strong emotional tie to an individual inhibits him/her from committing a crime for fear of damaging the emotional tie.

Crime prevention programs, such as the CJC's *Crimestop*, focus on targets and guardians, seeking to strengthen their anticrime potentials. Normally, these approaches have little to do with people who have criminal convictions. The community focus of the CJC enables them to work on the opportunity set in ways that include people convicted of crime as well. The relationship between fathers with criminal records and their children is strengthened through the *Too Legit to Quit* program, thereby increasing the presence of inhibitors in these fathers' lives. People who live in contact with formerly incarcerated people, when properly involved in the community safety agenda, serve the role of guardian as well. They can observe the person's conduct, with concern for behavioral irregularities (often thought of as "signals") that suggest a return to criminality, and this supports preemptive interventions.

Thus, the CJC conducts a comprehensive risk assessment, not only of the risk factors that are *present* in a person's life, creating risk problems that need to be controlled, but also the risk-abating factors that are *absent* from his/her situation. The ultimate result is a "risk management plan" that details the tasks of individual, family members and associates, and formal service delivery agencies, which constitute a strategy for maintaining the person in the community, not only at a reduced level of risk but also with sufficient promise that the community can anticipate a positive, crime free lifestyle from him/her.

### Victim Restoration Plan

The establishment of a realistic risk-management plan is a necessary, but not sufficient, condition for the CJC to accept a case. There must also be a victim-restoration plan that adequately provides for the alleviation of the damage suffered by the victim of the crime. An adequate plan to restore the victim has three elements:

- A full accounting of the costs of the crime, both in tangible losses of property, services, and income, and in emotional costs that are thought of as "quality of life" costs.
- A strategy for addressing those losses to which the victim assents.
- Contribution to the overall strategy by the person convicted of committing the crime.

A *full accounting* is necessary because too often victim compensation is thought of as applicable only to property losses. Going beyond property costs recognizes the way that crime damages the victim's sense of personal security as well as community quality of life for all residents. The CJC subscribes to the belief that there are very few truly "victimless" crimes—in many cases when there is no specific person to be restored, there is still a burden to speak to the community's expectation that it will be recompensed for criminality in its midst.

*Victim assent* to the restoration strategy is also important. Making the plan contingent upon victim approval is a fundamental way to elevate the status of the victim to that of a full player in the process. It also confronts the person convicted of a crime with the very real presence of a fellow citizen who has been harmed by the crime and must be considered in response to the crime.

This explains why the *contribution of people convicted of crime* to the strategy is essential. Their contribution, in time, financial resources, or services, symbolizes their resolve to treat fellow citizens as people who have the right to live free of victimization.

The CJC meets with victims (or in the case of "victimless" offenses, its community board) and develops an assessment of the full costs of the crime. It then convenes a sentencing circle open to all members of the community, especially those who are closely affected by the crime. The CJC describes the risk assessment of the person convicted of the crime in question, and outlines what might be done to manage this person under a sentence to the CJC. The alternative—what the criminal justice system will do if the individual is not accepted in the CJC—is also described. The CJC works with the community to develop a restorative package that might repay some of those costs of the crime. Until the victim and other members of the community are satisfied, the person convicted of the crime cannot expect to be accepted into the CJC's programs.

The elements of a compensation plan are also negotiated with the person convicted of the crime. There will often be several options for "paying" the community—labor, money, services, etc. The CJC sees its goals as compiling a plan that the potential participant finds superior to what will happen as a result of the normal justice process. By incorporating a series of supports, positive activities, risk-reduction services (such as employment and job training), and a reduction in the sanction's punitiveness, the CJC attempts to assemble a plan the individual would prefer to "straight punishment."

This system is used more frequently with people accused of more serious offenses, since the potential response of the justice system is more severe for these crimes. The harms suffered by victims of more serious offenses also gives the CJC a longer list of services that victims find attractive as an alternative to the traditional justice process.

Of course, extremely serious crimes are virtually exempt from the CJC, if only due to practical constraints. Victims of profoundly serious crimes typically find it impossible to construct a scenario that leads to their restoration. Those convicted of violent crime are often of such a risk that a satisfactory risk-management plan is not feasible. Finally, the community typically resists participation with the most serious offenses.

Community justice is a three-way proposition, and each party must feel the CJC's proposal is wise before it will be acceptable. When the stakes are small for any of the actors, little basis exists for a CJC initiated accommodation. As the stakes get larger, the potential for the CJC to develop an alternative to the justice process also grows. Because of these inherent pressures, the CJC makes no blanket exclusions based on prior record or current conviction; any case may be pursued if there seems a chance of working out agreements. This is not as chaotic as it might seem; over time, Bledsoe and McDowell have developed realistic expectations about which cases they will be able to work out.

### Community Contract

The community contract is an agreement by the community to accept the person convicted of crime into the CJC under the terms described in the risk-management plan and the victim-restoration arrangement. When the community accepts a CJC plan, it accepts the reasonable risks the plan involves and sanctions the arrangements in the risk and restoration plans as consistent with community values. The main body CJC uses for community actions is the sentencing circle. In some cases, victims' advocates are especially sought for participation, especially when the crime implies a class of victims, such as occurs in family violence offenses. The CJC has often found it helpful to include advocacy groups for the class of victims in its planning—victims' support groups, family violence service agencies, and the like can often provide valuable voice and helpful input as the circle considers a case.

It is the community contract that obligates the various parties to their tasks. The person convicted of crime has received permission to join in a community-sponsored justice initiative, and is obligated to certain actions that earn this permission. The victim has accepted this person's presence in the community as a part of a broader restorative possibility. The CJC, in order to make the complex arrangement sensible, agrees to monitor all parties' progress through the agreement, and report to the community board, which provides oversight, any problems in the system of agreements.

### Cost Sharing

The CJC receives referrals from three sources: the Department of Corrections, the Court, and the Public Defender's Office. The first two sources include people released from prison and referred by probation, respectively. The third source is important, because these referrals are used to calculate cost sharing, which funds the CJC.

Cost sharing is both a conceptual and practical essential to community justice. The conceptual basis for cost sharing is that people referred by the Public Defender face prison terms if they are not accepted into the CJC. Prison sentences, which average about 28 months for people from Megalopolis, cost the state's taxpayers an average of $45,000 in correctional costs per person. These are taxes taken from communities wealthier than Tocqueville Heights, and they are used to pay for the incarceration of Tocqueville Heights residents in state prisons. Once one of these individuals is accepted into a CJC program, this in effect means that the savings are being created by Tocqueville Heights' citizen willingness to assume a risk. The CJC believes the neighborhood's citizens should accrue some of the benefit.

The CJC recognizes that none of the existing criminal justice agencies can absorb its operating cost, and it sees programmatic value to being fiscally independent of traditional justice agencies. Yet unless a system can be devised that allows the existing agencies to get a benefit from community justice (and the benefits of support services described above for traditional agencies are paramount), then community justice will be at odds with criminal justice. Creating a separate funding stream for community justice helps alleviate this problem.

The CJC has to guarantee that clients it accepts would otherwise be sentenced to prison. This is done through inquiries about the prosecutor's sentencing recommendation as well as studies of past sentencing practices. For each person diverted from prison through acceptance in the CJC, $15,000—a third of the savings—is set aside for the CJC to use on program development. For each participant who completes a year under CJC supervision, the full amount is credited to the CJC's account. (The year's success is required in order to avoid credit for participants who quickly fail and end up in prison anyway.)

The math, then, is straightforward. Tocqueville Heights sends 500 residents a year to the state's prison system. Fifteen successful CJC participants a year fully pays the cost of the office; each additional participant helps to fund crime prevention in Tocqueville Heights. One successful participant each week generates $500,000 a year in excess of the CJC's operating budget. They can match this figure. And when they do, the community board has an operating budget to spend on various crime-prevention projects.

Spend they do. In the *Crimestop* program, $150,000 a year is spent on targeting locations that suffer from serious crime problems, and this project has been extremely successful at reducing crime. *Victims' Awareness* gets $80,000 a year. The rest is used for neighborhood reclamation projects and "banking" for a rainy day—some victims may require expensive services, and this fund will make them available.

### The Traditional Justice System

The CJC works closely with the criminal justice system. The fundamental requirement is that the system has confidence in the CJC's work. This is accomplished by hard work and attention to detail. The "detail" involves attending to the interests of the system: making sure that the judge is informed of the progress of participants under CJC, especially immediate information if there are problems.

That is why the CJC works in close partnership with the probation, parole, and police agencies. This is the secret to credibility with the justice system. Judges, after all, sentence. Their willingness to send people to the CJC is dependent upon their perception that the CJC is a responsible agency, and this depends upon the CJC's willingness to take their interests seriously. Therefore, the CJC caters to the system's needs. It wants Probation to know that Probation's clients will be monitored; it wants Parole to know that its clients' progress will be followed. Most important, it wants the system to know that reasonable plans will be developed for CJC participants, and that these plans will have a chance to succeed.

*Failures*

The linkage to the criminal justice system becomes most significant when the CJC experiences failure. There are two types of failure: the inability to develop a three-way agreement, and the failure of a participant to live up to the terms of the agreement.

The first type of failure—the inability to arrive at an agreement—has important implications for the criminal justice system, for the case goes forward as usual in that system. The CJC takes care to ensure that the failure to accept a case does not undermine an individual's processing by the criminal justice system. Studies of the nonacceptances provide the CJC with a basis for estimating the costs that might have been avoided had the case been accepted.

The second type of failure—participant program failure—is a far more serious matter. The CJC makes distinction between two versions of noncompliance with agreements on the part of the person convicted of crime: new criminality or other behavior that indicates a significant risk of new criminality, and the failure to live up to one of the requirements of an agreement (such as victim compensation or attendance at Tocqueville Heights Habitat). Though either of these types of program failure will result in return to court for sentencing, the CJC is particularly strict about risk-related failure. It defines community safety as a central concern for all of its programs, and stakes organizational credibility on its jealous adherence to an ethic of community safety. When the participant is failing to abide by elements of the agreements, reasonable efforts are made to support his/her need to comply. If these do not work, s/he is terminated from the CJC and returned to court (Clear and Karp 2000).

## Two More Ideas

This is just one kind of imagining of community justice. There are many such possibilities. A few months ago, I was on an AMTRAK train headed from New York to Washington, D.C. Passing through North Philadelphia, I saw once again street after street of vacant housing, boarded up, desolate, and depressing. I then thought of the homeless shelter a few blocks from my home in Hoboken. It seemed downright silly to have so many homeless people looking for places to live when there were so many vacant houses needing people to live in them. I then began to imagine something like what Susan Tucker and Eric Cadora (2003) have called a "justice corps": work crews of people who are coming home from prison and sentenced by the court to join with private citizens who volunteer their time to renovate these dilapidated Philadelphia houses, turning them from wasted space into private homes, building by building and block by block. Some of the workers would move their families into the places they helped renovate.

It would not be so hard for a community court to make community reclamation work a part of its agenda. Let us say that a community prosecutor brings cases against absentee landlords whose places are substandard (or owners of boarded-up property whose structures are deemed a public nuisance) to court. After the appropriate due process and fact-finding, the court holds them criminally liable (or civilly liable) and offers them a deal: renovate the property within six months under court-ordered specifications, sell the property to the court's nonprofit corporation at market values, or go to jail. (If this sounds coercive, it is in no important way different from the deal a standard community court offers every day to people convicted of drug possession: complete a treatment program or go to jail.) A public-private partnership can do the renovation at below cost on all work because some of the labor is done *gratis* by probationers who are performing court-ordered community service as a criminal sanction. They work 36 hours per week at prevailing wages, but the first 16 hours each week are unpaid labor to work off community service obligation. At $20/hour, they earn $400 per week and get health care and the other usual benefits of employment. Working beside them are both former probationers who learned their job skills on the job while working off their community service obligation and regular citizens of the neighborhood who have never been in trouble with the law. Nonprobationers who work for the nonprofit are eligible to purchase the renovated property from a local investment bank, which gives them a mortgage on the prerenovation value of the property. The down payment is the difference between the prerenovation and postrenovation values of the property; collateral is taken from the nonprofit corporation's account, held in the bank. To obtain the mortgage, the individual with a felony conviction (with family) has to agree to live in the property for at least five years before ownership goes from the nonprofit to the private citizen. If the person moves or gets rearrested and goes to prison, all bets are off. The community receives from the court sanctions for people who are convicted of crimes, renovated property, homeowners, and good jobs with fair wages. There are problems with such a scenario, of course. But all of these problems can be dealt with through creativity. And each of these problems is preferable to the vast and incapacitating difficulties we now face with the current justice system.

Dennis Maloney has shown how these problems can be seen as opportunities in his community justice work in Deschutes County, Oregon. Deschutes County emphasized service and got results. Within one year, the community service program reduced youth incarceration in state facilities by 72 percent—a national high according to the National Center for Juvenile Justice. Maloney knows this was no accident. The youth in the program average 204 hours of community service versus the average of four for incarcerated youth; and their restitution rate is four times higher than that of kids who serve time. Service is honorable, he says. "The public recognizes the contribution that they make and supports them."

Though the public traditionally has a higher tolerance for juveniles convicted of crime, the Deschutes County community soon realized that adults also deserve a second chance. And because many adults in the program brought technical skills to the table, the community saw results faster: a child advocacy center and a homeless shelter were built in weeks not months, and parks seemed to grow overnight. Each year, the United States pumps $54 billion into a correctional system that provides no tangible benefits to people who have been victimized by crime, those who have committed crimes, or to neighborhoods. In contrast, the community service program in Deschutes County creates public spaces, provides employers with a skilled workforce, and allows people to earn a place for themselves in the community. And these programs save state dollars. Oregon saved $17,000 per case when they granted Deschutes County flexible use of state funds, which now support schools, libraries, health care, and parks. (State funding ceased in July 2003, but because of the program's success, the local government provided the funding.) Maloney is confident that what he has accomplished on a local level will work nationally. His inspiration is the Civilian Conservation Corps (CCC) of the 1940s, which—hailed by experts as one of the most success- ful government programs ever—contributed billions of dollars to our nation's infrastructure by building bridges, national parks, hatcheries, and municipal auditoriums (Tucker and Cadora 2003:6).

So there it is: a small potpourri of community justice choices, free for those who want to solve the problems associated with mass incarceration concentrated among those from poor communities. These are, I think, attractive and reasonable alternatives to the current punishment system. They will not be easy to create nor to implement, and in putting such ideas into practice, there will be numerous practical and political adjust- ments. But the payoff will be enormous, far exceeding the value of an intensive supervision program or a reentry project, no matter how well run. I hope some of those who read these pages will be challenged to try this kind of work.

# Bibliography

American Friends Service Committee. 1971. *Struggle for justice.* New York: Hill & Wang.

Anderson, Elijah. 1999. *Code of the street: Decency, violence and the moral life of the inner city.* New York: W. W. Norton.

Andrews, Donald A. 2001. Principles of effective correctional programs. In Laurence L. Motiuk and Ralph C. Serin, eds., *Compendium 2000 on Effective Correctional Programming.* Ottawa, ON: Correctional Service Canada.

Austin, James, and John Irwin. 2006. A Blueprint for Reducing Crime and Incarceration in the United States. Unpublished report to the Open Society Institute.

Austin, James, Wendy Naro, and Tony Fabelo. 2007. The 2006 national prison population forecast. Report of the JFA Institute. Philadelphia: Pew Charitable Trust.

Barlow, Melissa H., David E. Barlow, and Theodore G. Chiricos. 1995. Mobilizing support for social control in a declining economy: Exploring ideologies of crime within crime news. *Crime and Delinquency* 41:191–204.

Bayley, David. 1997. *What works in policing.* New York: Oxford University Press.

Beck, Allen J. 2000. *State and federal prisoners returning to the community: Findings from the Bureau of Justice Statistics.* Washington, DC: Bureau of Justice Statistics.

Beckett, Kathryn, and T. Sasson. 2000. *The politics of injustice.* Thousand Oaks, CA: Pine Forge Press.

Bellair, Paul. 1997. Social interaction and community crime: Examining the importance of neighbor networks. *Criminology.* 35:677–704.

Bellair, Paul. 2000. Informal surveillance and street crime: A complex relationship. *Criminology* 38:137–170.

Benda, Brent B., and Nathaniel J. Pallone, eds. 2005. *Rehabilitation Issues, Problems, and Prospects in Boot Camp.* Binghamton, NY: Haworth Press.

Bennett, Susan F. 1995. Community organizations and crime. *Annals of the American Academy of Political and Social Science* 539:72–84.

Berman, Greg, and John Feinblatt. 2005. *Good Courts: The Case for Problem-Solving Justice.* New York: New Press.

Bernburg, Jon Gunnar, and Marvin D. Krohn. 2003. Labeling, life chances, and adult crime: The direct and indirect effects of official intervention in adolescence on crime in early adulthood. *Criminology* 41(4):1287–1318.

Besci, Zsolt. 1999. Economics and crime in the United States. *Economic Review of the Federal Reserve Bank of Atlanta* 84:38–56.

Bhati, Avi, James Lynch, and William Sabol. 2005. Baltimore and Cleveland: Incarceration and crime at the neighborhood level. Paper presented to the meetings of the American Society of Criminology, Toronto, November 18.

BJS. 2006. http://www.ojp.usdoj.gov/bjs/glance.htm. Accessed January 18, 2007.

Block, Richard. 1979. Community, environment and violent crime. *Criminology* 17:46–57.

Bloom, Barbara. 1995. Imprisoned mothers. In Katherine Gabel and Denise Johnston, eds., *Children of incarcerated parents*. New York: Lexington.

Blumstein, Alfred. 1993. Racial disproportionality of U.S. prison populations revisited. *University of Colorado Law Review* 64:743–60.

Blumstein, Alfred, and Allen Beck. 1999. Population growth in U.S. Prisons, 1980–1996. In Michael Tonry and Joan Petersilia, eds., *Crime and Justice: Prisons*. Vol. 26, 17–61. Chicago: University of Chicago.

Blumstein, Alfred, and Allen Beck. 2005. Reentry as a transient state between liberty and recommitment. In Jeremy Travis and Christy Visher, eds., *Prisoner reentry and crime in America*, 50–79. New York: Cambridge University Press.

Blumstein, Alfred, Jose A. Canelo-Cacho, and Jacqueline Cohen. 1993. Filtered sampling from populations with heterogeneous event frequencies. *Management Science* 39:886–99.

Blumstein, Alfred, and Jacqueline Cohen. 1973. A theory of the stability of punishment. *Journal of Criminology, Criminal Law, and Police Science* 63(2):198–207.

Bonczar, Thomas P., and Allen J. Beck 1997. *Lifetime likelihood of going to state or federal prison*. Washington, DC: Bureau of Justice Statistics.

Bontrager, Stephanie, William Bales, and Ted Chiricos. 2005. Race, ethnicity, threat and the labeling of convicted felons." *Criminology* 43(3):589–622.

Braga, Anthony, David Weisburd, Elin Waring, William Spelman, Lorriane Mazerolle, and Frank Gajewski. 1999. Problem-oriented policing in violent crime places: A randomized controlled experiment. *Criminology* 37(4):541–71.

Braithwaite, John. 1979. *Inequality, crime and public policy*. London: Routledge and Keegan Paul.

Braman, Donald. 2004. *Doing Time on the Outside: Incarceration and Family Life in America*. Ann Arbor: University of Michigan Press.

Brooks-Gunn, Jeanne, Greg J. Duncan, and J. Lawrence Aber, eds. 1997. *Neighborhood Poverty*. Vol. 2. New York: Russell Sage.

Browne, Irene. 1997. The black-white gap in labor force participation among women. *American Sociological Review* 62:236–52.

Bureau of Justice Statistics. 2006. Key crime and justice facts at a glance. http://www.ojp.usdoj.gov/bjs. Accessed January 18, 2007.

Burke, Peggy, and Michael Tonry. 2006. *Successful transition and reentry for safer communities: A Call to action for parole.* Silver Spring, MD: Center for Effective Public Policy.

Bursik, Robert J., Jr., and Harold G. Grasmick. 1993. *Neighborhoods and Crime: The Dimensions of Effective Community Control.* New York: Lexington.

Bushway, Shawn, and David McDowell. 2006. Here we go again: Can we learn anything form aggregate level studies of policy interventions? *Criminology & Public Policy* 5(3):461–70.

Cadora, Eric, Charles Swartz, and Mannix Gordon. 2002. Criminal justice and human services: An exploration of overlapping needs, resources and interests in Brooklyn neighborhoods. In Jeremy Travis and Michelle Waul, eds., *Prisoners Once Removed: The Impact of Incarceration and Reentry on Children, Families, and Communities.* Washington, DC: Urban Institute.

Canelo-Cacho, Jose A., Alfred Blumstein, and Jacqueline Cohen, 1997. Relationship between the offending frequency of imprisoned and free offenders. *Criminology* 35:133–75.

Carlson, Bonnie, and Neil Cervera. 1992. *Inmates and Their Wives.* Westport, CT: Greenwood Press.

CASES. 1998. *The Community Justice Project.* New York: Center for Alternative Sentencing and Employment Services.

Chen, M. Keith, and Jesse M. Shapiro. 2006. Does prison harden inmates? A discontinuity-based approach. *Criminology & Public Policy* 5(2):132–64.

Chiricos, Ted, Kelly Welch, and Marc Gertz. 2004. "The racial typification of crime and support for punitive measures." *Criminology* 42:359–90.

Cho, Rosa, and Robert LaLonde. 2005. The Impact of Incarceration in State Prison on the Employment Prospects of Women. Unpublished paper.

Christy Visher, and Jill Farrell. 2005. *Chicago Communities and Prisoner Reentry.* Washington, DC: Urban Institute.

Clark, John, James Austin, and D. Alan Henry. 1997. Three strikes and you're out: A review of state legislation. *NIJ Research in Brief.* Washington, DC: National institute of Justice.

Clear, Todd R., and Eric Cadora. 2001. *Community Justice.* Belmont, CA: Wadsworth.

Clear, Todd. R., and David R. Karp. 2000. *The Community Justice Ideal: Preventing Crime and Achieving Justice.* Boulder, CO: Westview.

Clear, Todd R., and Dina R. Rose. 2003. Individual sentencing practices and aggregate social problems. In D. F. Hawkins, S. Myers, and R. Stone, eds.,

*Crime Control and Criminal Justice: The Delicate Balance.* Westport, CT: Greenwood.

Clear, Todd R., Dina R. Rose, and Judith A. Ryder. 2001. Incarceration and community: The problem of removing and returning offenders. *Crime and Delinquency* 47(3):335–51.

Clear, Todd R., Dina R. Rose, Elin Waring, and Kristen Scully. 2003. Coercive mobility and crime: A preliminary examination of concentrated incarceration and social disorganization. *Justice Quarterly* 20(1):33–64.

Clear, Todd R., Elin Waring, and Kristen Scully. 2005. Communities and reentry: Concentrated reentry cycling. In Jeremy Travis and Christy Visher, eds., *Prisoner Reentry and Crime in America*, 179–208. New York: Cambridge University Press.

Clear, Valorous B., and Todd R. Clear. 1971. Two million dollars. Report to the Indiana Criminal Code Study Commission. Anderson, IN: Anderson College.

Cohen, Barbara E. 1992. *Evaluation of the Teen Parents Employment Demonstration.* Washington, DC: Urban Institute.

Cohen, Stanley. 1985. *Visions of Social Control.* Cambridge, UK: Polity Press.

Coleman, James. 1988. Social capital and the creation of human capital. *American Journal of Sociology* 94 (Suppl.):S95.

Coles, Catherine M., Brian Carney, and Bobbie Johnson. 2000. Crime prevention through community prosecution and community policing: Boston's Grove Hall Safe Neighborhood Initiative. In Corina Solé Brito and Eugenia E. Gratto, eds., *Problem-Oriented Policing: Crime-Specific Problems, Critical Issues and Making POP Work.* Vol. 3. Washington, DC: Police Executive Research Forum.

Covington, Jeannette, and Ralph B. Taylor. 1991. Fear of crime and urban residential neighborhood: Implications of between- and within-neighborhood sources of current models. *Sociological Quarterly* 32:231–49.

Crane, Jonathon. 1991. The epidemic theory of ghettos and neighborhood effects on dropping out and teenage childbearing. *American Journal of Sociology* 96(5):1226–59.

Crutchfield, Robert D. 1989. Labor stratification and violent crime. Social Forces 68(2):489–512.

Crutchfield, Robert D. 2005. Neighborhoods, Collective Efficacy, and Inmate Release: A Summary of Preliminary Analyses. Unpublished paper.

Crutchfield, Robert D., Michael R. Geerken, and Walter R. Gove. 1982. Crime rate and social integration: The impact of metropolitan mobility. *Criminology* 20:467–78.

Crutchfield, Robert D., and Susan R. Pitchford. 1997. Work and crime: The effects of labor stratification. *Social Forces* 76:93–118.

Darity, William A., and Samuel L. Myers, Jr. 1994. *The Black Underclass: Critical Essays on Race and Unwantedness.* New York: Garland.

Darling, Nancy, and Laurence Steinberg. 1997. Community influences on adolescent achievement and deviance. In Jeanne Brooks-Gunn, Greg J. Duncan, and J. Lawrence Aber, eds., *Neighborhood Poverty: Policy Implication in Studying Neighborhoods.* Vol. 2, 120–31. New York: Russell-Sage.

Dejong, Christina. 1997. Survival analysis and specific deterrence: Integrating theoretical and empirical models of recidivism. *Criminology* 35:561–75.

DiIulio, John. 1995. Arresting ideas: Tougher law enforcement is driving down urban crime. *Policy Review* 74(Fall):12–26.

DiIulio, John. 1999. Two million prisoners are enough. *Wall Street Journal,* March 12.

Donohue, John J., III, and Peter Siegelman. 1998. Allocating resources among prisons and social programs in the battle against crime. *Journal of Legal Studies* 27(1):1–43.

Doob, Anthony N., and Cheryl Marie Webster. 2003. Sentence severity and crime: Accepting the null hypothesis. In Michael Tonry, ed., *Crime and Justice: A Review of Research.* Vol. 30, 143–95. Chicago: University of Chicago Press.

Duff, R. A. 2001. *Punishment, Communication and Community.* New York: Oxford University Press.

Earles, Felton J., Jeanne Brooks-Gunn, Stephen W. Raudenbush, and Robert J. Sampson. 1994. *Project on Human Development in Chicago Neighborhoods.* Cambridge, MA: Harvard University Press.

Edin, Kathryn, and Laura Lein. 1997. Work, welfare, and single mothers' economic survival strategies. *American Sociological Review* 62(2):253–66.

Edin, Kathryn, Timothy Nelson, and Rechelle Paranal. 2004. Fatherhood and incarceration as potential turning points in the criminal careers of unskilled men. In Mary Pattillo, David Weiman, and Bruce Western, eds., *Imprisoning America: The Social Effects of Mass Incarceration,* 46–75. New York: Russell Sage.

Etzioni, Amatai. 1996. The responsive community: A communitarian perspective. *American Sociological Review* 61:1–11.

Fabelo, Tony, Wendy Naro, and James Austin. 2005. *Exploring the Diminishing Effects of More Incarceration: Virginia's experiment in sentencing reform.* Washington, DC: JFA Institute.

Fagan, Jeffrey A. 1990. Intoxication and aggression. *Drugs and Crime—Crime and Justice: An Annual Review of Research* 13:241–20.

Fagan, Jeffrey. 1997. Legal and illegal work: Crime, work and unemployment. In Burton Weisbrod and James Worthy, eds., *Dealing with Urban Crises,* 33–71. Evanston, IL: Northwestern University Press.

Fagan, Jeffrey. 2006. Incarceration and Voting. Unpublished memorandum to the Project on Concentrated Incarceration of the Open Society Institute.

Fagan, Jeffery, and Richard B. Freeman. 1999. Crime and work. In Michael Tonry, ed., *Crime and Justice: A Review of Research.* Vol. 5, 225–90.

Fagan, Jeffrey, Valerie West, and Jan Holland. 2003. Reciprocal Effects of Crime and Incarceration in New York City Neighborhoods. Unpublished paper, Center for Violence Research and Prevention, Colombia University.

Farkas, George, Paula England, Keven Vicknair, and Barbara Stanek Kilbourne. 1997. Cognitive skill, skill demands of jobs, and earnings among young European American, African American, and Mexican American workers. *Social Forces* 75:913–40.

Farrington, David, Patrick A. Langan, and Michael Tonry, eds. 2004. *Cross-National Studies in Crime and Justice.* Washington, DC: U.S. Bureau of Justice Statistics.

Farrington, David P., and Brandon C. Welsh. 2007. *Saving Children from a Life of Crime: Early Risk Factors and Effective Interventions.* New York: Oxford University Press.

Flanagan, Timothy J., and Dennis R. Longmire, eds. 1996. *Americans View Crime and Justice: A National Public Opinion Survey.* Thousand Oaks, CA: Sage.

Felson, Marcus. 1996. Those who discourage crime. In John E. Eck and David Weisburd, eds., *Crime and Place: Crime Prevention Studies.* Vol. 4, 53–66. Albany, NY: Harrow and Heston.

Felson, Marcus. 2003. The process of co-offending. In Margaret J. Smith and Derek B. Cornish (eds.), *Theory for Practice in Situational Crime Prevention.* Crime Prevention Studies. Vol. 16, 149–265. Monsey, NY: Criminal Justice Press.

Finckenauer, James O. 1982. *Scared Straight: Delinquency and the Panacea Phenomenon.* Englewood Cliffs, NJ: Prentice-Hall.

Fleisher, Mark S. 1995. *Beggars and Thieves: Lives of Urban Street Criminals.* Madison: University of Wisconsin Press.

Fleisher, Mark S. and Scott H. Decker. 2001. Going home, staying home: Integrating prison gang members back into the community. *Corrections Management Quarterly* 5(1):65–77.

Freeman, Richard B. 1992. Crime and unemployment of disadvantaged youth. In Adele Harrell and George Peterson, eds., *Drugs, Crime and Social Isolation: Barriers to Urban Opportunity.* Washington, DC: Urban Institute.

Freeman, Richard. 2003. Can We Close the Revolving Door? Recidivism vs. Employment of Ex-Offenders in the U.S. Unpublished paper.

Frieden, Terry. 2006. Violent crime takes first big jump since '91; Murder numbers climb in smaller cities. Available at: http://www.cnn.com/2006/LAW/06/12/crime.rate/index.html. Posted June 12, 2006.

Fritsch, T. A., and J. D. Birkhead. 1981. Behavioral reactions of children to parental absence due to incarceration. *Family Relations* 30:83–88.

Frost, Natasha. 2006. *The Punitiveness Report—Hard Hit: The Growth in Imprisonment of Women, 1977–2004.* New York: Women's Prison Association Institute on Women & Criminal Justice.

Frost, Natasha. 2006. *The punitive state: Crime, punishment and imprisonment across the United States.* NY: LFB Scholarly Publishing.

Gabel, Stewart, and Richard Shindledecker. 1993. Characteristics of children whose parents have been incarcerated. *Hospital and Community Psychiatry* 44(7):543–59.

Garfinkel, Irwin, Sara McLanahan, and Thomas L. Hanson. 1998. A patchwork quilt of non-resident fathers. Working paper no. 98-25. Princeton, NJ: Princeton University Press.

Garland, David, ed. 2001. *Mass Imprisonment: Social Causes and Consequences.* Thousand Oaks, CA: Sage.

Gebelin, Richard S. 2000. *The Rebirth of Rehabilitation: Promise and Perils of Drug Courts.* Papers from the Executive Sessions on Sentencing and Corrections, no. 6. Washington, DC: National Institute of Justice.

Geerken, Michael R., and Hennessey D. Hayes. 1993. Probation and parole: Public risks and the future of incarceration alternatives. *Criminology* 31(4):549–64.

George, Susan, Robert LaLonde, and Todd Schuble. 2005. Socio-Economic Indicators, Criminal Activity, and the Concentration of Female Ex-prisoners in Chicago Neighborhoods. Unpublished paper.

Gephart, Martha, and Jeaane Brooks-Gunn. 1997. In Jeanne Brooks-Gunn, Greg J. Duncan, and J. Lawrence Aber, eds., *Neighborhood Poverty: Policy Implication in Studying Neighborhoods.* Vol. 2, xiii–xxii. New York: Russell Sage.

Gibson, Christina, Katheryn Edin, and Sara McLanahan. 2003. High hopes but even higher expectations: The retreat from marriage among low-income couples. Working Paper 03-066-FF. Princeton, NJ: Center for Research on Child Wellbeing, Princeton University.

Good, Joshua, and Pamela Sherrid. 2005. *Ready4Work: A National Response to the Prisoner Reentry Crisis.* Philadelphia: Public/Private Ventures.

Goering, John, and Judith Feins, eds. 2003. *Choosing a Better Life? Evaluating the Moving to Opportunity Social Experiment.* Washington, DC: Urban Institute.

Goetz, Edward G. 1996. The U.S. war on drugs as urban policy. *International Journal of Urban and Regional Research* 20:539–50.

Gordon, Diana. 1990. *The justice juggernaut.* New Brunswick, NJ: Rutgers University Press.

Gottfredson, Don M. 1999. Effects of judges sentencing decisions on criminal careers. In *NIJ Research in Brief.* Washington, DC: U.S. Department of Justice.

Gottfredson, Don M., Leslie T. Wilkins, and Peter B. Hoffman. 1978. *Guidelines for Parole and Sentencing. A Policy Control Method*. New York: Lexington.

Granovetter, Mark. 1993. Strength of weak ties. *American Journal of Sociology* 78:1360–80.

Green, Judith, Kevin Pranis, and Jason Ziedenberg. 2006. *Disparity by Design: How Drug-Free Zone Laws Impact Racial Disparity–and Fail to Protect Youth*. Washington, DC: Justice Policy Institute.

Greenspan, Rosanne, Steve Mastrofski, Ann Marie McNally, and David Weisburd. 2000. Compstat and organizational change: A national assessment. Annual Conference on Criminal Justice Research and Evaluation, Washington, DC, July.

Greenwood, Peter W., and Allan Abrahamse. 1982. *Selective Incapacitation*. Santa Monica, CA: Rand.

Greenwood, Peter W., and Susan Turner. 1987. *Selective Incapacitation Revisited: Why the High Rate Offenders Are Hard to Predict*. Santa Monica, CA: Rand.

Grogger, Jeffrey. 1995. The effect of arrests on the employment and earnings of young men. *Quarterly Journal of Economics* 110(1):51–71.

Haapanen, Rudy, and Lee Britton. 2005. Drug testing for youthful offenders on parole: An experimental evaluation. *Criminology & Public Policy* 1(2):217–32.

Hagan, John. 1993. The social embeddedness of crime and unemployment. *Criminology* 31:465–92.

Hagan, John. 1994. *Crime and Disrepute*. Thousand Oaks, CA: Pine Forge Press.

Hagan, John. 1996. The next generation: Children of prisoners. In *The Unintended Consequences of Incarceration*, 19–28. New York: Vera Institute of Justice.

Hagan, John, and Ronit Dinovitzer. 1999. Collateral consequences of imprisonment for children, communities and prisoners. In Michael Tonry and Joan Petersilia, eds., *Prisons*, 121–162. Chicago: University of Chicago Press.

Hairston, Creasie. 1998. The forgotten parent: Understanding the forces that influence incarcerated fathers' relationships with their children. *Child welfare* 5:617–39.

Harcourt, Bernard E., and Jens Ludwig. 2006. Broken windows: New evidence from New York City and a five-city social experiment. *University of Chicago Law Review* 73:271–301.

Hawkins, Darnell, F. John H. Laub, Janet L. Lauritsen, and L. Cothern. 2000. *Race, Ethnicity, and Serious Violent Juvenile Offending*. Washington, DC: Office of Juvenile Justice & Delinquency Prevention.

Hay, Carter, Edward N. Forston, Dusten R. Hollist, Irshad Aletheimer, and Lonnie M. Schaible. 2006. The impact of community disadvantage on the relationship between the family and the juvenile court. *Journal of research on crime & delinquency* 43(4) 326–46.

Henig, Jeffrey R. 1982. *Neighborhood Mobilization: Redevelopment and Response.* New Brunswick, NJ: Rutgers University Press.

Herbert, Bob. 2006. An emerging catastrophe. *New York Times,* March 20, A-28.

Holzer, Harry, Peter Edelman, and Paul Offner. 2006. *Reconnecting Disadvantaged Young Men.* Washington, DC: Urban Institute.

Holzer, Harry, Steven Raphael, and Michael Stoll. 2001. Perceived criminality, criminal background checks, and racial hiring practices of employers. Discussion paper no. 1254-02, Institute for Research on Poverty, University of Wisconsin, Madison.

Hudson v. Michigan, S, Ct. 04-1360 (2006).

Huebner, Beth M. 2005. The effect of incarceration on marriage and work in the life course. *Justice quarterly* 22(3):281–301.

Hughes, Timothy A., Doris James Wilson, and Alan J. Beck. 2006. *Reentry Trends in the United States: Inmates Returning to the Community after Spending Time in Prison.* Washington, DC: Bureau of Justice Statistics.

Hughes, Timothy A., Doris James Wilson, and Allen J. Beck. 2001. *Trends in State Parole, 1990–2000.* Washington, DC: Bureau of Justice Statistics.

Hunter, Albert J. 1985. Private, parochial and public social orders: The problem of crime and incivility in urban communities. In Gerald D. Suttles and Mayer N. Zald, eds., *The Challenge of Social Control: Citizenship and Institution Building in Modern Society.* Norwood, NJ: Aldex Publishing.

Jacobs, David, and Ronald E. Helms. 1996. Toward a political model of incarceration: A time series examination of multiple explanations for prison admission rates. *American Journal of Sociology* 102:323–57.

Jacobson, Michael. 2005. *Downsizing Prisons: How to Reduce Crime and End Mass Incarceration.* New York: New York University Press.

Johnson, Elizabeth I, and Jane Waldfogel. 2004. Children of incarcerated parents: Multiple risks and children's living arrangements. In Mary Pattillo, David Weiman, and Bruce Western, eds., *Imprisoning America: The Social Effects of Mass Incarceration,* 97–134. New York: Russell Sage.

Johnson, Rucker C, and Steven Raphael. 2005. The Effects of Male Incarceration on Dynamics of AIDS Infection Rates among African-American Women and Men. Unpublished paper presented to the incarceration study group of the Russell Sage Foundation, July.

Johnston, L. D., P. M. O'Malley, J. G Bachman, and J. G. Schulenberg. 2004. *Monitoring the future survey results on drug use: 1973–2003.* Bethesda, MD: National Institute on Drug Abuse.

Jucovy, Linda. 2006. *Just Out: Early Lessons from the Ready4Work Reentry Initiative.* Philadelphia: Public/Private Ventures.

Kampfner, Christina Jose. 1995. Post-traumatic stress reactions of children of incarcerate mothers. In Stuart Gabel and Denise Johnston, eds, *Children of Incarcerated Parents*, 121–62. New York: Lexington.

Kane, Robert J. 2006. On the limits of social control: structural deterrence and the policing of suppressible crimes. *Justice Quarterly* 23(2):186–213.

Kaufman, Joanne. 2005. Explaining the race/ethnicity-violence relationship: Neighborhood context and social psychological processes. *Justice Quarterly* 22(2):224–51.

Kelling, George, and Catherine M. Coles. 1998. *Fixing Broken Windows: Restoring Order and Reducing Crime in Our Communities.* New York: Free Press.

Kennedy, David. 1997. Pulling levers: Chronic offenders, high-crime settings, and a theory of prevention. *Valparaiso University Law Review* 31(2):449–84.

Kennedy, David. 2007. *Deterrence and Crime: Reconsidering the Prospect of Sanction.* London: Routledge.

Kennedy, David. 2006. Taking Criminology Seriously: Narratives, Norms, Networks and Common Ground. Discussion draft prepared for the symposium in honor of Irving Spergel, University of Chicago School of Social Service Administration, January.

Kessler, Daniel, and Steven D. Levitt. 1999. Using sentence enhancements to distinguish between deterrence and incapacitation. *Journal of Law and Economics* 42:343–63.

King, Ryan S., and Marc Mauer. 2004. *The Vanishing Black Electorate: Felony Disenfranchisement in Atlanta, Georgia.* Washington, DC: Sentencing Project.

King, Ryan S., Marc Mauer, and Malcolm C. Young. 2005. *Incarceration and Crime: A Complex Relationship.* Washington, DC: Sentencing Project.

Kleck, Gary, Brion Sever, Spencer Li, and Marc Gertz. 2005. The missing link in general deterrence research. *Criminology* 43:623–60.

Klepper, Steven, and Daniel Nagin. 1989. The deterrent effect of perceived certainty and severity of punishment revisited. *Criminology* 27:721–46.

Kling, Jeffrey. 1999. The Effect of Prison Sentence Length on Subsequent Employment and Earnings of Criminal Defendants. Woodrow Wilson School discussion paper on Economics, no. 208, Princeton University.

Kornhauser, Ruth Rosner. 1978. *Social sources of delinquency: An appraisal of analytic methods.* Chicago: University of Chicago Press.

Kotloff, Lauren J. 2005. *Leaving the Street: Young Fathers Move from Hustling to Legitimate Work.* Philadelphia: Public/Private Ventures.

Kovandzic, Tomislav, and Lynne M. Vieraitis. 2006. The effect of county-level prison population growth on crime rates. *Criminology & Public Policy* 5:2:101–32.

Krivo, Lauren J. 2000. The structural context of homicide: accounting for racial differences in process. *American Sociological Review* 65:547–99.

Krivo, Lauren J., and Ruth D. Peterson. 1996. Extremely disadvantaged neighborhoods and urban crime. *Social Forces* 75:619–50.

Kurlychek, Megan, Robert Brame, and Shawn Bushway. 2006. Scarlet letters: Does an old criminal record predict future criminal behavior? *Criminology & Public Policy* 5(3):483–504.

Kurlycheck, Megan, and Cynthia Kempinen. 2006. Beyond boot camp: The impact of aftercare on offender reentry. *Criminology & Public Policy* 5(2):363–88.

Lalonde, Robert, and Susan George. 2003. *Incarcerated Mothers: The Project on Female Prisoners and Their Children*. New York: Open Society Institute.

Langan, Patrick, and David Levin. 2002. *Recidivism in Prisoners Released in 1994*. Washington, DC: Bureau of Justice Statistics.

Langan, Patrick A., Erica L. Schmidt, and Matthew R. Durose. 2003. *Recidivism of Sex Offenders Released from Prison in 1994*. Washington, DC: Bureau of Justice Statistics.

Laub, John, Daniel Nagin, and Robert Sampson. 1998. Trajectories of change in criminal offending: Good marriages and the desistence process. *American Sociological Review* 63(2):225–38.

Laub, John H., and Robert J. Sampson. 1993. Turning points in the life course: Why change matters to the study of crime. *Criminology* 31:301–25.

Lengyel, Thomas. 2000. Forcing welfare recipients to apply informal social resources in their transition to work: A policy of self-sufficiency or indifference? *The Roundtable* 3(9):11.

Lengyel, Thomas E. 2006. *Spreading the Pain: The Social Cost of Incarcerating Parents*. New York: Healing the Divide.

Leventhal, Tama, Jeanne Brooks-Gunn, and Sheila B. Kamerman. 1997. Communities as place, face and space: provision of services to poor, urban children and their families. In Jeanne Brooks-Gunn, Greg J. Duncan, and J. Lawrence Aber, eds., *Neighborhood Poverty: Policy Implication in Studying Neighborhoods*. Vol. 2, 182–205. New York: Russell Sage.

Levitt, Stephen D. 1996. The effect of prison population on crime rates. Evidence from prison overcrowding litigation. *Quarterly Journal of Economics* 111:319–51.

Levitt, Stephen D. 2001. Alternative strategies for identifying the link between unemployment and crime. *Journal of Quantitative Criminology* 17:377–90.

Liedka, Raymond V., Anne Morrison Piehl, and Bert Useem. 2006. The crime control effects of incarceration: Does scale matter? *Criminology & Public Policy* 5(2):245–76.

Lipsey, Mark W. 1999. Can rehabilitative programs reduce the recidivism of juvenile offenders? An inquiry into the effectiveness of practical programs. *Virginia Journal of Social Policy and the Law* 6:611–41.

Lofland, John, and Lyn H. Lofland. 1995. *Analyzing Social Settings: A Guide to Qualitative Observations and Analysis.* Belmont, CA: Wadsworth.

Logan, John R., and Harvey L. Molotch. 1987. *Urban Fortunes: The Political Economy of Place.* Berkeley: University of California Press.

Losen, Daniel L., and Johanna Wald, eds. 2003. *Deconstructing the School to Prison Pipeline.* New Directions for Youth Development #99. Canada: John Wiley & Sons.

Lynch, Allen K., and David W. Rasmussen. 2001. Measuring the impact of crime on house prices. *Applied Economics* 33(15):1981–89.

Lynch, James P., and William J. Sabol. 1992. Macro-social Changes and Their Implications for Prison Reform: The Underclass and the Composition of Prison Populations. Paper presented at the American Society of Criminology, New Orleans, November 5.

Lynch, James P., and William J. Sabol. 2004a. Assessing the effects of mass incarceration on informal social control in communities. *Criminology & Public Policy* 3(2):267–94.

Lynch, James P., and William J. Sabol. 2004b. Effects of incarceration on informal social control in communities. In Mary Pattillo, David Weiman, and Bruce Western, eds., *Imprisoning America: The Social Effects of Mass Incarceration,* 135–64. New York: Russell Sage.

Lynch, James P., William J. Sabol, Michael Plant, and Mary Shelley. 2001. Crime, Coercion, and Community: The Effects of Arrest and Incarceration Policies on Informal Social Control in Neighborhoods. Report to the National Institute of Justice. Washington, DC: Urban Institute Justice Policy Center.

MacKenzie, Doris Layton. 2006. *What works in corrections: Reducing the criminal activities of offenders and delinquents.* NY: Cambridge University Press.

Markowitz, Fred E., Paul E. Bellair, Allan E. Liska, and Jianhong Liu. 2001. Extending social disorganization theory: Modeling the relationships between disorder, cohesion and fear. *Criminology* 39(2):293–319.

Martin, S., B. Clifford, S. Christine, and J. Inciardi. 1999. Three-year outcomes of therapeutic community treatment for drug-involved offenders in Delaware: From prison to work release to aftercare. *The Prison Journal* 79(3):294–320.

Maruschak, Laura M. 2001. *HIV in Prisons and Jails, 1999.* Washington, DC: Bureau of Justice Statistics.

Maruschak, Laura M., and Alan J. Beck. 2001. *Medical Problems of Inmates, 1997.* Washington, DC: Bureau of Justice Statistics.

Marvell, Thomas B., and Carlisle E. Moody. 1997. The impact of prison growth on homicide. *Homicide Studies* 1:205–33.

Marvell, Thomas B., and Carlisle E. Moody. 1998. The impact of out-of-state prison population on homicide rates. Displacement and free rider effects. *Criminology* 36:513–53.

Mauer, Marc. 1999. *Race to Incarcerate.* Washington, DC: Sentencing Project.

Mauer, Marc. 2005. Thinking about prison and its impact in the twenty-first century. Walter C. Reckless Memorial Lecture, *Ohio State Journal of Criminal Law* 2:607–18.

Mauer, Marc, and Tracy Huling. 1995. *Young Black Americans and the Criminal Justice System: Five Years Later.* Washington, DC: Sentencing Project.

Mauer, Marc, Ryan S. King, and Malcolm C. Young. 2004. *The Meaning of Life: Long Prison Sentences in Context.* Washington, DC: Sentencing Project.

Meares, Tracey. 1997. Charting race and class differences in attitudes toward drug legalization and law enforcement: Lessons for federal criminal law. *Buffalo Criminal Law Review* 1:137–74.

Mears, Daniel P., and Avinash Bhati. 2006. No community is an island: The effects of resource deprivation on urban violence in spacially and socially proximate communities. *Criminology* 44(3):509–48.

Melossi, Dario, ed. 1998. *The Sociology of Punishment: Socio-Structural Perspectives.* London: Ashgate.

Miller, Jerome G. 1992. *Hobbling a Generation: Young African American Males in the Criminal Justice System of America's Cities.* Baltimore: National Center on Institutions and Alternatives.

Moore, Quinn, and Heidi Shierholz. 2005. Externalities of Imprisonment: Does Maternal Incarceration Affect Child Outcomes? Paper presented at the meeting of the American Society of Criminology, Toronto.

Morenoff, Jeffrey D., Robert J. Sampson, and Stephen W. Raudenbush. 2001. Neighborhood inequality, collective efficacy, and the spatial dynamics of urban violence. *Criminology* 39:517–61.

Morris, Norval. 1974. *The Future of Iimprisonment.* Chicago: University of Chicago Press.

Mumola, C. 2000. *Incarcerated parents and their children.* Washington, DC: National Institute of Justice.

Murray, Joseph. 2005. The effects of imprisonment on the families and children of prisoners. In Allison Liebling and Shadd Maruna, eds., *The Effects of Imprisonment*, 442–92. Cullompton, UK: Willan.

Murray, Joseph, and David Farrington. Forthcoming. Effects of parental incarceration on children. In Michael Tonry, ed., *Crime and Justice: A Review of Research*. Chicago: University of Chicago Press.

Murray, Joseph, and David Farrington. 2005. Parental imprisonment: Effects on boys' anti-social behaviour and delinquency through the life course. *Journal of Child Psychology and Psychiatry* 46(12):1269–78.

Murray, Joseph, Carl-Gunnar Janson, and David Farrington. 2007. Crime in adult offspring of prisoners: A cross-national comparison of two longitudinal samples. *Criminal Justice & Behavior* 34:133–49.

Musto, David F. 1999. *The American Disease: Origins of Narcotic Control*. New York: Oxford University Press.

Nagin, Daniel. 1998. Criminal deterrence research at the outset of the twenty-first century. In Michael Tonry, ed., *Crime and Justice: A Review of Research*. Vol. 25, 1–42. Chicago: University of Chicago Press.

Nagin, Daniel, and Greg Pogarsky. 2000. Integrating celerity, impulsivity, and extra-legal sanction threats into a model of general deterrence. *Criminology* 39:865–91.

Nagin, Daniel, and Joel Waldfogel. 1998. The effect of conviction on income through the life cycle. *International Review of Law and Economics* 18:25–40.

National Commission on Correctional Health Care. 2002. *The Health Status of Soon-to-Be-Released Inmates*. Washington, DC: National Institute of Justice.

National Corrections Reporting Program. 2002. *Spreadsheet*. Washington, DC: Bureau of Justice Statistics.

National Council of State Governments. 2005. *Report of the NCSG Reentry Council*. New York: NCSG.

Nurse, Anne M. 2004. Returning to strangers: Newly paroled young fathers and their children. In Mary Pattillo, David Weiman, and Bruce Western, eds., *Imprisoning America: The Social Effects of Mass Incarceration*. New York: Russell Sage.

O'Brien, Patricia. 2001. Just like baking a cake: Women describe the necessary ingredients for successful reentry after incarceration. *Families in Society: The Journal of Contemporary Human Services* 82(3):287–95.

Osgood, Wayne. 2000. Poisson-based regression analysis of aggregate crime rates. *Journal of Quantitative Criminology* 16:21–43.

Pager, Devah. 2003. The mark of a criminal record. *American Journal of Sociology* 108(5):937–75.

Pager, Devah. 2007. *Marked: Race, Crime, and Finding Work in an Era of Mass Incarceration*. Chicago: University of Chicago Press, 2007.

Parcel, Toby L., and Elizabeth G. Menaghan. 1993. Family social capital and children's behavior problems. *Social Psychology Quarterly* 56:120–35.

Paternoster, Raymond. 1983. Estimating perceptual stability and deterrent effects: The role of perceived legal punishments and the inhibition of criminal involvement. *Journal of criminal law and criminology* 74:210–97.

Paternoster, Raymond. 1985. Assessment of risk and behavioral experience: an exploratory study of change. *Criminology* 23:417–33.

Paternoster, Raymond. 1987. The deterrent effect of perceived certainty and severity of punishments: A review of the evidence and issues. *Justice Quarterly* 4:173–217.

Pattavina, April, James M. Byrne, and Luis Garcia. 2006. An examination of citizen involvement in crime prevention in high-risk versus low- to moderate-risk neighborhoods. *Crime & Delinquency* 52(2):203–31.

Petersilia, Joan. 2003. *When Prisoners Come Home: Parole and Prisoner Reentry.* New York: Oxford University Press.

Petersilia, Joan. Forthcoming. California corrections: A paradox of excess and deprivation. In Michael Tonry, ed., *Crime and Justice: A Review of Research.* Chicago: University of Chicago Press.

Petersilia, Joan, Peter Greenwood, and Martin Lavin. 1978. *Criminal Careers of Habitual Felons.* Santa Monica, CA: Rand.

Petersilia, Joan, and Susan Turner. 1990. *Intensive Supervision for High-risk Probationers. Findings from Three California Experiments.* Santa Monica, CA: Rand.

Petersilia, Joan, Susan Turner, James Kahan, and Joyce Petereson. 1985. *Granting Felons Probation: Public Risks and Alternatives.* Santa Monica: Rand.

Petersilia, Joan, Susan Turner, James Kahan, and Joyce Petereson. 1986. *Prison vs. Probation in California: Implications for Crime and Offender Recidivism.* Santa Monica: Rand.

Pettit, Becky, and Bruce Western. 2004. Mass imprisonment and the life course: Race and class inequality in U.S. incarceration. *American Sociological Review* 69:151–69.

Pettit, Phillip, and John Braithwaite. 1993. *Not Just Deserts: A Republican Theory of Criminal Justice.* New York: Oxford University Press.

Phillips, Susan, and Barbara Bloom. 1998. In whose best interest? The impact of changing public policy on relatives caring for children with incarcerated parents. *Child Welfare* 77(5):531–41.

Phillips, Susan D., Alaatin Erkanli, Gordon P. Keeler, E. Jane Costello, and Adrian Angold. 2006. Disentangling the risks: Parent criminal justice involvement and child's exposure to family risks. *Criminology & Public Policy* 5(4):101–206.

Piehl, Anne Morrison, and John J. DiIulio, Jr. 1995. Does crime pay? *Brookings Review* (Winter):21–26.

Piquero, Alex R., and Alfred Blumstein. Forthcoming. Does incapacitation reduce crime? *Journal of quantitative criminology.*

Podolefsky, Aaron, and Frederik DuBow. 1980. *Strategies for Community Crime Prevention: Collective Responses to Crime in Urban America.* Reactions to Crime Project, Center for Urban Affairs. Evanston, IL: Northwestern University Press.

Polikoff, Alexander. 2004. Racial inequality and the black ghetto. *Inequality & Race* 13(6):1–12.

Pope, Carl E. 1979. Victimization rates and neighborhood characteristics: Some preliminary findings. In William H. Parsonage, ed., *Perspectives in Victimology.* Beverly Hills, CA: Sage.

Pogarsky, Greg, Alan J. Lizotte, and Terence P. Thornberry. 2003. The delinquency of children born to young mothers: Results from the Rochester Youth Development Study. *Criminology* 41(4):1249–86.

Portes, A., and J. Sensebrenner. (1993) Embeddedness and immigration: Notes on the determinants of economic action. *American Journal of Sociology* 98:1320–50.

Powell, John A., Ruthe D. Peterson, Lauren J. Krivo, Paul E. Bellair, and Kecia Johnson. 2004. The Impact of Mass Incarceration on Columbus, Ohio. Unpublished paper.

Pratt, Travis C., Michael G. Turner, and Alex Piquero. 2004. Parental socialization and community context: A longitudinal analysis of the structural sources of low self-control. *Journal of Research in Crime & Delinquency* 41(3):219–43.

Rau, Jordan. 2007. Governor blames public indifference for prison ills. *Los Angeles Times,* January 18.

Reiss, Albert. 1988. Co-offending and criminal careers. In Michael Tonry and Norval Morris, eds., *Crime and Justice: A Review of Research.* Vol. 10, 117–70. Chicago: University of Chicago Press.

Renauer, B. C., S. Cunningham, W. Feyerherm, T. O'Connor, and P. Bellatty. 2006. Tipping the scales of justice: The effect of overincarceration on neighborhood violence. *Criminal Justice Policy Review* 17(3):362–79.

Rengifo, Andres, and Elin Waring. 2005. A Network Perspective on the Impact of Incarceration on Communities. Paper presented to the annual meetings of the American Society of Criminology, Toronto, November 17.

Reynolds, Morgan O. 1996. Crime and Punishment in Texas: Update. NCPA Policy Report No. 202, January. Dallas, TX: National Center for Policy Analysis.

Riley, Michael. 2006. Iowa law has sex offenders in parking lots, rundown hotels. *Denver Post,* January 10. Available at: http://www.denverpost.com/nation-world/ci_3382005. Accessed January 18, 2007.

Roberts, Dorothy. 2004. The social and moral cost of mass incarceration in African American communities. *Stanford Law Review* 56(5):1271–1305.

Rojek, Dean G., James E. Coverdill, and Stuart W. Fors. 2003. The effect of victim impact panels on DUI rearrest rates: A five-year follow-up. *Criminology* 41(4):901–22.

Roncek, Dennis. 1981. Dangerous places: Crime and residential environment. *Social Forces* 60:74–96.

Rose, Dina R., and Todd R. Clear. 1998. Incarceration, social capital and crime: Examining the unintended consequences of incarceration, *Criminology* 36(3):441–79.

Rose, Dina R., Todd R. Clear, and Judith A. Ryder. 2000. Drugs, Incarceration and Neighborhood Life: The Impact of Reintegrating Offenders into the Community. Final Report to the National Institute of Justice.

Rose, Dina R., Todd R. Clear, and Judith A. Ryder. 2001. Addressing the unintended consequences of incarceration through community-oriented services. *Corrections Management Quarterly* 5(3):69–78.

Rosenbaum, James E, and Stephanie DeLuca. 2000. *Is Housing Mobility the Key to Welfare Reform? Lessons from Chicago's Gatreaux Program.* Washington, DC: Brookings Institution.

Rosenfeld, Richard, Joel Wallman, and Robert Fornango. 2005. The contribution of ex-prisoners to crime rates. In Jeremy Travis and Christy Visher, eds., *Prisoner Reentry and Crime in America*, 80–104. New York: Cambridge University Press.

Sabol, William J., and James P. Lynch. 2003. Assessing the longer-run effects of incarceration: Impact on families and employment. In Darnell Hawkins, Samuel Myers, Jr., and Randolph Stine, eds., *Crime Control and Social Justice: The Delicate Balance.* Westport, CT: Greenwood Press.

Saegert, Susan, J. Phillip Thompson, and Mark R. Warren, eds. 2001. *Social Capital and Poor Communities.* New York: Russell Sage.

Sampson, Robert J. 1985. Neighborhoods and crime: The structural determinants of personal victimization. *Journal of Research in Crime and Delinquency* 22:7–40.

Sampson, Robert J. 1991. Linking the micro- and macro-level dimensions of community social organization. *Social Forces* 70:43–64.

Sampson, Robert J. 2001. Crime and public safety: Insights from community-level perspectives on social control. In Susan Saegert, J. Phillip Thompson, and Mark R. Warren, eds., *Social Capital and Poor Communities*, 89–114. New York: Russell Sage.

Sampson, Robert J. 2002. Transcending tradition: New directions in community research, Chicago-style. *Criminology* 40(2):213–30.

Sampson, Robert J., and W. Byron Groves. 1989. Community structure and crime: Testing social disorganization theory. *American Journal of Sociology* 94:774–802.

Sampson, Robert J., and John H. Laub. 1993. *Crime in the Making: Pathways and Turning Points Through Life.* Cambridge, MA: Harvard University Press.

Sampson, Robert J., Jeffrey D. Morenoff, and Thomas Gannon-Rowley. 2002. Assessing neighborhood effects: Social processes and new directions for research. *Annual Review of Sociology* 28:443–78.

Sampson, Robert J., and Stephen W. Raudenbush. 1999. Systematic social observation in public spaces: A new look at disorder in urban neighborhoods. *American Journal of Sociology* 105:603–51.

Sampson, Robert J., Stephen W. Raudenbush, and Felton Earls. 1997. Neighborhoods and violent crime: A multilevel study of collective efficacy. *Science* 277:918–24.

Samuels, P., and Deborah Mukamal. 2004. *After Prison: Roadblocks to Reentry.* New York: Legal Action Center.

Sanders, Jimy M., and Victor Nee. 1996. Social capital, human capital and immigrant self-employment. *American Sociological Review* 62:231–49.

Sharp, Susan F., and Susan T. Marcus-Mendoza. 2001. It's a family affair: Incarcerated women and their families. *Women & Criminal Justice* 12(4):21–49.

Shaw, Clifford R., and Henry D. McKay. 1942. *Juvenile Delinquency and Urban Areas.* Chicago: University of Chicago Press.

Shepherd, Joanna. 2006. The imprisonment puzzle: Understanding how prison growth affects crime. *Criminology and Public Policy* 5(2):285–98.

Sherman, Lawrence. 1992. Attacking crime: Police and crime control. In Michael Tonry and Norval Morris, eds., *Modern Policing*, 159–230. Chicago, IL: University of Chicago Press.

Sherman, Lawrence. 1993. Defiance, deterrence and irrelevance: A theory of criminal sanctions. *Journal of Research in Crime & Delinquency* 30(4): 445–73.

Sherman, Lawrence W., Denise Gottfredson, Doris MacKenzie, John Eck, Peter Reuter, and Shawn Bushway. 1997. Preventing Crime: What Works, What Doesn't, What's Promising! Report to the U.S. Congress. Washington, DC: National Institute of Justice.

Silverman, Eli. 1999. *NYPD Battles Crime: Innovative Strategies in Policing.* Cambridge, MA: Northeastern University Press.

Simons, Ronald L., Leslie Gordon Simons, Callie Harbin Burt, Gene H. Brody, and Carolyn Cutrona. 2005. Collective efficacy, authoritarian parenting, and delinquency: A longitudinal test of a model integrating community- and family-level processes. *Criminology* 43(4):989–1029.

Skogan, Wesley G. 1990. *Disorder and Decline: The Spiral of Decay in American Neighborhoods.* New York: Free Press.

Smith, Linda G., and Ronald L. Akers. 1993. A comparison of recidivism of Florida's community control and prison: A five-year survival analysis. *Journal of Research in Crime and Delinquency* 30:267–92.

Smith, Michael. 2001. What future for public safety and restorative justice in a system of community penalties? In Anthony Bottoms, Loraine Gelsthorpe, and Sue Rex, eds., *Community Penalties: Change and Challenges*, 200–25. Devon, UK: Willan Publishing.

Smith, Paula, Claire Goggin, and Paul Gendreau. 2002. *The Effects of Prison Sentences and Intermediate Sanctions on Recidivism: General Effects and Individual Differences.* Ottawa: Public Works and Government Services of Canada.

Solomon, Amy L., Vera Kachnowski, and Avi Bhati. 2005. *Does Parole Supervision work?* Washington, DC: Urban Institute.

Spaulding, Shayne. 2005. *Getting Connected: Strategies for Expanding the Employment Networks of Low Income People.* Philadelphia: Public/Private Ventures.

Spelman, William. 1994. *Criminal Incapacitation.* New York: Plenum.

Spelman, William. 2005. Jobs or Jails? The crime drop in Texas. *Journal of policy analysis and management* 24:133–65.

Spelman, William. 2000. The limited importance of prison expansion. In Alfred Blumstein and Joel Walman, eds., *The Crime Drop in America*, 97–129. New York: Cambridge University Press.

Spohn, Cassia, and David Holleran. 2002. The effect of imprisonment on recidivism rates of felony offenders: A focus on drug offenders. *Criminology* 40(2):329–58.

Stemen, Don, Andres Rengifo, and James Wilson. 2005. *Of Fragmentation and Ferment: The Impact of State Sentencing Policies on Incarceration Rates, 1975–2002.* New York: Vera Institute of Justice.

Stemen, Don. 2007. *Reconsidering Incarceration: New Directions for Reducing Crime.* New York: Vera Institute of Justice.

Stewart, Eric A., and Ronald Simons. 2006. Structure and culture in African American adolescent violence: A partial test of the code of the street hypothesis. *Justice Quarterly* 23(1):1–33.

Stretesky, Paul, B, Amie M. Schuck, and Michael J. Hogan. 2004. Space matters: An analysis of poverty, poverty clustering, and violent crime. *Justice Quarterly* 21(4):817–41.

Sullivan, Mercer L. 1989. *Getting Paid: Youth, Crime and Work in the Inner City.* Ithaca, NY: Cornell University Press.

Swartz, Charles. 2007. New York City Criminal Justice Maps. Justice Mapping Center, Columbia University.

Taylor, Ralph, and Jeanette Covington. 1988. Neighborhood changes in ecology and violence. *Crimnology* 26:553–89.

Taylor, Ralph. 1997. Social order and disorder of street blocks and neighborhoods: Ecology, microecology and the systemic model of social disorganization. *Journal of Research in Crime and Delinquency* 34(1):113–55.

Taylor, Ralph, John Goldkamp, Phil Harris, Peter Jones, Maria Garcia, and Eric McCord. 2006. Community Justice Impacts over Time: Adult Arrest Rates, Male Serious Delinquency Prevalence, Rates within and between Philadelphia Communities. Presentation to the Eastern Sociological Society meetings, Boston, February.

Thomas, Adam. 2005. The Old Ball and Chain: Unlocking the Correlation between Incarceration and Marriage. Unpublished manuscript.

Thomas, James C., and Elizabeth Torrone. 2006. Incarceration as forced migration: Effects on selected community Health outcomes. *American Journal of Public Health* 96(10):1–5.

Tonry, Michael. 1996a. *Malign Neglect*. New York: Oxford University Press.

Tonry, Michael. 1996b. *Sentencing Matters*. New York: Oxford University Press.

Tonry, Michael. 2004. *Thinking about Crime: Sense and Sensibility in American Penal Culture*. New York: Oxford University Press.

Travis, Jeremy. 2005. *But They All Come Back: Facing the Challenges of Prisoner Reentry*. Washington, DC: Urban Institute.

Travis, Jeremy, and Kirsten Christiansen. 2007. Failed Reentry: The Unique Challenges of Back-End Sentencing. Unpublished paper.

Tremblay, Richard. 2006. Tracking the origins of criminal behaviour. *The Criminologist* 31(1):1, 3–7.

Tucker, Susan B., and Eric Cadora. 2003. Justice reinvestment: To invest in public safety by reallocating justice dollars to refinance education, housing, healthcare, and jobs. *Ideas for an Open Society* 13(3):1–8.

Turner, Margery Austin, and Delores Acevedo-Garcia. 2005. Why housing mobility: The research evidence today. *Poverty & Race* 14(1):1–3.

Tyler, Tom. 1990. *Why People Obey the Law*. New Haven, CT: Yale University Press.

Tyler, Tom R., and Jeffrey Fagan. 2005. Legitimacy and Cooperation: Why Do People Help the Police Fight Crime in Their Communities? Columbia Public Law Research Paper No. 06-99. Available at SSRN: http://ssrn.com/abstract=887737.

Uggen, Christopher. 2000. Work as a turning point in the life course of criminals: A duration model of age, employment, and recidivism. *American Sociological Review* 67:529–46.

Uggen, Christopher, and Jeff Manza. 2002. Democratic contraction? The consequences of felon disenfranchisement in the United States. *American Sociological Review* 67(6):777–803.

Uggen, Christopher, and Jeff Manza. 2005. Lost voices: The civic and political views of disenfranchised felons. In Mary Pattillo, David Weiman, and Bruce Western, eds., *Imprisoning America: The Social Effects of Mass Incarceration*, 165–204. New York: Russell Sage.

Uggen, Christopher, and Jeff Manza. 2006. *Locked Out: Felon Disenfranchisement and American Democracy.* New York: Oxford University Press.

Uggen, Christopher, Sara Wakefield, and Bruce Western. 2005. Work and family perspectives on reentry. In Jeremy Travis and Christy Visher, eds., *Prisoner Reentry and Crime in America*, 209–43. New York: Cambridge University Press.

U.S. Department of Justice, Bureau of Justice Statistics. 1997. *Survey of Inmates in State and Federal Correctional Facilities.* Ann Arbor, MI: ICPSR.

Vacha, Edward F., and T. F. McLaughlin. 1992. The social structural, family, school and personal characteristics of at-risk students: Policy recommendations for school personnel. *Journal of Education* 174(3):9–25.

Van den Haag, Ernest. 1975. *Punishing Criminals: Concerning a Very Old and Painful Question.* New York: Basic Books.

Veiraitis, Lynne M., Tomislav V. Kovandsic, and Thomas B. Marvell. 2007. The Criminogenic Effects of Imprisonment: Evidence form State Panel Data, 1974–2002. Unpublished paper.

Venkatesh, Sudhir Alladi. 1997. The social organization of street gang activity in an urban ghetto. *American Journal of Sociology* 103:82–111.

Viboch, Marcy. 2005. *Childhood Loss and Behavioral Problems: Loosening the Links.* New York: Vera Institute of Justice.

Visher, Christy, and Jill Farrell. 2005. *Chicago communities and Prisoner Reentry.* Washington, DC: The urban Institute.

Vito, Gennaro. 1986. Probation and recidivism: Replication and response. *Federal Probation* 50:17–25.

Wacquant, Loic. 2007. *Urban Outcasts.* Cambridge, UK: Polity.

Walker, Samuel, Cassia Spohn, and Miriam Delone. 2006. *Sense and Nonsense about Crime and Drugs.* Belmont, CA: Wadsworth.

Waring, Elin, Kristen Scully, and Todd R. Clear. 2005. Coercive Mobility in an Eight-year Tallahassee Sample: A Follow-up of the Original Tallahassee Coercive Mobility Study. Unpublished paper presented to the consortium to study concentrated incarceration in poor communities, a project of the Open Society Institute.

Warner, Barbara D., and Glenn L. Pierce. 1993. Reexamining social disorganization theory using calls to the police as a measure of crime. *Criminology* 31:493–517.

Weatherburn, Don, and Bronwyn Lind. 2001. *Delinquency-Prone Communities.* New York: Cambridge University Press.

Webster, Cheryl Marie, Anthony N. Doob, and Franklin E. Zimring. 2006. Proposition 8 and crime rates in California: The case of the disappearing deterrent. *Criminology & Public Policy* 5(3):1501–28.

Wellman, Barry. 1979. The community question: The intimate networks of East Yorkers. *American Journal of Sociology* 84:1201–31.

Western, Bruce. 2006. *Punishment and Inequality in America.* New York: Russell Sage.

Western, Bruce, and Katherine Beckett. 1999. How unregulated is the U.S. labor market? The penal system as a labor market institution. *American Journal of Sociology* 104(4):1030–60.

Western, Bruce, Jeffrey Kling, and David Weiman. 2001. The labor market consequences of incarceration. *Crime and Delinquency* 47(3):410–38.

Western, Bruce, Leonard M. Lopoo, and Sara McLanahan. 2004. Incarceration and the bonds between parents in fragile families. In Mary Pattillo, David Weiman, and Bruce Western, eds., *Imprisoning America: The Social Effects of Mass Incarceration.* New York: Russell Sage.

Western, Bruce, Mary Patillo, and David Weiman. 2004. In Mary Pattillo, David Weiman, and Bruce Western, eds., *Imprisoning America: The Social Effects of Mass Incarceration,* 1–18. New York: Russell Sage.

Whitman, James. 2003. *Harsh Justice.* New York: Oxford University Press.

Widom, Kathy Spatz. 1989. Does violence beget violence: A critical examination of the literature. *Psychological Bulletin* 106(1):3–28.

Widom, Kathy Spatz. 1994. Childhood victimization and risk for adolescent problem behaviors. In Robert D. Ketterlinus and Michael E. Lamb, eds., *Adolescent Problem Behaviors: Issues and Research,* 127–64. New York: Lawrence Earlbaum.

Williams, Diane, Jodina Hicks, Shelli Rossman, and Christy Visher. 2006. *Safer Return: A Community Empowerment Reentry Initiative.* Chicago: Safer Foundation.

Wilson, James Q. 1975. *Thinking about Crime.* New York: Basic Books.

Wilson, James, and Robert C. Davis. 2006. Good intentions meet hard realities: an evaluation of project green light. *Criminology & Public Policy* 5(2):303–38.

Wilson, James Q., and George E. Kelling. 1982. Broken windows: The police and neighborhood safety. *Atlantic Monthly* 249(3):29–38.

Wilson, William Julius. 1987. *The Truly Disadvantaged: The Inner City, the Underclass, and Public Policy.* Chicago: University of Chicago Press.

Wilson, William Julius. 1996. *When Work Disappears: The World of the New Urban Poor.* New York: Alfred Knopf.

Wool, Jon, and Don Stemen. 2004. *Changing Fortune or Changing Attitudes: Sentencing and Corrections in 2003.* New York: Vera Institute of Justice.

Wooldredge. 2002. Examining the (ir)relevance of aggregation bias in multilevel studies for neighborhoods and crime with an example comparing census tracks and neighborhoods in Cincinnati. *Criminology* 40(3):681–710.

*World Fact Book.* 2006. https://www.cia.gov/cia/publications/factbook/index.html.

Worrall, John. 2006. Does targeting minor offenses reduce serious crime? A provisional, affirmative answer based on an analysis of county-level data. *Police Quarterly* 9(1) 47–72.

Wright, Richard, and Scot Decker. 1994. *Burglars on the Job*. Cambridge, MA: Northeastern University Press.

Zedlewski, Edwin. 1987. Making confinement decisions. *Research in Brief*. Washington, DC: U.S. Department of Justice.

Zimring, Franklin E., and Gordon Hawkins. 1988. The new mathematics of imprisonment. *Crime and Delinquency* 34(4):425–36.

Zimring, Franklin E., and Gordon Hawkins. 1997. *Incapacitation*. Chicago: University of Chicago Press.

Zimring, Franklin, Gordon Hawkins, and Susan Kamin. 2001. *Punishment and Democracy: Three Strikes and You're Out in California*. New York: Oxford University Press.

# Index

community (*contd.*)
  stigmatized by high levels of
    incarceration, 128–130
  supervision of released inmate, 19
  and voting, 113–15
  *See also* neighborhoods
community justice, 13, 190–201
  and adjudication, 203–205
  the appraisal of, 205–207
  the funding of, 200–2001
  in high-incarceration places, 195–196
  and law enforcement, 201–207
  norms and values of, 196–198
  philosophies of, 191–195
  and policing, 202–203
  as a reinvestment of funds, 200–201
  strategies of, 195–201
  targets of, 198–200
Concentrated Incarceration Consortium, ix
correctional officers, 12
corrections, 40
cost/benefit analysis. *See* risk/reward
courts, 32, 40. *See also* community justice
Crane, Robert, xi
crime, vii–viii, 4, 5, 16–17, 40, 83
  cost of committing, 21–22
  displacement of, 7
  as impacted by group crime, 36
  as impacted by incarceration, 5, 6, 7,
    16–17, 18–20, 21–24, 37, 189
  patterns of, 24
  pleasure of, 21
  prior to incarceration, 35
  violent, 6, 13, 23, 39, 44, 52, 54, 72, 75, 90,
    105, 160, 163, 197, 199
crime control, 16, 19–20, 90, 149, 178–179,
  180, 187, 191
crime prevention, vii, 6, 7, 41, 46–47, 56, 189
criminal history, 26
criminals. *See* inmate(s); offenders
Crutchfeld, Robert, ix, 113
Curtis, Ric, xi
cycling in and out of prison, 9, 58–60, 67,
  75–76, 78, 83, 84, 137

Daley, Mayor Richard, 12
Defiance Hypothesis, 23
Democrats, 4

deterrence, 6–7, 15, 16, 19–23, 25, 29–34, 43,
  46, 47, 125, 149, 165, 193, 197
  failure of, 21–23, 25–27, 31
  general, 28, 33
  specific, 25, 30, 33, 45
DiIulio, John, 176
disadvantaged places. *See* community;
  impoverished neighborhoods;
  neighborhoods; poverty
disorder theorists, 152
disparity, racial, 4
displacement of crime, 6
dropouts, 8, 65, 70, 95, 195, 198
drug courts, 203–205
drug crimes, 19, 20, 27, 36, 51, 180, 187, 195,
  199, 203, 207
drug laws, 12, 18, 45, 51–52, 54–56, 62, 63, 64,
  67, 114, 143, 187–188. *See also* legislation
drug use, 54, 77, 106, 196
  in blacks as compared to whites, 8
due process, 23
Duff, R. A., 191
Dukakis, Michael, 57

economic stress-induced offender
  motivation. *See* ESIOM paradigm
economists, 29
economy, 11, 81, 115, 130–135
  and incarceration, 5, 10, 11, 28, 36, 37–38,
    62, 63, 87, 94, 106–111
  and labor market, 108–110
  and property values, 110–111
  strength of, 5
education, 8, 58, 62, 63, 64, 76, 80, 102,
  198–200, 200–201
employment, 62, 101, 106–110, 113, 130–135,
  198, 206
  difficulties in obtaining, 9, 58, 63, 77
England, 21
epidemic model of offender population
  growth, 157
ESIOM paradigm, 156–158
ethnography, ix

Fagan, Jeffrey, ix, 114
faith-based organizations, 199
Families Against Mandatory Minimums,
  12, 61

UCR. *See* Uniform Crime Report
Uggen, Chris, xi
unemployment. *See* employment
Uniform Crime Report (UCR), 16–17
unions, 12
Urban League, 123
U.S. Centers for Disease Control and
　　Prevention, 105
U.S. Sentencing Commission, 55

van den Haag, Ernest, 21, 25
Vera Institute of Justice (Vera Institute), vii,
　　13, 45, 53
Viboch, Marcy, 102
victims, victimization, 22–23, 194
Vietnam War, 4
Visher, Christy, x

Wacquant, Loic, 176
War on Crime, 50
War on Drugs, 54, 112
Waring, Elin, viii, ix, x, 78
Wattenberg, Ben, 15
Weatherburn, Don, 156–158
Weed and Seed programs, 194, 195
Western, Bruce, xi, 8
Wilson, James Q., 202
Wilson, William Julius, 70–71, 196
women, 65, 81, 88, 97, 104, 171, 175
　　effects of their incarceration, 10, 74, 164
　　incarceration of, ix, 54, 62, 63
　　*See also* marriage(s)

Zedlewski, Edwin, vii, 36, 38, 42
Zimring, Franklin, 36